A Short History of
the English Language

Torben Kisbye

A Short History of
the English Language

Edited by
Knud Sørensen

AARHUS UNIVERSITY PRESS

Copyright: Aarhus University Press, 1992
Typesetting by Werks Fotosats, Aarhus
Printed on acid-free paper by Bogtrykkeriet, Skive

ISBN 87 7288 406 1

AARHUS UNIVERSITY PRESS
Building 170, Aarhus University
DK-8000 Aarhus C, Denmark

Preface

At his sudden death on April 27, 1990, my friend and colleague Torben Kisbye left an almost finished manuscript, which I have been asked to prepare for publication. Drawing on his previous book from 1975, *A Short History of the English Language*, of which the present volume is a revision, I have added a number of missing sections and notes plus an index, corrected some obvious slips in the manuscript, and endeavoured to remove ambiguities. I have not, however, tampered with Torben Kisbye's approach to his subject, and I trust that this book appears in substantially the form it would have had if the author had lived to put the finishing touches to his work himself.

June 1990
Knud Sørensen

Contents

Abbreviations

A = accusative
AN = Anglo-Norman
AV = The Authorised Version
D = dative
Dan. = Danish
EMnE = early Modern English
fem. = feminine
G = genitive
IE = Indo-European
inf. = infinitive
masc. = masculine
ME = Middle English
MnE = Modern English
N = nominative
neut. = neuter
OE = Old English
OF = Old French
OHG = Old High German
ON = Old Norse
PE = Present-Day English
pret. = preterite
WGerm = West Germanic
WSax = West Saxon
> = develops into
< = is developed from
* denotes inferential (reconstructed) forms

CHAPTER I

Backgrounds and developments common to all Indo-European languages

The Indo-European family of languages

The term Indo-European (IE) has been invented to conveniently identify a family of languages, which on the basis of correspondences of sound and structure (inflexion,[1] gender, etc.) and to some extent vocabulary can be shown to have originated from one common ancestor, usually referred to as proto-Indo-European.

Far beyond the dawn of recorded history, however, this common base began to split up into a number of subgroups. When exactly this division took place we do not know, but some time before 2000 B.C. seems a fair conjecture, since we have at that date definitely lost trace of even the most ancient languages that have descended from the common proto-Indo-European base. The IE language family is divisible into the following principal subgroups (see diagram p. 10).

Satem languages[2]

The *Indo-Iranian* group consists of Indian (about 1500 B.C.) and Iranian (about 1000 B.C.).

The most ancient literary monuments of Indian are the Vedas written in *Sanskrit*. The modern languages of India (Hindi, Bengali, Punjabi, Urdu, etc.) derive from the colloquial dialects known as Prakrits, which developed alongside of Sanskrit.[3]

The *Iranian* branch comprises Old Persian and Avestan, the language of the sage Zarathustra (Zoroaster). Of these, however, only the former has survived to the present day. Chief modern representatives are Iranian, Afghan and Kurdish.

Armenian (5th c. A.D.), spoken along the eastern shores of the Black Sea, like Albanian (below) takes up a somewhat isolated position. The vocabulary shows a heavy admixture of Iranian, Greek and Arabic elements.

Albanian (14th c. A.D.) is probably the last vestige of ancient Illyrian. The vocabulary, however, testifies to extensive borrowing from Slavic, Italian, Turkish and Greek.

The *Balto-Slavic* group. The Baltic branch comprises Lettish, Old Prussian (extinct since 17th c.) and Lithuanian. These languages, and in particular Lithuanian, are heavily inflected and marked by extreme conservatism. Lithuanian is the language that has preserved into modern speech most of the structural features that are considered typical of parent IE.

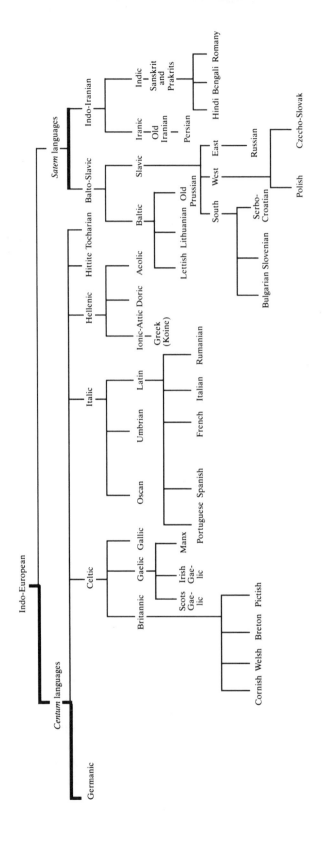

The *Slavic* branch (9th c. A.D.) is also though less consistently archaic in structure. It contains three main divisions, East Slavic including Russian, Ukrainian, and White Russian, West Slavic including Polish, Czech, Slovakian, and Wendish (still spoken in small pockets in the Bautzen-Cottbus area of Germany). Finally there is South Slavic including Bulgarian, Serbo-Croatian and Slovenian.

Centum languages

The *Italic* group has Latin (about 300 B.C.), the language of Latium and Rome, as its most prominent member. Side by side with Latin, which was to become the koine of the far-flung Roman Empire, there existed a popular spoken variety commonly known as Vulgar Latin. From this language of the masses have sprung what we today know as the Romance languages, whose most important representatives are Italian, French, Spanish, Roumanian and Portuguese.

The *Hellenic* group consists of numerous dialects, chief of which are Doric, Aeolic, Arcadian and Ionic. It fell to Attic, however, a sub-dialect of Ionic spoken in and around Athens, to form the basis of the koine of the entire Greek world. The most ancient literary monuments were until recently believed to be the Homeric poems, assumed to go back to the 8th century B.C. (but see p. 12).

The *Celtic* group (8th c. A.D.). The Celts were once one of the most powerful and expansive branches of the IE family, numerically as well as geographically. A few centuries before the Christian era their language had come to be spoken throughout the greater part of Europe (France, Spain, Great Britain, Germany, northern Italy), extending for a time even into Greece, Russia, and Asia Minor (cf. Paul the Apostle's letter to the Galatians).

Wedged in between the expanding Roman Empire and the pressure of the Germanic hordes, however, their culture soon collapsed, and their language was superseded by those of their conquerors, primarily Latin and Germanic.

Celtic falls into three main divisions, Gallic (the extinct language of ancient Gaul), Britannic, including Welsh, Cornish (extinct since the 18th century), and the Breton of north-western France,[4] and finally Gaelic with Irish, Scots-Gaelic and Manx (extinct since the 1950's) as its modern representatives. In spite of more or less nationalist efforts to revive them, the Celtic languages of Britain are spoken now practically only as secondary tongues.

The *Germanic* group is represented today primarily by English, German, Dutch, Flemish, Frisian, Danish, Norwegian, Swedish, Icelandic and Faroese. The first five belong to the West Germanic (see p. 19) and the rest to the North Germanic branch (see p. 18). There is also an East Germanic branch, which includes languages like Gothic, Vandalic and Burgundian, all long extinct. Apart from the Scandinavian runic inscriptions, some of which go back to the 3rd century A.D., Gothic constitutes the earliest recorded

Germanic dialect. It has been handed down to us mainly through the fragmentary translation of the New Testament by Bishop Wulfila (311-83) of the Visi (or West) Goths. The first West Germanic records date from about the 8th century A.D. However, a few runic inscriptions antedate the earliest manuscripts.

Newly discovered IE languages
Hittite (about 1500 B.C.) until fairly recently had been known only through accidental reference in the Old Testament (e.g. Gen. 23.10 'Ephron the Hittite'; II Sam. 11.3 'Uriah the Hittite'). In 1907, however, archaeologists excavated the ancient Hittite capital at Bogkazköi near Ankara in Asia Minor, and their finds included a vast number of clay tablets with a hitherto unknown language, later deciphered and identified as either of IE extraction or co-ordinate with IE. The linguistic structure of Hittite suggests that IE may have been a less homogeneous language than we have so far supposed.

Tocharian (7th c. A.D.) The identification of Tocharian in Chinese Turkestan is likewise a 20th-century achievement. Tocharian is an IE centum language but located in the eastern satem area (see p. 9).

Linear B, the ancient speech of Mycenae, was discovered in Crete and the Peloponnese and not deciphered until the 1950's. Recent research has proved it to be Greek in its most archaic form. Since it probably goes back to about 1500 B.C., we must now push the history of Greek some 800 years further back in time.

Non-Indo-European languages in Europe.
The Indo-European family does not include all the existing languages of Europe. Outside the family we find Finnish, Hungarian, Estonian and Lappish. Some linguists, on the basis of common features, have placed them in a separate group called Finno-Ugric.

Basque, spoken in pockets astride the Pyrenees, is an enigmatic language, which seems to have no affiliations with any other known language.

The Indo-European parent language
It is generally agreed that proto-IE was spoken by nomadic tribes somewhere in Central Europe about 3-4000 B.C. In the millennium before 2000 B.C., however, the dialectal differences that must naturally have existed in a language spoken over such a vast area were further accentuated when these tribes began to wander in successive migrations across the continent of Euro-Asia. Linguistically the encounter with languages they met on their way and the many centuries of separation from their sister dialects caused these variants of one original tongue to gradually become so diversified that they evolved into what could now be called wholly separate languages.[5] When the recorded history of the oldest known IE languages begins (Sanskrit, Hittite, Linear B), proto-IE had thus long ceased to be a unified speech.

Of proto-IE we possess no first-hand knowledge since no written records are extant. What we do know is only what can be inferred from reconstruction based on a comparative study of the earliest attested or most conservative descendant languages, primarily Hittite, Sanskrit, Greek and Lithuanian. Such reconstructed or hypothetical forms are marked by an asterisk*.

Reconstruction along such lines, however, reveals to us a language of extreme inflexional complexity. The noun had elaborate declensions for case, number and gender, there was a highly complicated verbal system, and rigid concord between noun, adjective and pronoun was observed.

The IE noun boasted no less than eight cases (nominative, vocative, accusative, genitive, dative, locative, ablative, and instrumental), three numbers (singular, dual and plural) and three genders (masculine, feminine and neuter). The verb was equally complex with heavily inflected tense and mood systems like those we know from Latin and Greek. There were not only three numbers (singular, dual and plural), three voices (passive, active and medium), but also additional moods like optative and injunctive, and additional tenses like the aorist. Verbal aspect,[6] as in the Slavic languages, played a prominent part, tenses or distinctions in time, as we know them, being secondary or derived functions.

Vestiges of this basic structure are preserved in varying degrees in all modern IE languages, most conservative in character being the languages of the Balto-Slavic group.

The Indo-European habitat

The common ancestry of the IE languages presupposes a common homeland in the period prior to their dispersion over the continent of Euro-Asia. So far there has been little consensus of opinion concerning the exact location of such a parent community. The fact that many migrations (e.g. the Huns, the Mongols, etc.) had surged into Europe from the east and the early discovery of Sanskrit (Sir William Jones 1786) with its strong affinity with the structure of Proto-IE long spoke in favour of Central Asia as the possible pre-dispersion home of the Indo-Europeans (Schlegel 1808), and the Church for obvious reasons was also strongly in favour of an eastern cradle for mankind.

More recent scholarship, basing its conclusions on evidence converging from both language and archaeology, however, has focused its attention on Europe as the more plausible centre of dispersion. But a narrower geographical delimitation has so far been a matter for dispute. There are theories pointing to Asia, Southern Russia, the Carpathians, Central Europe, Northern Europe, and even Scandinavia.

In what follows we shall give a brief sketch of the more or less convincing arguments that have been deployed in the attempt to assign a homeland to our IE ancestors.

Racial arguments have largely been given up now. IE is diffused over such a vast belt (stretching from Great Britain to India) and spoken by peoples of such ethnic diversity that it is pointless to try to identify the

13

Indo-Europeans with certain racial characteristics like e.g. tall stature, blond hair, etc. and placing them in Northern Europe.

With purely linguistic arguments, however, we are on safer ground. Not only do the IE languages have many structural features in common, but also, as we have seen, a basic vocabulary. By selecting words with a well-defined prehistoric geographical distribution (e.g. names for plants, animals, climatic conditions, etc.) and which are common property to all IE languages, it is possible to get some clues as to the location of a homeland.

They knew trees like the oak, the beech, the willow, the birch, the fir and the apple-tree, and their animal names included 'lax' (salmon), bear, hare, wolf, horse, dog, eagle, cow, sheep (and the word *wool*), boar, dog, goose, beaver, honey-bee. Particularly the word *wool* is culturally interesting, for it suggests that at least one of the animals was domesticated. Further, their vocabulary indicates that they were familiar with snow, winter, ice and frost. If such words are present in all or most of the sub-members that constitute the IE family, there is every reason to assume that they formed part also of the ancestral speech.

On the basis of such and similar evidence it has been suggested and is widely accepted that the IE homeland should be sought somewhere in the cold climate of Northern Europe[7].

Some of the words ('lax', beech[8] and honey-bee[8]), however, may warrant a somewhat narrower delimitation of their homeland, and some authorities have suggested that the territory between such salmon-bearing streams as the Vistula and the Elbe could be a probable centre of dispersion.

Place-names may also afford some clues. It is an established fact that they constitute the most archaic linguistic material in any given area, so the fact that Central and Northern Europe lack place-names that are pre-IE has been taken by some to indicate that the Indo-Europeans must have been the first to inhabit these areas. The place-name argument, however, does not seem altogether convincing because some river-names appear to fit less well into the picture.

Some authorities try to be equally specific, attempting to locate the IE homeland somewhere along the centum-satem split (see p. 9), possibly the area around Lithuania, which, as we have seen, has a language very close in structure to the IE base[9].

To a more eastern homeland points the fact that the Semitic languages show many grammatical features (e.g. the concept of gender, perfect and imperfect aspect (see note 6), case forms, and originally also dual forms, etc., which probably derive from very early contact with IE.

The interdisciplinary efforts of comparative linguistics, anthropology and archaeology, however, may shed further light on the vexed question of the primordial home of the Indo-Europeans. On the basis of shared vocabulary attempts have been made to establish the culture stage attained by them prior to their dispersion and then seek help from archaeology.

Archaeologists seem to agree that the Indo-Europeans should be identified with the neolithic so-called cord-impressed pottery and stone battle-axe culture (also known as the single-grave culture), which about 2000 B.C. prevailed in Central and Northern Europe. But again views are diverging as to where these tribes may have come from. Areas from the eastern fringes of Central Europe to somewhere beyond the Ural Mountains have been suggested, but there is no consensus.

Quite recent excavations, however, have unearthed traces of an ancient civilization which may well have been the original pre-dispersion centre of the Indo-Europeans, namely the so-called Kurgan Culture, which flourished north of the Caspian Sea between the 5th and the 3rd millennia B.C. Archaeology and palæobotany show that many of the items of flora and fauna mentioned above as known to the Indo-Europeans (p. 14) were present in that region, so for the moment much seems to speak in favour of accommodating the Indo-Europeans slightly further to the east, probably somewhere between Central Europe and the steppes of southern Russia.

CHAPTER II

The Germanic languages

The Germanic migrations

The original homeland of the Germani is supposed to have been the region along the south coast of the Baltic and southern Scandinavia. Their neighbours were the Celts to the west and south and the Balto-Slavs to the east. From this northern seat they gradually expanded their territory not only to where Germanic languages are heard today, but also, as we shall see, to more exotic lands.

The Goths, who linguistically belong to the East Germanic sub-group, pushed south from their earliest known home, the shores of the Baltic, and had by the early third century reached the regions north of the Black Sea. In the middle of the same century they must have split up, for there are now reports of two tribes, the Ostrogoths in the region between the Don and the Dniester and the Visigoths between the Dnieper and the Danube.

The Visigoths, dislodged from their home by the neighbouring Huns, however, began to move west, made incursions into Greece and Italy and sacked Rome in 410 under Alaric. In the 5th century they conquered Spain and Portugal, where they established a kingdom, which lasted till 711 when it succumbed to the increasing power of the Muslims. In these regions their language was soon superseded by Latin.[1]

The Ostrogoths extended their empire from the Black Sea to the Baltic. Reinstalled in their former territory after the collapse and retreat of the Huns in the 5th century, they moved into Italy, where their king Theodoric ruled from 493 to 526.

The Vandals have traditionally been assumed to derive their name from Vendsyssel in northern Jutland. A southward drive had by the beginning of the Christian era taken them as far as to what is now southern Poland. From there they were soon dispelled by the advancing Huns, and in a series of migrations they traversed Gaul and Spain and eventually founded a kingdom in Northern Africa, which survived till the 6th century. Place-names such as *Andalucia* in Spain and *Gandalon* in France may point to former Vandalic presence there.

Apart from place or personal names and some scanty inscriptions the only substantial linguistic legacy handed down from these powerful East Germanic tribes is the Codex Argenteus, a fragmentary Bible translation from the Greek by Bishop Wulfila (see p. 12), written in the period when the Visigoths, before their great thrust westwards, had temporarily settled in what is now Bulgaria.[2]

The West Germanic tribes, pushing the Celts before them, had settled in areas roughly corresponding to what is now Germany, the Netherlands and part of Jutland.

Essential for the history of England, however, are three contiguous tribes, the Saxons, the Angles and the Jutes, who according to Bede's 'Historia Ecclesiastica Gentis Anglorum' (731) were settled in a region between the Elbe and the Rhine, in Schleswig-Holstein and in southern Jutland respectively. However, the evidence is conflicting and particularly the original homeland of the Jutes poses unsolved problems.

From their ancestral homelands these pagan West Germanic tribes had long been ravaging the southern shores of Romano-Celtic Britain. In 410, however, when the Roman legionaries were withdrawn from the island, the former Roman province was left defenceless against the inroads of the Picts and the Scots in the North, and the Celtic King Vortigern solicited their assistance as mercenaries. His heathen auxiliaries arrived around 450, and according to Bede, the Jutes under the two chieftains Hengest and Horsa came first. They soon made short shrift of the Pictish and Scots aggressors, but, mission accomplished, refused to leave the country again and rebelled against the Celts. The following years were to see a full-scale invasion of other Continental tribes, Frisians, Saxons and Angles, and the Celts in successive retreats were slowly pushed back into the barren mountainous fringes of the west,[3] some over the Channel to France, where they have maintained themselves as a linguistic minority in Brittany till the present day (see p. 11).

The North Germanic expansion is of later date. After a short period of desultory pillage and plundering chiefly along the coasts of the Channel and the North Sea in the 7th and 8th centuries, the Viking attacks came to assume the nature of more organized settlement, resulting in the establishment of kingdoms in many parts of Europe from Ireland to southern Russia.

They obtained possession of the northern and eastern parts of England (the Danelaw, see p. 30), and in the period from 1014 to 1035 there were four Danish kings ruling over the entire country. Ireland was conquered by Norwegian Vikings, who as early as 839 had founded a kingdom in Dublin, from which base they later planted several colonies in Cumberland and Westmorland.

The 10th century settlement of the Danes in northern France under Rollo (Rolf) is testified to not only by the word *Normandy*, but also by numerous other place-names.[4] The rest of France saw no permanent settlement, but towns like Paris, Tours, Bordeaux, Arles, Nîmes were repeatedly sacked and ravaged.

The Vikings pushed further south, clashed with the Muslim caliphate and devastated Cadiz, Lisbon and Seville, and through what they called Nørvasund (Gibraltar) proceeded along the North African coast, penetrating in 861 as far as to Italy, where they established kingdoms in Naples and Sicily.

The eastern Vikings were also on the move and following the inland waterways thrust deep into Russia (ON Garðariki), where they set up principalities at Novgorod (ON Homgarðr) and Kiev (ON Kænugarðr) in the 9th century. In Russia they also left an impressive legacy of place and personal names behind.[5]

Other Vikings pressed south until they reached Constantinople (ON Miklagarðr), some crossed the Caspian Sea and were reported as far away as Bagdad in what they called *Serkland* ('silk country').

In the North Atlantic Vikings had possessed themselves of the Faroe Islands and Orkneys as early as 795, and in the following centuries Iceland and Greenland were colonized. In the year 1000 a small band of Vikings led by Leif set out and reached the American coast, which they called Vinland, and where they planted a colony, which seems to have survived for a couple of hundred years. Traces of their material culture have recently been unearthed at l'Anse aux Meadows (New Foundland).

The dialectal distribution of Germanic

Proto-Germanic (also referred to as Primitive or Common Germanic) is the usual term for the more or less unified language spoken during the last centuries B.C. As in the case of proto-IE (see p. 9) we are also here dealing with a hypothetical speech whose structure and vocabulary can only be inferred through a comparative study of its oldest documented descendants, e.g. Gothic and the runic inscriptions.

During the centuries around the beginning of our era, however, Germanic tribal movements must have led to an increase of dialectal divergence, and we must now distinguish three main varieties of proto-Germanic, namely what is traditionally known as East, North and West Germanic.

East Germanic. The dialects constituting this branch (Gothic, Vandalic, Burgundic) are all extinct (see p. 11). The oldest literary monument is the Visigothic Bible translation by Bishop Wulfila (4th c.), see p. 12.

North Germanic. This branch may be diagrammatically represented as follows:

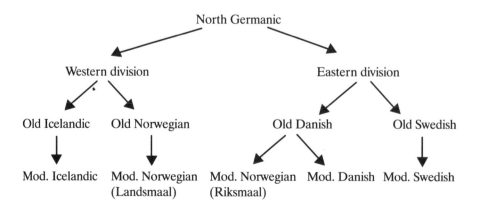

It will be observed that Danish and Norwegian belong to two different divisions. Their conspicuous similarity today is due to the fact that Danish was the official and cultural language in Norway between the 15th and 19th centuries, and has since withstood attempts to revive the old national tongue (Landsmaal).

The much greater divergence (yet mutually intelligible) between Swedish and Danish of the eastern sub-division is likewise politically conditioned (separation, warfare, etc.).

While the close relationship between Danish, Swedish and Norwegian is evident, Icelandic differs appreciably from the three, being extremely archaic and conservative of ancient speech-forms.

West Germanic. This branch may be diagrammed as follows:

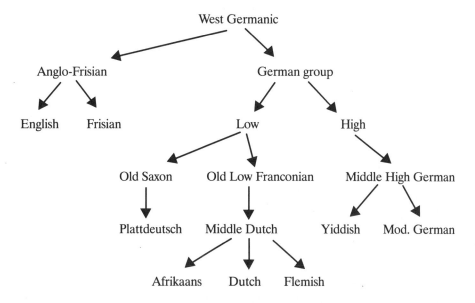

Within the West Germanic branch English and Frisian are bound together by so many striking affinities that most authorities have now set up Anglo-Frisian as a theoretical common ancestor. The German group is split up into Low and High by the operation about 600 A.D. of the so-called High German sound shift.[6]

Yiddish (i.e. Jüdisch) is the language of the Jews of Eastern Europe, who migrated from Germany during the Middle Ages. It has retained many features of the Middle High German dialects.

Afrikaans is the language of the descendants of Dutch settlers in South Africa and highly illustrative of 16th-century Dutch.

It should be borne in mind, however, that West Germanic, through which English links up with proto-Germanic, also constitutes a purely theoretical speech, there being no written evidence of it, so here again we must rely on reconstruction.

19

Principal characteristics of the Germanic languages

A number of important features have given Germanic an identity of its own, but have also obscured its relationship to the other IE languages.

I. The twofold adjective declension

In parent IE the adjective seems to have had nominal endings, i.e. it agreed in gender, number and case with the noun as we remember from Latin (e.g. *mensa magna, templum magnum, domini magni, domino magno*).

This former regularity is preserved to some extent in the Germanic so-called strong declension (see p. 89), which is inherited from IE.

The setting up of an additional weak declension characterized by the distinctive formative element *-n-* (see p. 89), on the other hand, is a specific Germanic innovation, traces of which can be observed in all descendant languages today, except in English, where the adjective has become invariable (but cp. German *ein guter Mann; der gute Mann – den guten Mann,* etc.; Danish *en god mand, den gode mand*).

The weak form is used mainly after the definite article, the strong when no such word precedes (OE *gōde fiscas* but *þa gōdan fiscas*).

II. The verbal system

This has undergone a series of radical changes since IE. Most important is the dramatic simplification of its highly complex tense and aspect system (see p. 13). Another significant innovation is that all Germanic languages develop and extend a so-called dental preterite (the *-ed* of English and the *-te* of German)[7] in what have been classed as the weak verbs (see p. 114).

a. Strong and weak verbs

The basic pattern inherited from the IE parent language is that represented by the so-called strong verbs, i.e. verbs that form their tenses by means of an internal change in the root vowel, commonly called *ablaut,*[8] e.g. *drink – drank – drunk,* German *helfen – half – geholfen*. These primary verbs have come to constitute a dwindling category in all Germanic languages. English can register a loss of more than half of its OE inventory of about 300 strong verbs, many of which (about 80) having become absorbed by the much more consistently patterned weak conjugation (e.g. *help, step, walk, climb, crow*).

The so-called weak verbs, as we have mentioned above, are a unilaterally Germanic departure. They are all secondary or derived verbs, formed chiefly from nouns by the addition of a *-jan* suffix and characterized by the dental suffix in the preterite: OE *dēman* 'deem', *dēmde* < * *dōm-jan,* * *dōm-ida*.

These consistently formed verbs came to make up a highly productive and expanding category in all Germanic languages. Verbs imported from other languages or formed to express new concepts are almost invariably assigned to this group *(blitzed, vamoosed, computerized, shanghaied,* etc).

b. The two-tense system

As we have already noted (see p. 13), the IE parent tongue possessed an extremely elaborate system of six aspects, which later also evolved tense-implications. One glance at the verb in Greek, Latin or the Slavic languages will give us an idea of the former complexity.

From this system Germanic has preserved only two inflexional or synthetic tenses, one to express the present (and future) and one to express all past time. The refinement of this basic Germanic two-tense system through the formation of analytic tenses by means of auxiliaries, however, belongs in much later periods (see p. 117).

c. Other important simplifications

– were incurred by the Germanic verb. Of the original total of three voices (see p. 13) Germanic has retained only one, namely the active, and the passive must be formed analytically by means of auxiliaries (cp. *amatur* vs. *he is loved, er wird geliebt*[9]). Of the IE elaborate mood system (see p. 13) Germanic has preserved only the indicative and the subjunctive, besides rudiments of the imperative.

The indicative-subjunctive contrast, however, is relatively well preserved in some Germanic languages today, e.g. German and Icelandic, whereas others, e.g. English and the Scandinavian languages, have gone very far in expressing the subjunctive analytically by means of the so-called modal verbs (see p. 118).

Other simplifications are later. The loss of dual inflexion in the verb (still alive in Gothic) and the levelling under one form of all persons of the plural are probably West Germanic departures.

III. The Germanic initial accent

At an early stage in its development the IE accent was probably a pitch (tonal, 'musical') accent, which is still reflected by many descendant languages, e.g. in the Balto-Slavic group.

In the Germanic group, however, the inherited accent became prevailingly a matter of stress, although some sub-languages, e.g. Swedish and Norwegian, have preserved vestiges of the original pitch pattern. Danish, however, reflects it only secondarily in the characteristic glottal stop ('stød').

The IE accent was mobile, i.e. it might rest on any syllable of a word and shift down through the declensions and conjugations, as is handily illustrated e.g. by Latin: 'amo- 'amas- 'amat, but a'mamus- a'matis- 'amant; o'rator- ora'toris; 'dominus- domi'norum, etc. We shall return to this free IE accent later when we account for the operation of Verner's Law.

In Germanic, it should be noted, the IE accent was shifted on to the first syllable, unless this was a mere prefix (e.g. over'come, zer'reissen, be'fale). This accentual shift affects all Germanic languages and has come to influence their morphology more radically than any other phonetic change. One penetrative effect is the tendency inherent in Germanic though differing in intensity (cp. English, Danish vs. German, Icelandic) to weaken and ultimately shed inflexional endings and express grammatical relations by other, chiefly analytic means.

The impact of the accent shift on Germanic has left indelible marks on its modern descendants, and will be obvious if we compare native words with words imported from such IE languages as have preserved the original free accent. Note how the accent remains stable in the Germanic word, but shifts with the adding of suffixes in the imported word: 'love, 'lover, 'lovely, 'loveable, 'lovingly, 'lovelessness, but 'photograph, pho'tographer, photo'graphic; com'pare, 'comparable, compara'bility).

IV. The Germanic consonant shift

The Germanic languages have come to stand apart from the other members of the IE language family by reason of a fairly systematic shifting of their IE heritage of stop consonants.

The regularity or 'law' behind this series of consonant changes was first discovered by the Danish linguist Rasmus Rask in 1814 and later codified by Jakob Grimm in 1822 (hence the often-used misnomer Grimm's Law). By establishing regular recurrent consonantal correspondences between the Germanic and the non-Germanic members of the IE family, Rask was able to demonstrate scientifically what was unknown to his time, namely the historical relationship between these languages and their descent from one common ancestor.

It will take us too far to give anything but the very broad outlines of this important criterion of a Germanic language.

a. Unvoiced series

IE *p*	shifting to	Germanic *f*
as reflected by:		as reflected by:
Welsh *pump,* Greek *penta,*		English *five,* German *fünf,*
Russian *pjatj,* Sanskrit *pancha,*		Danish *fem,* Icelandic *fimm*
Lithuanian *penki,*		

Similarly Latin *piscis* vs. *fish,* Iranian *pidar* vs. *father,* Hittite *pitar* 'wing' vs. *feather,* Lithuanian *padas* vs. *foot,* etc.

IE *t*	shifting to	Germanic *þ*
as reflected by:		as reflected by:
Latin *tres,* Sanskrit *tri,* Greek *treis,* Russian *tri,* Irish *tri,* Lithuanian *trys.*		English *three,* Icelandic *þrir* (the other Germanic dialects have developed *d-* or *t-* through later changes)

Similarly Latin *tenuis* vs. *thin,* Sanskrit *tarsah* vs. *thirst,* Latin *tonare* vs. *thunder,* Russian *tern* vs. *thorn,* etc.

IE *k*	shifting to	Germanic *h*
as reflected by:		as reflected by:
Latin *cornu*, Irish *corn*, Greek *keras*, Sanskrit *çṛṅgam*		English, German, Danish, Swedish *horn*

Similarly Latin *centum* vs. *hundred*, Russian *suka* vs. *hound*, Greek *cannabis* vs. *hemp*, Irish *cridhe* vs. *heart*, Latin *quis* vs. Danish *hvem*, English *who* (< OE hwā).

b. Voiced series

IE *b*	shifting to	Germanic *p*
as reflected by:		as reflected by:
Lithuanian *troba*, Latin *turba*, Irish *treabh*		*English thorpe*, Dutch *dorp*, Swedish *torp*, Danish *-(s)trup* (in place-names)

Similarly Lithuanian *dubus* vs. *deep*, Greek *cannabis* vs. *hemp*, Russian *slabuii* vs. *sleep*, Latin *(s)lubricus* vs. *slippery*, etc.

IE *d*	shifting to	Germanic *t*
as reflected by:		as reflected by:
Latin *dentem* (acc.), Sanskrit *danta*, Lithuanian *dantis*, Greek *odont-*, Welsh *dant*		English *tooth*, Danish *tand*, German *Zahn* (see p. 19), Icelandic *tönn*

Similarly Russian *dva* vs. *two*, Greek *edein* vs. *eat*, Latin *decem* vs. *ten*, etc.

IE *g*	shifting to	Germanic *k*
as reflected by:		as reflected by:
Latin *genu*, Greek *gonu*, Hittite *genu*		Danish *knæ*, English *knee*, German *Knie*

Similarly Latin *ager* vs. *acre*, Sanskrit *yuga* vs. *yoke*, etc.

c. Aspirated series

In Germanic the heritage of IE voiced aspirated stop consonants lost their aspiration.

IE *bh*	shifting to	Germanic *b*
as reflected by:		as reflected by:
Sanskrit *bhrátar*, Irish *brathair*, Russian *brat*, Iranian *birādar*, Lithuanian *bralis*[10]		English *brother*, Danish, Swedish *broder*, German *Bruder*, Icelandic *broðir*

IE *dh*	shifting to	Germanic *d*
as reflected by:		as reflected by:
Sanskrit *dhwar*, Lithuanian *duris*, Welsh *drws*, Russian *dver*[11]		English *door*, Danish *dør*, Dutch *deur*, Icelandic *dyrr*

IE *gh*	*shifting to*	Germanic *g*
as reflected by:		as reflected by:
Latin *hostis*, (< * *ghostis*),		English *guest*, German *Gast*,
Russian *goste*		Danish *gæst*

It should be observed, however, that no shifting takes place in the combinations *sp*, *st*, *sk*. Hence correspondences like Latin *spuo* – *spit*, Latin *sto* – *stand*, Latin *piscis* – Danish *fisk*.

The Germanic consonant shift has provided us with an excellent test of borrowed words in all Germanic languages, the original unshifted consonant indicating a later loan, usually from Latin or Greek: *foot* – *pedal*, *five* – *penta(gon)*, *fee* – *pecuniary*, *father* – *paternal*; *three* – *triangle* – *Trinity*, *thunder* – *intone*, *thin* – *tenuous*; *hound* – *canine*, *hundred* – *(per)cent*, *hearty* – *cordial*, *while* – *tranquil*; *slippery* – *lubricate*, *purse* – *bursary*, *lip* – *labial*; *tooth* – *dental*, *ten* – *decimal*, *eat* – *edible*, *two* – *dual*; *cold* – *gelid*, *knee* – *genu(flexion)*, *acre* – *agrarian*, *kind* – *gender*, *quean* – *gynae(cology)*; *brother* – *fraternal*, *break* – *fragile*, *bear* – *(con)fer*; *death* – *funeral*, *do* – *facile*, *garden* – *hort(iculture)*, *guest* – *host* ... and countless others.

Dating the shift
Various attempts have been made to date the Germanic consonant shift, but none of the arguments adduced can alone be considered conclusive evidence. The earliest recorded Germanic, namely the Scandinavian runic inscriptions from the third century A.D., have all shifted consonants, so the shift must antedate them.

But it is difficult to establish a terminus ante quem non. Germanic loanwords in Finnish and Lappish (see p. 12) show both shifted and unshifted consonants, but unfortunately we do not know from exactly what period in the long pre-historic contact between these two peoples they date. Some have suggested that the earliest loans may go back to 5-400 B.C.

The Celtic loan-words in Germanic may provide a more reliable criterion, for we have every reason to assume that these words were adopted by the Germanic tribes during the great Celtic expansion in the last five centuries before the Christian era.

These loans from Celtic display a curious mixture of shifted and unshifted consonants, e.g. * *ambaktos* 'servant' (cp. OE *ombeht*, where we would have expected something like * *ompeht*).

The collective weight of such and similar evidence, however, seems to point to the last three or four centuries B.C. as the most plausible operational period of the consonant shift, though of course it could have taken place somewhat earlier.

V. Verner's Law
Already Rask and Grimm were puzzled by the fact that some of the consonants in going through the shift might be voiced in the process. These cur-

ious exceptions were not explained until 1875 when the Danish linguist Karl Verner discovered what was later to be published in his 'Eine Ausnahme der ersten Lautverschiebung'.

The consonants in question were the unvoiced stops *p, t, k*, which for reasons unknown sometimes appeared with the expected *f, þ, h* values, but sometimes as the voiced counterparts *b, ð, ʒ*. IE *s* also seemed to take part in the change and became *z*, which in all recorded Germanic (except Gothic) is represented graphically by <r>, in ON by <R>.

The appearance of these enigmatic voiced variants where we would have expected their unvoiced counterparts *f, þ, h* was explained by Verner as being due to the influence of the IE mobile or free accent (see p. 21), which must have existed for some time in early proto-Germanic, before it came to be permanently fixed on the first syllable. The voiced fricative appeared, he found out, when the preceding vowel was unaccented. If it was accented, we would get the unvoiced fricative.

Once explained, it is easy to understand what actually happened. If the accent rested on the vowel immediately preceding the consonant, this consonant became protected from the influence of the voiced vocalic surroundings (see examples below) and therefore remained unvoiced. If these conditions were not present, the consonant became voiced.[12] It also explains why voicing never took place when the consonant occurred in initial position.

This important discovery can be exemplified directly in Gothic,[13] and to some extent also in modern German:

Sanskrit	Gothic
(note position of accent)	
pitár	fadar [faːðar]
bhrátar	broþar

The impact of Verner's Law has manifested itself most strikingly in the comparison of adjectives (e.g. *taller – tallest*, reflecting an original shift of accent from the comparative to the superlative) – and in the verbs, where it can be seen not only in *was – were* (<* wæzun*), but also in seemingly anomalous forms like *seethe – sodden, lose – (for)lorn, rear – raise, freeze – frore, see* (cp. German *sehen*) *– sight, flee* (cp. German *fliehen*) *– flight*, etc. where the consonant alternation therefore must be traced back to differences in the IE accentual pattern. The *was – were* change is due to an original shift of accent from the singular to the plural as still reflected e.g. by Latin (see p. 21).

We might turn to other Germanic languages for additional illustration. German *schneiden – geschnitten, (vier)zig – (vier)zehn, war – gewesen, verlieren – Verlust*, Danish *glas – glar, hest* (<* hanhista*) *– hingst*, etc.

We are now able to establish the relative chronology of the three important Germanic sound-changes discussed above. Verner's Law must have been in operation after the consonant shift, involving as it does the results of it, whereas the fixation of the Germanic accent on the first syllable must have followed after Verner's Law, which, as we have seen, presupposes the operation of the IE mobile accent.

Sources of our knowledge of proto-Germanic
As we have already mentioned, Germanic recorded speech can be traced no further back than the scanty Scandinavian runic inscriptions of the third and the Gothic Bible translation of the fourth century of our era. To form an idea of the linguistic situation antecedent to these, however, we must, as in the case of IE (see p. 13), resort to 1) reconstruction on the basis of a comparative study of the earliest attested forms, or to 2) secondary evidence.

1) An example of *reconstruction:* The Germanic word for e.g. *stone* appears in its earliest recorded stages with the following forms: OE *stān*, OHG *stein*, ON *steinn*, Gothic *stains*, showing the diphthong *ai* to be the most plausible representative of the ancestral form, and OE *ā* to be a secondary development. The safety of such an assumption is further borne out by runic *stainaR*, with *R* < *z (see p. 25).

Germanic loan-words in Finnish (see p. 24) like e.g. *kuningas* 'king' make * *staināz* a possible proto-Germanic ancestor of *stone,* and that the vocalic element in the suffix *-āz* is not a wild guess, is suggested by Latin *-us* (from earlier *-os*), Greek *-os* (cp. Latin *hostis* – runic *gastiR*).

2) Secondary evidence is primarily scattered proper names on coins and in inscriptions of other cultures, or stray Germanic words reported by Roman and Greek authors (e.g. Pytheas of Massilia (4th c. B.C.), Caesar (1st c. B.C.), Pliny and Tacitus (1st c. A.D.)). But unfortunately the evidence culled from such sources is far from reliable, since we can rarely exclude the possibility of sound substitution. When Caesar in his 'De Bello Gallico' wonderingly describes a stiff-legged animal which the Germani called *alces* 'elk' (OE *elh*, German *Elch*), dare we then take it to indicate that *-k-* was still unshifted when he heard it (which would indeed be a most welcome terminus ante quem non for the dating of the consonant shift, see p. 24) – or is he simply trying to render Germanic fricative *h* by the closest substitute he could find?

That the Germanic tribes must have had a long and intimate contact with the Finns and the Lapps in the centuries around the beginning of our era is evident from the adoption of numerous Germanic loan-words by these non-IE languages. As ascertained by the Danish linguist Vilhelm Thomsen (1869), there are in West Finnish about 400 words and in Lappish about 600 words of Germanic origin.

It is a remarkable fact that these loans have undergone so few sound-changes that they appear even today in forms which reflect a pre-historic stage – more archaic in fact than any surviving record of Germanic – with such fidelity that they can often be used to confirm hypothetical forms arrived at through reconstruction, as we have just shown above. A few examples will suffice: *kuningas* 'king' (proto-Germ. * *kuningaz*, ON *konungr*), *kulta* 'gold' (Goth. *gulþ*), *rengas* 'ring' (* *hrengaz*, ON *hringr*).

CHAPTER III

The external history of English

The Old English period

General background

By 600 the invading Angles, Saxons and Jutes (see p. 17) had established their power firmly in England, and were slowly relegating its former Celtic-speaking population to the mountainous extremities of the west. The coming of the three West Germanic tribes marks the beginning of the OE period.

The Jutes, on the authority of Bede's Iuti, settled in Kent, Hampshire and on the Isle of Wight. The regional distribution of the Saxons and the Angles is reflected by place-names like Essex (: East Saxons), Sussex, Wessex and (East) Anglia. From the latter tribe is also derived what was later to become the name of the entire nation (*Englisc, Englalond*), probably because the name Saxon was too often confused with the Saxons on the Continent.

There is nothing but scant and vague documentary evidence for this early phase of the settlement, so we must rely primarily on information drawn from archaeology and the place-name material to estimate the character of the Anglo-Saxon penetration of the island.

Here we should consult such items of the place-name inventory as can be assigned exclusively to the period of earliest settlement. Place-names in *-ing(s)* (OE *-ingas*) provide important clues, suggesting as they do not only the pressure inland of the Anglo-Saxon invaders and the settlement areas first chosen by them, but also how these tribes were socially organized. The first component of this name-type is usually a personal name probably once borne by some tribal chieftain, the *-ing* suffix denoting 'descendants from' or 'followers of' that man. *Hastings* thus means 'area where the followers of Hæsta had settled'. Similarly *Reading* (: *Reada*), *Gipping* (: *Gyppa*), *Wittering* (: *Withere*), etc.

Equally suggestive are place-names in *-ingham*, containing the genitive suffix *-inga* + *-hām* 'homestead', which are supposed to be of similar antiquity, e.g. *Birmingham* 'homestead of the followers of Beorma', *Ellingham* (: *Ella*), *Whittingham* (: *Hwita*), etc.[1] Not surprisingly, the heaviest concentration of these names is found in Sussex, Kent and Essex, from where the Anglo-Saxon expansion radiated westward.

Of the social life, traditions and pagan deities of these Anglo-Saxon tribesmen we have very little first-hand knowledge. Archaeology can tell us something, but much must be deduced from secondary sources like Tacitus'

'Germania' or through the indirect evidence of place-names or Old Norse mythology.

As their poetry was probably handed down from generation to generation through oral delivery, its vocabulary and imagery may reflect some aspects of their life back in the pagan epoch. Their poems, no matter whether they celebrate glorious victory (Brunanburh) or glorious defeat (Maldon) or heroic adventure (Beowulf), are homage to martial valour and unflinching loyalty. A passion for the sea and its hardships looms large in their imagery (they have 24 synonyms for 'sea' and 50 for 'ship') and their love of battle, weapons and personal courage is reflected by an equally specialized lexicon. Of heathen sentiment the poems tell us little, however, since they owe their preservation to Christian clerks, who wrote them down in the 9th and 10th centuries and sometimes in the process gave them a varnish of Christian morality or interpolated new passages or edifying conclusions.

The great number of place-names associated with Anglo-Saxon paganism include *Weedon* (OE *wīg* 'place of heathen worship'), *Harrowick* (OE *hærg* 'heathen temple'). West Germanic deities like Woden and Thunor 'the Thunderer' (corresponding to Scand. Odin and Thor) linger on in *Wednesbury*, *Woodnesbury*, *Thundridge*, *Thundersfield*. The war-god Tiw (Scand. Tyr) is found in *Tuesley, Tysoe*.[2, 3]

Later these heathen tribes were to merge for protection into a number of kingdoms of fluctuating political supremacy and cultural importance. The most important of these were Wessex (the kingdom of King Alfred the Great), Northumbria (with Christian centres of learning like Lindisfarne and Jarrow), Mercia (the kingdom of Offa), Kent, East Anglia, Sussex and Essex. They are sometimes referred to collectively as the Anglo-Saxon Heptarchy.

Christianity was brought to Anglo-Saxon England in 597 when St Augustine landed in Kent with his Roman missionaries, but by then the northern kingdoms of the country had already for some time been exposed to the influence of Celtic Christianity, which had extended its missionary field from Ireland to Scotland (St Columba in Iona 563). By the close of the 7th century, however, the new faith seems to have been firmly established everywhere in its Roman garb.

In the years after England's conversion to Christianity it became a European centre of learning with such leading figures as Bede, Ealhwine (better known as Alcuin), Aldhelm and Benedict Bisceop. St Boniface, alias Wynfrith, a Wessex monk, brought Christianity to pagan Germany, and Willebrord of Northumbria became the apostle of the Frisians and the first Christian missionary in Denmark.

Among important innovations brought by the Christian missionaries were the Roman alphabet, parchment, and the habit of writing. We are now able to follow the development of English on much safer ground.

Another important linguistic effect of English cultural contact with Continental Christianity was a growing need to borrow words, and it started with a substantial import of Latin words into the vocabulary (see p. 40).

Periods

For practical reasons we may divide Anglo-Saxon (now usually referred to as OE) into the following periods 1) Pr(imitive) OE, i.e. the period prior to the emergence in the 7th century of written documents (another reconstructional phase), 2) early OE, i.e. the period down to about 900 and 3) late OE from 900 to about 1100. These dates, it should be emphasized, are (like those we shall be using later in distinguishing OE, ME, and EMnE) conventional and arbitrary, dependent as they are upon what linguistic or cultural features we select as decisive criteria.

Dialects

The tribal settlement pattern and some of the most powerful Anglo-Saxon kingdoms are reflected by the names of the four principal dialectal areas. Two of these are known as Anglian, namely Northumbrian (north of the Humber) and Mercian (between the Humber and the Thames), the south-Thames area being divided between West-Saxon and Kentish (the latter descending from the language of the Jutes, see p. 17).

Far and away the most important dialect, however, is *West Saxon,* the language in which nearly all recorded OE literature has come down to us. It is the language of great prose-writers like King Alfred, Wulfstan and Ælfric. The ascendancy of that dialect is due to various convergent causes. Wessex was a kingdom of political unity and stability under such powerful rulers as Ecgberth (802-39) and Alfred (871-900) – a fact which enabled it to withstand with some success the incursions of the heathen Vikings, who with their sacking of the monastic centres of learning had caused a permanent setback to all literary and scholarly activity in the North.

Another important factor is the endeavours of King Alfred to re-establish Christian culture and learning in Wessex. He reformed education and tried to extend literacy beyond the clerical professions and for that purpose recruited scholars wherever they were available, many Northumbrian, Irish, Frankish or Continental Saxon scholars.

Through his inspiration and personal involvement King Alfred's West Saxon vernacular came to be the medium of an impressive array of prose works, chief of which are a national history (the Parker manuscript of the Anglo-Saxon Chronicle was written here), translations or paraphrases mainly from Latin sources (e.g. Orosius, Cura Pastoralis, Bede's Historia Ecclesiastica) and the transcription of works – mainly poetry – of Northumbrian origin.

A vast circulation throughout the country of documents, charters and letters from the royal scriptoria at Winchester also helped West Saxon to achieve the status of what we may call a written standard for OE. This early use of the vernacular and not Latin for official purposes gives English a unique position among the languages of Europe.

What we know about OE, it should be noted, is therefore bound to derive mainly from that West Saxon standard, though, as we shall see later, Anglian dialects have contributed much more significantly to the shaping of modern English.

The next time we shall witness the emergence of a written standard is nearly 500 years later and in a quite different part of the country (see p. 35).

The Vikings

As we have mentioned in a previous chapter (see p. 17), inroads by aggressors the Anglo-Saxons usually referred to as Danes started as early as the closing decades of the 8th century with the sacking of the Northumbrian monasteries. Later, however, the attacks assumed a different character. What had started as plunder and harassment ended in conquest. In 865 the Anglo-Saxon Chronicle records the landing of 'a mycel hǣþen here' (: a big heathen army), which in a succession of brilliant campaigns led by the sons of Regnar Lodbrog obtained possession of most of eastern England. Only the powerful King Alfred of Wessex was able to withstand their onslaught and in 886 bought peace by ceding all territory north of Watling Street (following a line running roughly from London to Chester), which came to be known as *the Danelaw* (i.e. the territory where Danish law was imposed).

Important for the future history of English, however, is the fact that 'the big heathen army', unlike their many precursors, remained in the country, abandoned their predatory ways, and, to quote the Chronicle again, 'shared the land amongst them and began to plough and eke out a livelihood for themselves'. In other words the Vikings became farmers (as they had probably also been at home) and slowly assimilated with the native population. As they, unlike their kinsmen in Normandy, Ireland and Russia, were not linguistically isolated, their language probably survived for a couple of centuries. English and Scandinavian were at that time no further differentiated than that they must still have been mutually intelligible with some patience and forbearance.

The linguistic legacy of this conquest, penetrating as we shall see later even into the grammatical structure of the language (p. 107) and with a contribution of loan-words (p. 42) that seems redundant in that it more often than not overlaps with native and already perfectly adequate vocabulary, points to a peaceful and intimate fusion of the two population groups in the Danelaw. There is nothing in the Scandinavian linguistic contribution to English that suggests that the Vikings ever came to constitute a ruling aristocracy as the Normans did. The linguistic evidence testifies to intimate contact over an extended period and on a broad social level.

In the following century Alfred's son, Edward the Elder, and his grandson Athelstan embarked upon a gradual, systematic, but not very violent reconquest of the territories that had been ceded to the Danes, and by 924 when Edward died, almost the entire Danelaw was back in English hands, its population now recognizing the Wessex king as their overlord.

Hostilities, however, gradually took on a new aspect, turning now into national and highly organized warfare when Svein Forkbeard, the king of

Denmark, completed the conquest of the island in the early years of the 11th century. In 1014 Svein became king of England, having thrown the Anglo-Saxon king Æthelred and his French queen into exile in Normandy, and until 1042 England was now ruled by a dynasty of Danish kings (Svein, Canute the Great, Harold and Hardecanute).

Again it is the place-names which, used with caution, may give us an idea of the extent and the geographical distribution of the Scandinavian settlement. They are nearly all located north of the Danelaw boundary with the heaviest concentration in Lincolnshire and Yorkshire. Most commonly represented are Scandinavian place-names containing the elements -by, -thorpe (Danish -trup), -toft, -thwaite (Danish -tved). These and many others will be dealt with in more detail in a later chapter (see p. 44).[4]

The Scandinavian language, no doubt reinforced by later influxes of settlers under Canute, survived in the British Isles for a thousand years. In England it probably died out in the 12th century, but in isolated Shetland and Orkney the language of the Scandinavian landnamsmen preserved its integrity much longer. It was spoken until as recently as about 1800 and was called *Norn*.

Scandinavian came to leave a lasting imprint on English as we shall see in later chapters, not only lexically (see p. 42), but also phonologically (see p. 43), semantically (see p. 43), and grammatically (see p. 107).

The ME period

The Norman Conquest
After the extinction of the Danish dynasty of Viking kings with the death of Hardecanute in 1042, Edward (the Confessor) acceded to the throne. He had been brought up in Normandy where his father Æthelred had lived in exile since the Danish seizure of his throne in England. The French-speaking monarch introduced a great number of Norman prelates, artists and nobles with whom he surrounded himself during the 24 years of his reign.

The linguistic influence emanating from this short pre-conquest period of French culture will be dealt with later p. 46.

Edward the Confessor died in 1066, but his time on the throne spent in monastic self-denial and prayer had left the country with no successor. The actual ruler of the country had long been Godwin, the powerful Earl of Wessex. It was the succession to the throne of Godwin's son Harold in 1066 that set the stage for the Norman invasion. William, Duke of Normandy, was second cousin to the late king, and claimed to have been promised the throne.

The Normans were direct descendants from Vikings, who as early as 912 under Rollo (Rolf) had established their own 'Danelaw' in northern France, but they had since given up their language and were by 1066 French, or more precisely, Norman-speaking.

The Norman victory at Hastings was decisive, and William firmly established his sovereignty in the following years by also subduing the northern provinces. His Normans with astonishing efficiency proceeded to turn Anglo-Saxon England into a feudal state modelled on their highly organized homeland. The archbishoprics of Canterbury and York were taken over by Normans and only two of the English bishops (Wulfstan of Worcester and Giso of Wells) outlived William's short reign. By 1070 only one of the twelve earls of the realm was English. The contact with the Norman cultural hinterland, however, remained uninterrupted, and most of the nobility, lay as well as ecclesiastical, held offices and estates on both sides of the Channel. John of Salisbury, the most learned classical scholar of the time, died as bishop of Chartres in 1180.

The impact of the Norman conquest on Anglo-Saxon England was extensive. There was hardly any field of human activity unaffected by it. Innovations took place in all walks of life, architecture, letters, art, devotion, commerce, social manners, military organization, government and institutions, etc., and were reflected by a wholesale adoption of loan-words into the language. We shall deal with these in some detail in a later chapter (see p. 46).

During the first centuries after the Conquest two languages were spoken side by side – English and Norman-French, the latter the language of status and prestige, that of the Law Courts, the learned professions and the ruling feudal aristocracy. The first king to use English as his native speech was Henry Bolingbroke, who died in 1413.

Assimilation of the two peoples, however, appears to have been slow. The intake of loan-words bears this out. French words do not appear in records in any great number until after 1200.

The reign of Henry II (1154-89) marks the climax of Anglo-Norman culture. Oxford University was founded in 1167 and Cambridge University in 1209. A number of important literary works were written in Anglo-Norman, including the 'Lais' of Marie de France, the 'Roman de Brut' by Wace, 'Merlin' by Robert de Boron and the 'Tristan' of Thomas of Brittany. The Provençal tradition of troubadour poetry and the conventions of the continental mediaeval romance *(amour courtois)* were introduced in this period.

The co-existence of two languages in any given area (diglossia) always exposes one to the risk of being eventually elbowed out by the other. The language that prevails is not necessarily that spoken by the majority, but usually the prestige-carrying one, that used by the economic upper classes, by those in charge of government, church, and education. The result is that the use of the two languages now shifts from being ethnically to being socially conditioned. The fates of the Celtic languages in the British Isles provide abundant illustration.

The speech situation in the early Middle Ages indeed boded ill for English, and it cannot be pictured more concisely than Robert of Gloucester did in his 'Chronicle' (c. 1300): 'vor bote a man conne Frenss, me telþ of him lute, ac lowe men holdeþ to engliss and to hor owe speche'. The necessary pre-conditions, socially and linguistically, thus seem to have been present for an eventual triumph of French in England. That English long before 1400, however, had emerged victorious, though by no means unscarred, from this battle of tongues, will appear to be due to the interaction of several factors, linguistic as well as socio-political, as we shall see now.

An important factor was that John, King of England and Duke of Normandy, in 1204 forfeited his dukedom to his liege lord, the French king. The loss of Normandy severed the contact of the Norman aristocracy with their cultural hinterland. It was no longer possible to possess land and hold offices on both sides of the Channel. Feudalism did not countenance allegiance to two different crowns.

Further, the period of protracted warfare against France commonly known as the Hundred Years' War (1338-1455) conduced to sparking a spirit of growing nationalism in England, causing in its wake also a permanent setback to the use of French, which had come to be increasingly associated with the language of the enemy.

About 1350 most of Europe was harassed by what is known as the Black Death, which caused incredible fatalities notably among the lower classes, who were less able to isolate themselves. The long-term effect of the depletion of the ranks of the working classes was an acute shortage of labour, resulting again in rising wages and, concomitantly, a steadily increasing economic importance and social prestige for the English-speaking section of the population. Their language could now slowly free itself from the stigma of being the language of the uneducated and unprivileged.

A fourth factor tending to make English an eligible alternative to French is purely linguistic. In France the dialect of Paris, also known as Central French, had become the standard of culture and fashion as early as 1200, and the cultural ascendancy of France in the 13th century made her language universally admired all over Europe.

But the Normans in England spoke Norman-French, at the time of the Conquest an independent, prestige-neutral dialect, but after the rise of Parisian French slowly relegated to a provincial substandard. Moreover Anglo-Norman, after two centuries of wear and tear in the mouths of often bilingual speakers, had undergone so much change that it was no longer readily understood by Continental Frenchmen.[5]

There was thus no incentive for the Norman aristocracy in England to cling to their original tongue. Instead some tried, and there is ample evidence for that, to learn to master the now more prestigeful Parisian standard, which had become the fashion.

The French loan-words bear witness to this whole change in the linguistic situation (see p. 46). Before 1300 they were adopted chiefly through Anglo-Norman spoken idiom, but from the 14th century onwards Parisian French begins to be the primary source, now entering mainly through academic and literary channels.

French was gradually disused as a spoken upper-class language in the 13th century. In 1362 the Law Courts officially abandoned French,[6] and in 1363 Parliament was opened for the first time with a speech in English, though statutes continued to be enrolled in French (or Latin) till as late as the 1420's. About 1350 English began to be reinstated in the schools and soon superseded French there.

Dialects

The language spoken in England from about 1150 down to about 1500 is customarily referred to as *Middle English*. The term, however, does not cover any self-contained unified speech, but is rather the common denominator for a continuum of equally important and prestige-neutral dialects, none of which was to achieve universal acceptance till after 1400 when standardization was active again and the East Midland or London variety began to assume the status of a recognized educated standard.

The whole development may be crudely diagrammed like this:

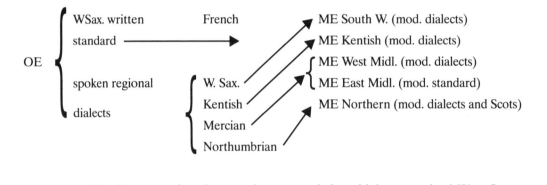

The Normans, in other words, removed the widely recognized West Saxon standard (see p. 29) by taking over the offices of those who used and cultivated it in church and administration and imposing French (or Latin) in its stead.

With the growing recognition of English, however, there was no longer a recognized standard, and with no such norm to guide them, vernacular writers found themselves compelled to resort to their own dialects, which they rendered graphically as best they could. John Barbour wrote his 'Bruce' in Northern (Scots) dialect, Langland his 'Piers Plowman' in West Midland, John of Trevisa his Higden translation in South Western dialect, Michael of Northgate his 'Ayenbyte of Inwyt' in 'engliss of kent', and Chaucer, Gower, Wiclyffe and Mandeville their work in the up and coming East Midland dialect.

It is only natural that such efforts would often be inconsistent and contain wide scope for individualism and experiment (as in the case of Orm c. 1200), but the picture these crude and tentative phonetic spellings present of ME speech is much more revealingly true to life than that which must be inferred from behind some conventional scribal standard.

The Modern English period

The ascendancy of East Midland, a direct descendant not of the old West Saxon standard but of Mercian as we have just shown above, is due to many chiefly geographical, social and cultural factors. It became the dialect of London, the centre of cultural and intellectual activity, the seat of the Court, of Parliament and the entire central administration. In the late Middle Ages London had grown to become the centre of industry and commerce and as such attracted rural migration from all parts of the country, whose speech, as we shall see, soon came to leave its provincial imprint on the new rising standard.

Of great importance for the growing status of East Midland was also the presence of the universities of Oxford and Cambridge and of the leading public schools in that same speech area. It was also the dialect used and perfected by great poets like Chaucer and Gower (a Kentishman born) for their literary work and by Wiclyffe (a Yorkshireman born) for his Bible translation and pamphleteering[7].

In 1476 the art of printing was introduced from the Netherlands by *William Caxton,* who set up his wooden press at Westminster. Before 1500 an astonishing number of incunabula had spread all over the country. Though many of these early products of moveable type were in Latin, their importance for the standardization and spread of the dialect of London and of a growing uniformity of spelling (see p. 60) can hardly be overestimated.

The language of London, like Parisian French much earlier (see p. 33), was no longer confined to a specific geographical area, but in process of becoming a widely diffused educated class-dialect.

A spoken standard, however, was much later than the one that applied to spelling. When Sir Thomas Elyot in 1531 complains of the 'corrupte and fowle pronuntiation' which sons of gentlemen might pick up from their nannies, he is probably referring to sociolect and not to regional speech, but there is some evidence that upper-class London and southern speech already by the 16th century had begun to serve as a model for many. The first dictionaries attempting to 'fix pronunciation' began to appear in the latter half of the 18th century.

About 1500 the full tide of what is known as the Renaissance reached England. In 1453 Constantinople, a Mecca for students of classical antiquity, had been sacked by the Ottoman Turks and the 'refugee' scholars were warmly welcomed to the courts and universities of Western Europe, particularly in Germany and Italy. The libraries and expertise of these scholars were disseminated to ever increasing numbers of people through the invention of printing.

The impact of Renaissance Latinity is noticeable in all European languages, but English seems to have been much more strongly affected than the others. It is probably the vast number of cognate French words adopted in ME that paves the way for what now looks like an almost reckless introduction of Latin vocabulary (see p. 41).

The influence of the Classical Renaissance, led by scholars like John Colet, Thomas More, Thomas Linacre and Erasmus, culminated in England between 1500 and 1650. The most outstanding works of the early period, More's 'Utopia' and Erasmus' 'Praise of Folly', were in Latin. Bacon wrote all the works to which he attached importance in Latin. To write in English was 'to wryte in sand'.

Latin, with its asset of universal currency, became to the learned world a kind of second tongue, the only fit medium for scientific and scholarly endeavour. Admired for its expressiveness, flexibility and above all consistent orthography, it successfully supplied the demands for vocabulary created by a dramatic expansion of knowledge and by the opening up of the frontiers of the known world.

The use of English for scholarly achievement, however, was continued in this period, but was tentative and experimental (Ascham, Elyot, Bacon, Mulcaster), and it was not until the 17th century that there was a real incentive for the learned to 'prostitute their muse in the vulgar tongue'. The reason was largely commercial. By about 1600 literacy had been extended to between one third and half of the population. For the 'mercenary stationer' the profitable market provided by an increasingly influential inquisitive middle class was a factor now to be reckoned with.

Conducive to the gradual disuse of Latin as the language of international currency, in England as well as abroad, was also the rise of nationalism in the 17th and 18th centuries, which not only greatly enhanced the prestige of using the vernacular, but also contributed to an increased preoccupation with questions of correctness and standardization, as we shall see later.

But the position of English as the medium of drama and poetry had, however, remained unchallenged by Latin. The work of such towering figures as Spenser, Shakespeare, Ben Jonson, and Milton established English once and for all as one of the great literary languages of the world. More influential than any single factor in diffusing a literary standard to all corners of England, however, were the Bible translation of William Tyndale (1524) and that of 1611, known as the Authorised Version.

This period also saw the first feeble beginnings of the scholarly study of the English language itself. The imposition of prescriptive grammar, the dabbling with new spelling systems, the compilation of dictionaries and spelling books all have their roots in the 16th and 17th centuries (see p.61).

The overall desire was to refine and stabilize the language, to give it a rational and permanent form by eradicating the aberrations of 'fowle and corrupt usage'. The rationalistic spirit of the 18th century gave further impetus to the sustained efforts of cultivating a standard of correctness (Swift, Dryden, Sheridan, Dr Johnson), and there were urgent requests for the establishment of an English Academy on the model of France to legislate in linguistic matters. Language should in no way be allowed to take care of itself. The idea of an Academy, however, petered out after the death of its royal votary Queen Anne in 1714. Her successor on the throne George I spoke German.

The 18th century was the heyday of prescriptive grammar. The preoccupation of the age with 'ascertainment' and stabilization would naturally provide a market for grammars whose aim was to prescribe and proscribe and not to describe. Reason and authority (largely by appealing to Latin models) now for the first time began to seriously dispute the claim of usage to be 'the only certain mistress of language'. Unlike the 16th and 17th century grammarians (Bullokar, Wallis, Ben Jonson), who left little or no imprint on contemporary or later grammatical practice, the 18th-century prescriptive school laid down rules which in many cases have survived to this day, e.g. the regulation of the use of *shall* and *will* (see p. 133), the condemnation of double negatives (see p. 94) and of *you was* for the singular (see p. 149, note 11). By far the most influential normative grammar was Bishop Lowth's 'A Short Introduction to English Grammar' (1762), which went through no less than 22 editions.

By the end of the 18th century the English language was in the main fixed in its present form, grammatically, orthographically, and, apart from a few minor details, also in pronunciation. But in the area of lexical borrowing there are important accretions to take note of. The 17th and 18th centuries were a period of great colonial expansion, which was to spread the English language to all continents of the world.

The opening up of the new world to European colonization was owed chiefly to Spanish and Portuguese initiative (Columbus 1492, Vasco da Gama 1498), but England was slow to seize her share, and long seemed content to waylay the Spanish galleons when they returned from the Spanish Main. In 1600, however, Elizabeth granted a charter to the East India Company, and in 1607 Virginia, the first colony in America, was founded and others followed in rapid succession.[8] Canada, held by the French, passed into British hands subsequent on the capture of Quebec by Thomas Wolfe in 1759.

In 1770 the British flag was planted in New Zealand and Australia (Thomas Cook), which latter territory served for many years as a penal settlement.

British control over South Africa began as early as 1795 with the seizure of the Cape province from Dutch settlers, whereas the opening up of the rest of Africa is largely a 19th-century achievement, with England taking the lion's share from France.

In India, the East India Company had established settlements and trading stations at Bombay and Calcutta early in the 17th century in keen competition with the French and the Dutch. After a series of successful campaigns against the French the victory ultimately fell to the British, and India became part of the Empire after the state had taken over the rights of the East India Company. In India English became the language of business and administration, and it is today, as in all the former African colonies, a second language for almost everybody.

The influx of words from this vast colonial empire is enormous (see p. 53) and has reached the English language either directly through personal contact, trade or barter with the native populations or indirectly through the languages of the nations that vied with Britain in the acquisition of overseas domains, notably French, Spanish and to some extent Dutch.

Particularly the number of words entering English through the intermediary of Spanish is great, and some of the earliest can be traced back to the prolonged period of piratical harassment of the Spanish colonies on the Central and South American shores (Hawkins, Drake, Raleigh).

Centuries of isolation from developments in the mother tongue and the encounter with other languages, native or immigrant, have caused the English language spoken in this far-flung colonial Empire to gradually diverge and later develop what could today be called regional standards in their own right. Common to all of these, however, is that they still retain a number of features, lexically, grammatically, as well as phonologically, that were characteristic of the language of the first settlers, but which have since disappeared from the standard language in England.[9]

English, which a few centuries ago was what Florio in one of his Anglo-Italian Dialogues (1603) characterized as 'worthless beyond Dover', is now not only the most widespread language in the world, but also the language spoken by most people if by 'language' we mean self-contained unitary speech. But it has ceased to be a national tongue which serves to identify the English.

CHAPTER IV

The growth of the vocabulary

The Celtic element

The fact that the original language of Britain was Celtic (see p. 11) might lead us to assume that substantial elements of that language would have been absorbed into that of the Anglo-Saxon conquerors.

But the influence of the Celtic aborigines upon OE is negligible. Only about a dozen words can with reasonable certainty be ascribed to them, such as *brocc* 'badger', *binn* 'basket', *bratt* 'cloak', *cumb* 'valley', *ass* 'ass' (though ultimately from Latin *asinus*). A few loans owe their introduction to Celtic Christianity (see p. 28). They include *clugge* 'bell', *drȳ* 'sorcerer' (< *druid* through i-umlaut), and possibly *cursian* 'curse'. The long vowel in OE *crīst* 'Christ' also seems to point to Celtic rather than to Roman Christianity. Latin has a short vowel.[1]

But Celtic place-names abound and increase in density as we move west over the island, reflecting a gradual expansion of Anglo-Saxon territory. There are comparatively few in the southeast where the Anglo-Saxons first landed, which seems to suggest that if the Celts were anywhere exterminated by the invaders, it could only have been in those areas. Important Celtic place-names are *Cornwall, Kent, Devon, London, Leeds, Carlisle, Dover*. Celto-Latin hybrids like *Win(chester), Don(caster), Glou(cester)* contain as second element Latin *-castra* 'military camp' (see p. 40). *Lincoln* probably reflects a latinized Celtic form (the Romans called it *Lindum Colonia*). Well-known Celtic river names include *Thames, Severn, Avon, Trent, Wye, Esk, Usk*. Ancient Celtic tribal names are contained in *Cornwall* (: Cornubian Welsh), *Cumberland* (: land of the Cymru), *Devon* (: land of the Dumnonii).

It is important to note that the vast majority of Celtic words in English are late imports. A good many owe their introduction to Walter Scott.

From Welsh we have *flannel, clutter, maggot, coble, eisteddfod*. From Scots Gaelic are *bog, clan, slogan, collie, banshee, claymore, macintosh, whisky, plaid, ptarmigan, reel*, and the Irish contribution includes *brogue, bard, galore, hooligan, shamrock, colleen* 'girl', *shanty, Tory* (first used in its political sense about 1680; the original meaning was 'robber').

The Latin element

The Continental period

The Anglo-Saxons who invaded Britain in the 5th century had already in their vocabulary many Latin words acquired through an early commercial contact of the Germani with Roman trading posts on the Continent. These words are easily recognizable because they are a) typically cultural borrowings denoting phenomena novel to the more primitive Germanic civilization, and b) common property to all (or most) Germanic languages.

Continental loans from Latin, here cited in their OE form, include *mīl* 'mile' (Lat. *mille (passuum)* = a thousand double paces), *pund* 'pound' (Lat. *pondo*, abl. '(by) weight'), *weall* 'wall' (Lat. *vallum*), *pīl* 'spear' (Lat. *pilum*), *strǣt* 'street' (Lat. *(via) strata*), *mynet* 'mint, coin' (Lat. *moneta*), *wīn* 'wine' (Lat. *vinum*), *must* 'unfermented fruit juice' (Lat. *mustum*), *cytel* 'kettle' (Lat. *cutillus*), *cīese* 'cheese' (Lat. *caseus*), *pipor* 'pepper' (Lat. *piper*), *senep* 'mustard' (Lat. *sinapis*), *butere* 'butter' (Lat. *butyrum*), *cieres* 'cherry' (Lat. *cerasus*), *cealc* 'chalk' (Lat. *calx*).

The Celto-Roman period
The Roman conquest of what came to be Britannia started with Caesar's ill-starred expedition to the island in 55 B.C., but there was no actual occupation (and linguistic influence) till about a century later under the Emperor Claudius. The Britons under Roman rule adopted hundreds of Latin words into their vocabulary, but most of them disappeared with the gradual submersion of their language in the centuries after the Anglo-Saxon invasion of their country.

A few, however, lingered on and must have passed into OE through Celtic substratum, i.e. the Anglo-Saxons must have learnt them from the language of the Celts. They include *munt* 'mount' (Lat. *mont-em*), *port* 'harbour' (Lat. *portus*), *wīc* 'village' (Lat. *vicus*).

An important place-name element from this period is *-castra* 'military camp' (OE *ceaster* 'town'), which today appears, locally distributed, as *-chester* in the South (*Winchester, Rochester*) and *-caster* in the North (*Lancaster, Doncaster*). Note, however, that many of our present-day *-chesters* and *-casters* do not mark sites of ancient Roman camps. The Anglo-Saxons early interpreted the element as 'town'.

The Christian period
After the introduction of Christianity in Britain late in the 6th century (see p. 28) it is only natural that there would be a heavy influx of words pertaining to ecclesiastical activity and learning. Typical words are *abbot, altar, angel, anthem, candle, canon, cleric, deacon, martyr, mass, minster* (Lat. *monasterium*) as in *York Minster, monk, nun, pope, priest* (Lat. *presbyter*), *psalter, noon* (Lat. *nona (hora)*), *shrive, temple*.[2] However, a few of these words, including *church* and *bishop*, may be earlier and reflect early Germanic contact with Christianity on the Continent.

To Christian learning and education we owe *school, master* (Lat. *magister*), *grammatical, gloss*.

In the ME period the influence of Latin was continuous, but was now exerted largely through the intermediary of French. But since Latin was considered a sacred not a secular medium of expression, its impact on spoken idiom was bound to be limited.

It is often difficult if not impossible to determine whether a word has been adopted directly from Latin or circuitously through French. Words like *form, miserable, nature, consist, modest, grave, solid, explore, position, sublime* and adjectives in *-able*, to mention only a few, may derive from either source. Typically, however, the words that have taken the way through French are marked by sound changes there as well as in ME, cp. *colour* vs. *discoloration, machine* vs. *machination, example* vs. *exemplary, blame* vs. *blaspheme. Fact* is from Latin, but *feat* has reached us through French.

The chief effect of the Renaissance (see p. 35) is upon the vocabulary, and most of the innovations started out in the language of erudition, with such humanists as Sir Thomas More and Sir Thomas Elyot as the most inventive and proliferous coiners of new words and phrases. Most of these learned coinages have remained in the academic world, but some have become fully naturalized and are now an indispensable part of every-day idiom.

The majority of the loans were from Latin. Greek words were in some cases taken over directly (such as *criterion, anonymous, pathos, lexicon, polemic, acme*), but usually they were adopted through Latin or French.

In what form were words adopted?
Some were introduced raw like *apparatus, climax, major, minor, exterior, stratum, chaos, autograph, epitome, catastrophe, axis*. Others were brought into alignment with English simply by clipping the suffix, e.g. *exult* (Lat. *-are*), *dispel* (*-lere*), *capital* (*-is*), *denunciation* (*-em*).

Nouns in Latin *-tas* had their suffix changed to *-ty* on the analogy of earlier French loans where it had appeared as *-té*, e.g. *velocity, longevity, dexterity*. Similarly, the analogy of French has given correspondences like *-antia/-ance*, e.g. *tolerance, sufferance* and *-bilis/-ble* as in *tolerable, detestable*.

A great number of verbs were derived from Latin participle forms. *Terminate* (Lat. *terminatus*) is a typical instance. The infinitive form *terminare* has through French given us *(de)termine*.

From this period date also the many technical and encyclopedic adjectives often corresponding to a Germanic noun of the same root (see also p. 24) e.g. *hound – canine, brother – fraternal, horse – equestrian, father – paternal, heaven – celestial, foot – pedestrian, eye – ocular, sun – solar, king – regal* (but *royal* is from French).

The unrestrained import of classical words met with stiff opposition from many purists (Cheke, Ascham, Wilson), who contemptuously referred to them as 'ynkhorne termes'. And it is true that many of these learned neologies were indeed ephemeral, including such as *annect, deturpate, obstupefact, suppeditate, obtestate, contiguate, oblatrant, lapidifical, immorigerous, anacephalize, adminiculation, temulent*. But it is easy to see what prompted these enthusiastic coiners of inkhorn terms. To many Renaissance humanists the

41

vernacular was an unfit and inelegant vehicle for scientific or abstract thinking, so it was tempting for them to try to remedy its deficiencies by borrowing or adapting from a language with whose subtlety and wealth of connotation they were all familiar. It was not all wanton affectation.

Later Latin loans

The influence of the classical languages is by no means confined to the Renaissance, but has been continuous ever since to supply the demands of science and technology for specialized nomenclature. The Latin-Greek vocabulary of anatomy and zoology is largely a product of the 17th century, that of chemistry, physics and botany (Linnaeus) is about a century later. In the 19th century biology, bacteriology, biochemistry, geology and in the 20th psychology, dentistry, nuclear science, exploration of space (*astronaut, cosmonaut*) and computer technology have drawn their nomenclatures from the same source.

This Latin-Greek terminology has become a supranational, precise and highly efficient tool for scientific communication, and every new conquest will demand linguistic expression and add to it.

The Scandinavian element

As would be expected, the earliest stratum of loans, in evidence already in OE, is the so-called cultural borrowings, i.e. words denoting objects or concepts with which the Anglo-Saxons were unfamiliar or which they tried to imitate. To this early category belong a few items mainly concerned with ships, warfare and territorial organization, e.g. OE *barda* 'viking ship', OE *cnearr* 'warship', OE *scegþ* 'small, slender ship',[3] OE *dreng* 'warrior', OE *hofding* 'chieftain', OE *bȳ* 'small settlement', *wapentake*,[4] *Riding*.[5] A few terms relating to law and justice are also of early occurrence, e.g. *law* (ON *log*), *outlaw*, OE *niðing* 'criminal', *husting* 'tribunal', OE *stefnan* 'summon' (cp Dan. *stævne*), OE *māl* 'agreement, suit' (cp. Dan. *(søgs)mål)*,[6] OE *saclēas* 'innocent' (cp. Dan. *sagesløs*). Few of these legal terms survived the ME period. They were soon ousted by Norman terminology (see p. 46).

But the bulk of Scandinavian loans appear much later, most of them being first attested in early ME records. The reason why we find so few loans in OE is that practically all manuscripts have come down to us in the dialect of Wessex (see p. 29), an area long left undisturbed by the Vikings. But in the Anglian dialects of the Danelaw Scandinavian words must have existed in much larger numbers, only the lack of records in these dialects makes us unable to prove their existence. It is only when the language of the Danelaw begins to find expression in writing in early ME that the Scandinavian impact becomes really visible, and in texts like Ormulum (c. 1200), 'Genesis and Exodus' (c. 1250), 'The Lay of Havelok the Dane' (c. 1300) it appears overwhelming.

Before we go on to estimate the extent and depth of the influence of Scandinavian upon OE, it is important to note how close the similarity was between the two languages. Hundreds of words were identical or nearly so, belonging as they do to the common Germanic heritage: *will, can, come, see, ride, bring, send; house, land, strand, man, folk, father, mother, town, winter, summer*... to mention only a few. OE and ON differed more in points of grammar than they did lexically, and there seems to be general agreement that the two languages were to a certain extent mutually intelligible.

If we compare the Scandinavian contribution with any other lexical innovation of earlier or later date, we will be struck by one important difference. Apart from a small handful of cultural borrowings mentioned above, the Scandinavian words do not seem to supply any real need in the English vocabulary. They are as it were superfluous, overlapping with perfectly adequate native designations. A few examples will suffice: *call, take,[7] cast,[8] die,[9] thrive, want, scrape, scare, scowl, scream, bask, ransack, gape, cut,[10] drown, get, lift, raise;* nouns include *husband, fellow, sky, skill, skin, wing, window, loan,* OE *brȳdhlōp* 'wedding' (Dan. *bryllup*), *anger, birth, bloom, keel, down* (Dan. *dun* 'soft plumage'), *egg, loft, sister, want, skirt, skull, steak, slaughter, Thursday* (supplanting OE *þunresdæg*, see p. 140, note 3). Adjectives include *low, loose, wrong* (Dan. *vrang*), *meek* (Dan. *myg*), *ill, ugly, scabby, bleak* (Dan. *bleg*), *awkward, flat, odd, scant, weak* (Dan. *veg*), *same*.

In some cases a Scandinavian word imposed its meaning upon an OE cognate. OE *drēam* usually denoted 'joy, revelry', but the present sense 'dream' is from Scandinavian (ON *draumr*). OE *blōma* meant 'ingot, molten metal', but the present sense 'bloom' derives from ON *blomi* 'flower'. OE *eorl* meant 'man, warrior' but owes its present sense to ON *jarl*.

Identificatory criteria

It is difficult to identify the Scandinavian element in English because, as we have already made clear, numerous words were very similar in the two languages, namely those of the common Germanic heritage.

If a word which looks suspiciously Scandinavian turns up in early ME and is unattested in OE, it is no proof of Scandinavian origin. It could still be one of the common Germanic heritage, which only accidentally had escaped being recorded in writing, or was recorded in manuscripts now lost.

A phonological criterion, it should be emphasized, remains our only absolutely reliable test. North Germanic words are bound to have undergone certain sound changes unshared by the West Germanic dialects and vice versa. Germanic *ai* for instance became ā in OE, but remained unchanged in ON as shown in this diagram:

$$\text{Germ. *ai} \nearrow \text{OE ā} > \text{ME ǭ} > \text{PE ou}$$
$$\searrow \text{ON ei (later Dan. and Swed. ē)}$$

Hence we can with reasonable certainty ascribe PE *nay* to Scandinavian, whereas PE *no* (OE *nā*) must be the native variant. Similarly *swain* must be

Scandinavian, for OE had *swān,* which would have given PE **swoan,* had it survived.

Germanic **au* became *ēa* in OE but remained unchanged in ON. PE *-less* *(noiseless, childless)* thus presupposes OE *-lēas,* whereas the cognate *loose* owes its existence to ON *lauss.* For place-name pairs, see p. 142, note 15.

The consonants also offer important distinguishing criteria. Germanic **sk* became palatalized in OE to [ʃ] (see p. 67), but remained unchanged in ON. Hence words like *skin, skill, scale, sky, score, skulk, skirt* (cp. the native *shirt*).

The retention of the velar stop in words like *kid, gift, get, give* (where a native development would have given something like **yieve,* cp. OE *giefan*) is another reliable criterion of Scandinavian background.

In the absence of such phonological criteria (and there are a few more than those exemplified), identification should be attempted by resorting to a convergence of as many other criteria as possible (non-existence of the word in OE or any other West Germanic language, a perfectly adequate word for the same concept in OE, appearance for the first time in the ME dialects that represent the old Danelaw, survival in such dialects today, etc.).

Because of the difficulties which beset the identification of the Scandinavian loan-words in English we can only arrive at very rough estimates of their number. Conservative expert opinion has taken it to be somewhere in the region of 700-900 words, not including those that are now archaic or characteristic of regional dialect.[11]

Later Scandinavian loans

The Scandinavian influence since the Viking period has been negligible. Of 16th-century introduction are words like *batten* 'to grow fat', *skoal!,*[12] *scud, scrag, smelt* (probably from Swed. *smälta*), *rowan, rug* (Swed. *rugg* 'shaggy hair'), *slag.* The 17th and 18th centuries gave *troll, oaf* (Dan. *alf*), *keg* (Swed. *kagge*), *rune, cosy* (prob. from Norw. *koslig*), *tungsten,* with the 19th and 20th centuries contributing *floe, ski, nag,* and *ombudsman* (March 1967) as the latest acquisition.

Scandinavian place-names

The Scandinavian place-names are with few exceptions located north of the old Danelaw boundary with the heaviest concentration in Lincolnshire, in the North and East Ridings of Yorkshire, and in Leicestershire, where in some areas up to 75% of the place-name inventory may be of Scandinavian extraction. In Cumberland, Westmorland and Lancashire we find a number of place-names prevailingly Norwegian in character and suggesting settlement activity from Ireland.

Place-names with the element *-by* (ON *byr*)[13] constitute the most proliferous group, this element alone accounting for about 850 names (which is about 200 more than in Denmark). About half of these names contain a Scandinavian personal name, probably the owner of the settlement when its name was first recorded. Examples are *Ormsby, Grimsby, Thirkleby* (ON *Þorkell*), *Asselby* (ON *Asketill*), *Throxenby* (ON *Þorsteinn*), *Haconby* (ON *Hakonn*), *Cowesby* (ON *kausi* 'tomcat')[14], *Grisby* (ON *griss* 'pig').

Place-names containing the element *-thorpe* (corresponding to Dan. *-(s)trup, -drup, -rup*) are the second most frequent: *Osgathorpe* (ON *Asgautr*), *Hasthorpe* (ON *Haraldr*), *Swainsthorpe* (ON *Sveinn*), *Birkthorpe, Owsthorpe* (ON *austr* 'east').

Less frequent are the elements *-toft* (ON *topt*) as in *Sibbertoft* (ON *Sigbiorn*), *Moortoft, Langtoft* and *-thwaite* (ON *Þveit* 'clearing', Dan. *-tved*): *Applethwaite, Rounthwaite* (ON *raunn* 'rowan'), *Lingthwaite* (ON *lyng* 'heather'), *Inglethwaite* (ON *Ingolfr*).

Minor elements, though quite common in certain areas, include *-beck*, (*Skirbeck, Holbeck*), *-dale* (*Uldale, Grisdale, Lonsdale*), *-holm* (*Haverholme, Kettlesholme, Stockholme*), *-scough* (*Myerscough, Litherscew, Scowgarth*) [15].

Very numerous are the hybrids of the so-called 'Grimston' type, consisting of an ON personal name + the native place-name element *-ton* (OE *tūn*): *Grimston, Aslacton* (ON *Aslakr*), *Knuston* (ON *Knutr*), *Oulston* (ON *Ulfr*). These were probably Anglo-Saxon settlements taken over by the Vikings, who planted their names in them to indicate the change of ownership.[16].

Personal names
One of the primary sources for place as well as personal names is *Domesday Book* (1086), William the Conqueror's survey to list the economic resources of the country for fiscal purposes. Important are also early ME tax lists and legal documents (Pipe Rolls, Assize Rolls, cartularies). Besides, as we have just seen, numerous Scandinavian personal names are found imbedded in the place-name material. In such and similar sources we find about 600 different Scandinavian names[17], of which a few examples will be given: *Orm, Grim, Gamel, Frode, Fin, Esbern, Asgar, Elge*[16] and on the distaff side names like *Inga, Thore, Ragenel* (ON *Ragnhildr*), *Guede* (ON *Gyða*). Nicknames like *Crokebayn* (ON *krokbeinn* 'crow's leg'), *Leot* (ON *ljotr* 'ugly'), *Galman* (ON *galmann* 'loony'), *Broclos* (ON *broklauss* 'trouserless'), etc. abound.

Today's patronymic suffic *-son* 'son of' (*Richardson, Johnson, Thomson*) does not owe its existence, but much of its survival and later proliferation to Scandinavian *-son*. This suffix was known to the Anglo-Saxons, but they did not use it much and seem to have preferred another patronymic suffix *-ing* (*Wilding, Browning, Worthing*). Names like *Henderson, Donaldson, Hanson, Christison, Adamson* are still typical of the Scottish Lowlands, Lancashire and Cumberland.

The Scandinavian element in English names is rapidly on the decline already about 1200 when they begin to be crowded out by the Norman names.

In the course of ME they disappear completely.[18]

Modern names like *Eric, Harold, Gudrun, Karen, Thora, Ingrid*, it should

45

be noted, are not reminiscent of Viking name-giving, but reflect a recent influence from literature and film.

Curiously enough, many Scandinavian personal names seem to have survived only as family names, e.g. *Osborne* (ON *Asbiorn), Osgood* (ON *Asgautr), Havelock* (ON *Hafleikr), Swinburne* (ON *Sveinnbiorn), Haldane* (ON *Halfdan), Hasting* (ON *Hasteinn), Swain* (ON *Sveinn), Turpin* (ON *Þorfinnr)*[19] – and from the realm of nicknames: *Brockliss* (ON *broklauss* 'trouserless'), *Corey* (ON *kari* 'curly'), *Coe* (ON *ka* 'jackdaw'), *Skeat* (ON *skjotr* 'swift').

The French element

The introduction of French words in English is not confined to the post-Conquest period, but started when Edward the Confessor returned from his father's exile in Normandy (see p. 31).

But the linguistic influence that can be traced back to this French-speaking monarch and his Norman entourage is a mere trickle besides being extremely difficult to distinguish from potential Latin loans, the two languages being so closely related. But to this early period of French influence has been assigned a small handful of words like *castle, tower, market, capon, service, proud, bacon* – to pick some of the least disputed.

The French influence after 1066 is overwhelming, but it affects mainly the vocabulary and only to some extent grammar and orthography. Unlike the Scandinavian contribution the words adopted from French in this period belong to a category we may conveniently call *cultural borrowings*, i.e. they generally denote phenomena for which the Anglo-Saxons had inadequate or no words in their own language.

The weight of the French contribution to English is so massive and revealing that even if we had no first-hand historical sources from the period, the lexical loans alone would convey a fairly accurate picture of what happened in England after the Norman seizure of power not only in the feudal organization of the country in all its aspects (government, justice, Church, administration, army), but also in their social life and tastes.

Below we shall present a selection of French loans, classified according to the technical and cultural spheres that came under Norman dominance.

Law and justice

The Norman rulers made French and Latin the medium of all legal proceedings, and today most terms pertaining to that sphere are of French origin: *justice, judgment, judge, jury, court, assize, plaintiff, defendant, accuse, complaint, inquest, indictment, evidence, proof, sentence, verdict, fine, punishment, prison, crime, pardon, case, appeal.*

The same applies to names of crimes like *adultery, arson, burglary, treason, fraud, perjury, libel, assault and battery.*

Terms connected with wills and property: *assets, heir, heritage, legacy, estate, chattels, property.*

Many French law-terms are still highly technical: *issue male, heir apparent, fee simple, proof positive* (note the postposed adjectives and see p. 91), *petty larceny, lése majesté, puisne* 'judge inferior in rank to chief justice' (which in popular usage developed into *puny*). The royal assent to bills in Parliament is still worded in French *(le roi le veult)*.

Legal survivals from OE are *thief, theft, steal,* and *law* (the last is ultimately Scandinavian, see p. 42). It applies to these as well as to many other OE survivals in the categories to come that they were probably too deeply rooted in popular idiom to resist replacement by French equivalents.

In 1362 English was restored in the law courts because French was so rapidly on the decline as to be no longer understood by the vast majority of people.

Royalty and nobility

Basic concepts such as *king* and *queen* are native, and the same applies to *lord, lady* and *earl* (the last though with modified meaning through Scandinavian).

But apart from these, nearly all designations for the members of the ruling classes are French-derived: *duke, marquis, viscount, baron, count, prince, peer* including the titles of their wives.

A title of respect like *madam* still reveals its French morphology. *Sir* is an abbreviation of French *sire,* originally used in address to royalty.[20]

Norman feudalism accounts for words like *vassal, fief, liege, feudal(ism), allegiance, loyalty, homage, domain.*

Heraldic nomenclature is still today so heavily imbued with French terms and grammar that it is inaccessible to the uninitiated *(gules with a fesse, lions rampant and passant, two crosslets gold).* French is still retained in the Royal Arms *(Dieu et mon droit)* and in the crest of the Garter *(Honi soit qui mal y pense).*

War and military organization

Here belong loans like *war, peace, defence, army, garrison, soldier, troops, guard, company, battle, enemy, arms, archer* and names of military rank like *sergeant, lieutenant, general, officer.*

A few every-day words pertaining to this sphere, however, have survived from OE, primarily *sword, helmet, shield, spear, weapon* and the verb *to fight.*

Ways and manners

Words illustrating the manners and conventions of the Norman aristocracy in England include *chivalry, courteous, honour, grace, noble, fine, gracious, agreeable, debonair, courage, valour, glory, manners, amiable.* And to this category we might add *joy, comfort, ease, delight, pleasure, dance, feast, luxury.*

To polished table manners testify loans like *table, plate, goblet, saucer, fork* and names of meals like *dinner, supper, repast* (but *breakfast* is native).

Clothes and fashion

A large number of words and terms connected with fashion and dress were absorbed into ME, e.g. *cloak, gown, robe, garment, frock, costume, habit, collar, lace, embroidery, button, buckle, plume, garter, kerchief.* The Norman aristocracy could afford *satin, sable, ermine* and precious stones like *ruby, diamond, sapphire, jewel, amethyst.*

Plain and basic colours like *white, black, red, green* and *yellow* are native, but the more sophisticated blends have French names, e.g. *vermilion, saffron, tawny, russet, tan.*

Food

The Normans are responsible for the names of a great variety of dainties on the mediaeval menu. They must have introduced condiments like *mustard, thyme, vinegar, cinnamon, nutmeg, clove,* besides exotic fruits like *fig, date, olive, orange* and *lemon.*

Among names of fish we find *salmon, sardine, sturgeon, mackerel, oyster, sole.* To refinement in culinary techniques testify verbs like *broach, broil, stew, grate, mince, grill, souse, toast* and nouns like *pastry, soup, dainty, jelly.*

The superiority of the French cuisine is also reflected by word pairs like e.g. *calf – veal, swine – pork, ox – beef, sheep – mutton, deer – venison,* where the names of the domestic animals are native but the names of their meats for cooking are French[21].

Hunting and games

These were the favourite pastime of the leisured Norman aristocracy, and there is a large-scale introduction of words pertaining to that predilection, e.g. *chase, quarry, couple, brace, terrier, retrieve(r), kennel, falcon, leash, scent, warren, track, blow a mort. Tally-ho!* is still the cry raised by the huntsmen when the quarry is in sight. *Soho!* (< French *ça ho!*) is a similar hunter's call to indicate position of game.

To the sphere of games belong *ace, trumps, suit, dice, chess, tennis* (probably from the French imperative *tenez* 'catch'), *tournament, joust.* Until quite recently it was customary for dice players to count the spots on a die as *ace, deuce* (also used in tennis[22]), *tray, cater, cinque, size.* The word *sport* is a shortened form of French *desport* 'fun, pleasure' which in 16th-century England acquired the sense that has since been exported to all European languages.

Things ecclesiastical

As we have already mentioned, the Normans totally reorganized the Anglo-Saxon church, and foreign clergy were installed in all leading ecclesiastical offices. In the monasteries French was spoken throughout the ME period. Among the large number of words pertaining to this sphere are *religion, theology, service, prayer, sermon, preach, baptism, communion, confession, trinity, angel, saint, mercy, salvation, divinity, vice, virtue, faith, anoint, cardinal, chaplain, vicar, parson, friar, hermit.* Too deeply rooted in popular usage to be replaced by French equivalents, however, were *priest* and *bishop.*

The ecclesiastical monopoly of learning in the Middle Ages is responsible

48

for *study, treatise, grammar, logic, lesson, compilation, parchment, pen* and *paper*.

The Normans introduced an era of splendid church architecture reflected in *image, sculpture, figure, lattice, wicket, tower, arch, choir, altar, column, pillar, vault, turret, ceiling, porch, aisle, nave, cloister, abbey, chapel, palace, cathedral, convent*.

Government and administration

This would quite naturally be a field of strong Norman influence. Words that come under this head range from fundamental concepts such as *state, empire, crown, administration, government, reign, majesty, council, parliament, assembly, office(r), public, subject* ... to titles of high rank in the Norman administrative hierarchy, e.g. *chancellor, marshal, governor, minister, mayor, constable, chamberlain, treasurer, warden, bailiff*.

Provenance and dating

It is evident that most of the French words that were introduced into English in the first couple of centuries after the conquest must have come from a *Norman-French source*, a dialect with some admixture of Germanic elements. But after about 1300, for reasons touched upon p. 33, they were mainly drawn from the *Parisian-French (Central French) standard*. This dual provenance of the French loans in ME is reflected primarily by their consonant inventory, to some extent also by the vowels.

Words of Germanic origin with *w-* have retained this sound in Norman to the present day, whereas in Parisian French it early became *gu-*. This difference enables us to stratify French words in ME into early Norman and later Parisian-French strata, examples like *wasp, war, wicket, waste, wafer* reflecting introduction through Norman (cp. French *guepe, guerre, guichet, gater, gauffre*). In some cases the same word seems to have been borrowed first from Norman and then again from Parisian French, witness pairs like *warden – guardian, warranty – guarantee, wile – guile, wage – gage, wallop – gallop* (all with later semantic differentiation).

Latin *c* before *a* was usually retained as [k] in Norman, but developed into an affricate [tʃ] in Parisian French. English reflects borrowing through both channels in doublets like *catch – chase* (< late Lat. *captiare*), *cattle – chattel(s), car – chariot, cark(ing care) – charge*. Only the Norman variant has survived in *carpenter, carrion, carry* (but cp. the proper name Charrier).

Latin *-ti-, -ci-* became Norman [tʃ] but in Parisian-French [s]. Hence doublets like *catch – chase, launch – lance, pinch – pincers*. Cp. also *March* with French *mars* (Lat. *Martius*).

French loans like *master, feast, beast, forest, wasp* etc. must belong to an early stratum, because the *s* in French ceased to be pronounced in this position about 1200 (cp. *maître, fête, bête, forêt, guêpe*). A doublet like *hostel – hotel* illustrates both phases of the French development.

Before 1300 the French pronunciation of *j, ch* and *-ge* was similar to that which we see reflected by PE *just* and *charge*. This distinction enables us to identify words like *journey, jest, join, majesty, chance, chart, chief, age, large, judge,* etc. as early loans and words like *jabot, champagne, machine, chef, chamois, mirage, rouge* as later deposits. The same applies to the proper names *Charles* and the much later *Charlotte*.

Vocalic criteria are fewer. The OF diphthong *ei* was retained in Norman, but became *oi* in the Parisian standard, hence doublets like *display – deploy, convey – convoy. Loyal* is from Parisian French, but its archaic doublet *leal* is Norman. To *royal* corresponds an earlier form *real* now obsolete.

In what form were the French words adopted?

In verbal loans it was usually the French present plural that served as the model. This fact explains English forms like *survive* (cp. French *je survis, nous survivons*), *resolve* (cp. *je resous, nous resolvons*), *prove* (cp. *je preuve, nous prouvons*), *move* (cp. *je meuve, nous mouvons*), etc. and it is the same principle that accounts for the frequency of suffixes in *-ish* (cp. *je finis, nous finissons; je punis, nous punissons*), etc.

French infinitives underlie imports like *render, tender, saunter* and nouns like *dinner, remainder, rejoinder.*

Since French nouns and adjectives were usually taken over in their accusative form (which in OF had zero in most cases), they were easily absorbed into the ME declensional system. The OF nominative form, whose suffix was typically *-s* (e.g. *fils* (Lat. *filius*), acc. *fil*), is rarely preserved in the loans, but is seen e.g. in *fitz,* common in patronymic names of the type *Fitzgerald, Fitzsimmonds.*

The adjective *fierce* also derives from an OF nominative (OF *fiers* (Lat. *ferus*), acc. *fier*).

Later French loans

Almost half of the French-derived vocabulary in English was adopted between 1250 and 1400, but French influence has been continuous ever since. Loans in early Mod. Eng. and later, however, are typically less thoroughly anglicized in sound and spelling.[23] Sometimes, it will appear, even the French pronunciation and diacritics have been retained, suggesting a distinctive upper-class background rooted in the Restoration period when the Stuarts returned from France 'more French than English'. As the medium of international diplomacy French was slowly superseding Latin in post-Renaissance times.

Most of these late imports are concerned with things military, with diplomacy, art, fashion, food and social manners. Words from this period are (no temporal stratification attempted): *corps,*[24] *brigade, morale, parole, barricade, fanfare, ration, camouflage, colonel, commandant, cartridge, carbine; communiqué, laissez-faire, rapport, liaison, attaché, bureau, chargé d'affaires, entente, envoy, diplomacy, financial, representation* (in its political sense); *critique, ballet, burlesque, travesty, genre, amateur, memoirs, repertoire, cliché, baroque, pre-*

miere, resumé; crinoline, nuance, négligé, tricot, crepe, muslin, blouse, corduroy, chenille; soup, champagne, hors d'œuvre, café, chef, mayonnaise, bouillon, menu, restaurant, salon, soufflé, cigarette; savoir faire, nonchalance, facade, sangfroid, etiquette, embarrass, decor, routine, prestige, blasé, naive.

The French Revolution contributed *aristocrat, democrat, royalism, Liberal, Conservative, despotism.*

Place-names

Names of the type *Rickerby* (: Richard), *Etterby* (: Etard), *Thorpe Mandeville, Thorpe Morieux, Williamston, Walterstone,* etc. do not indicate settlement activity on the part of the Norman invaders, but should rather be looked upon as existing settlements with the French name suggesting change of ownership.

Compared to the Scandinavian contribution there are few Norman place-names in England. Some names of castles and monasteries seem to have been transplanted directly from France (*Beaumont, Richmond, Grosmont, Egremont, Mount Grace,* etc.).

As would be expected, many Norman place-names are distinctly aristocratic in character, indicating that the site was chosen primarily for its scenic beauty (*Beaulieu, Beaurepaire, Beauvale, Bellasis, Belvoir, Belgrave,* etc.).

Personal names

Like the names of the Scandinavian conquerors, the impact of the Normans on native personal nomenclature was bound to be swift and dramatic. About 1200 it was in process of sweeping away the indigenous Anglo-Saxon as well as the Scandinavian name-stock (see p. 45). Names like *Henry, William, Roger, Robert, Richard, Ralph, Hugh, Walter; Alice, Maud, Emma,* etc. begin to appear in the sources in ever increasing numbers – names taken over from the new ruling classes, names with prestige[25].

The Norman Church brought further pressure to bear on the English name-inventory by introducing a vast number of the so-called scriptural names (*John, Thomas, Paul, Simon, Peter, Matthew, Michael, James, Andrew, Luke, Mark; Mary, Anne, Joan, Elizabeth, Catherine,* etc.)[26].

The Spanish and Portuguese elements

The Spaniards and the Portuguese were unremitting explorers, and England's early contact and clashes with them in the 16th and 17th centuries started the introduction of a large number of exotic words, many denoting phenomena from the New World. Many of them appear for the first time in Hakluyt's 'Voyages' (1589). They include *negro, mulatto, potato* (ultimately Haitian), *mosquito, vanilla, tomato* (ult. Mexican), *alligator, banana* (ult. Guinean), *anchovy* (ult. Basque), *cannibal* (ult. Caribbean), *maize* (ult. Cuban), *lime, chocolate* (ult. Mexican), *tobacco* (ult. Haitian), *cork, sherry,*[27] *chili* (ult. Mexican), *cigar.*

To warlike or maritime contact with Spain testify *armada, galleon, desperado, renegade, embargo, stevedore, cask, tornado, cargo.*

More recent imports are *silo, lasso, bronco, canyon, hacienda, mustang, poncho, ranch, rodeo, siesta, vamoose* (Span. *vamos* 'let's go!') and the quite recent *cafeteria* – most of which have come into English via American.

Of Portuguese extraction are *caste, albino, flamingo, coco*(nut), *molasses, buffalo, yam, mandarin* (ult. Malay), *madeira, port* (wine from Oporto), *guinea* (coin made of gold from G.).

The Dutch and Low German elements

Of the Low German dialects it is Dutch which has contributed most significantly to the growth of English vocabulary, but many words were also introduced through trade relations with the German Hanseatic League, which had established commercial enclaves in London (the Steel Yard) and many other ports as early as the 15th century, and from about 1600 the English Merchant Adventurers obtained a permanent footing in Hamburg. Many Flemish craftsmen, particularly weavers, settled in great numbers in England in the Middle Ages.

From this early period date a small deposit of loans like *boor*,[28] *booze, pickle, hop* 'plant for flavouring beer', *luck, kit, sled, snap.*

Navigation and exploration in the 17th century, however, brought England into particularly close contact with the Dutch. Their status as one of the greatest sea-faring nations of Europe and until the Navigation Act of 1651 dominant in the freight trade has made them responsible for a large number of more or less international words pertaining to ships and the sea, e.g. *dock, sloop, yacht, schooner, yawl, bowline, bowsprit, jib, reef, cruise, deck, luff, skipper, freight, buoy.*

A few military words remind us of English expeditions to the Netherlands in the 16th century and of William II's Dutch regiments: *onslaught, drill, furlough, tattoo*,[29] *boot, blunderbuss, knapsack.* The contribution from the Dutch school of painting in the 17th century includes *easel, sketch, landscape,* etc.

Words like *commandeer, commando* and the recent *apartheid* have reached English through Afrikaans Dutch. The same goes for words like *trek* and *veldt,* which became popularized through the boy scout movement with its background in the Boer War (Baden-Powell).

Words like *boss, bowery, waffle, cookie,* and *Santa Claus* are Americanisms, but beyond that they are ultimately of Dutch origin.

The Italian contribution

Already in the Middle Ages the Italians were leading in the world of banking, and it is from that early period that we find the first recordings of monetary terms like *ducat, florin, million.* The word *bank* (ultimately identical with *bench*) is from the 16th century and *bankruptcy* about a century younger.[30]

As in all European languages, the musical vocabulary of English is largely derived from Italian. Of 16th-century introduction are *duo, allegro, fugue, violin, madrigal,* while later centuries have given *solo, opera, piano, spinet, stanza, concerto, duet, adagio, virtuoso, andante, soprano, alto, prima donna.*

Terms pertaining to architecture and the fine arts have been imported since the 16th century and include *citadel, villa, corridor, portico, frieze, stucco, pergola, colonnade, arcade,* and in the fields of painting and sculpture *fresco, pastel, miniature, cameo, torso, terra cotta, bust.*

The German element

The Germans were famous in the fields of mining and metallurgy already in the 16th century, and many terms relating to minerals and metals are of German origin, e.g. *quartz, feldspar, gneiss, meerschaum, zinc, nickel, cobalt, wolfram* – all from the 18th century.

The German influence, however, is most potent in the 19th century with Carlyle and Coleridge as the great intermediaries. The leading position of Germany in philosophy and literary criticism has contributed *enlightenment (: Aufklärung), Weltanschauung, leitmotif, folksong, gestalt.* Kant is ultimately responsible for *subjective, objective, nihilism, organic, pluralism, transcendental, intuition,* and Nietzsche for *superman.* German pioneer work in philology (primarily Grimm) has given *ablaut, umlaut, schwa, strong* and *weak* (declension).

To the military sphere belong *howitzer (: Haubitzer), minenwerfer, drumfire (: Trommelfeuer), sharpshooter (: Scharfschütze), U-boat* and the recent *blitzkrieg (the Blitz).*

Certain developments in German history are reflected by *Kaiser, Kulturkampf, the mailed first (: die gepanzerte Faust), the Third Reich, Fuehrer, anschluss, hetz, world power (: Weltmacht).*

Achievements in medicine, physics and chemistry have contributed *Roentgen-ray* (now usually X-ray), *heroin, pepsin, aspirin, seltzer, inferiority complex* and *psychoanalysis* (both from Freud), *uranium, relativity* (Einstein), *ohm* (Ohm), *molecule, dynamo, saccharine, aniline, cadmium, ether, filter, protein.*

German *'wanderlust'* has left its imprint in *rucksack, alpenstock, yodel, zither, alpinism.*

To the culinary vocabulary belong *sauerkraut, noodle, schnitzel, zwieback, pumpernickel, hamburger* (later to generate absurdities like *cheeseburger, fishburger), frankfurter, delicatessen, lager, schnapps.*

Miscellaneous loans include *kindergarten, semester, seminar, swan-song (: Schwanengesang), fuchsia, dachshund, poodle, handbook (: Handbuch), Diesel, iceberg (: Eisberg).*

Various minor elements

A good deal of political and cultural history is implicit also in the following lists of foreign vocabulary – the building of the Empire, commercial supremacy, England as 'the workshop of the world'. Some of the contributions have come into English directly, but as often as not they have arrived circuitously through other European languages, loans of OE or ME introduction usually through Latin and later loans chiefly through French and Spanish.

Indian loans began to appear from about 1600 as a result of the activities of the East India Company (see p. 37). Among such early words are *calico, chintz, bungalow* (Hindi *bangala* 'from Bengal'), *cowrie, indigo, punch,*[31] *jute, rupee, shampoo.* Later contributions include *dinghy, cashmere, jungle, khaki* (Hindi *khaki* 'dusty'), *puttee, pyjamas, swastika* (Sanskrit *svastis* 'welfare'), *juggernaut, thug.* From Tamil we have *copra, mango, curry, teak, pariah.* Many of the Indian words became known through the works of Kipling.

Of *Chinese* origin are *tea, ketchup, japan* 'varnish', *ginseng,*[32] *tycoon* (but borrowed through Japanese), and *silk.*[33]

Turkish words include *coffee, horde, kiosk, tulip, jackal* (the last two ultimately Persian).

Arabic words have often preserved the definite article *al-* (*almanac, alcohol, alchemy, algebra,* etc.). Other loans are *admiral, assassin,*[34] *mufti, hash(ish), carat, lemon, magazine, apricot, mohair, lute, sherbet, giraffe, tariff, zenith, cipher, damask, saffran, cotton.* Many of these, it should be noted, were adopted as early as ME.

Persian loans are *scarlet, arsenic, borax, caravan, bazaar, paradise, tiger, shawl, chess.*[35]

Russian has given *tundra, pogrom, samovar, mammoth, cossack.* From the post-Revolution period *bolshevik, soviet, commissar, intelligentsia,* and the quite recent *glasnost, perestroika.*

From *American Indian* are imported *tomahawk, squaw, moccasin, totem, wigwam, hickory, moose, skunk, (ra)coon, pemmican,* most of which have been recorded since the 17th century. We might here also include *kayak* from Eskimo.

On earlier loans (*tobacco, potato,* etc.) through Spanish, see p. 51.

CHAPTER V

Orthography

Four scripts

During the first one thousand years or so of the Christian era Britain was to see the use of four distinct modes of writing. The first was that introduced by the Romans after the conquest of the island and later also adopted by the romanized Celts, but given up again when the Roman legions were withdrawn early in the 5th century (see p. 17). There are numerous Latin inscriptions and graffiti illustrative of this initial phase.

Alongside the Latin script there existed the native so-called *ogham writing*, a special Iro-Celtic system developed by the druids for ritualistic purposes and which died with the coming of Christianity. Its symbols are in the form of notches or strokes carved under, above or through a central horizontal line:

The number of strokes (up to five and thus in origin probably a sign language based on the five fingers) and their orientation to the base line determine their value. In this alphabet there are over 300 inscriptions preserved.

The *runic script*, probably derived by migratory Germanic tribes (Goths) from the Etruscan alphabet of Northern Italy, was brought to Britain by the Anglo-Saxon invaders. The runic alphabet is chiefly inscriptional and characterized by angular letters well suited for chipping on wood.[1] As the name denotes (OE *rūn* 'secret, mystery'), its original use was ritualistic or sacral. The runic inscriptions represent the earliest recorded Germanic; a few in Denmark probably date as far back as the 3rd century A.D.

The runic alphabet, or *futhark* as it is also called,[2] is found throughout the Germanic world, but on the Continent, except in Scandinavia, it soon went out of use. Already Wulfila (see p. 12) exchanged it for an adapted form of the Greek alphabet in his Bible translation.

The runic script, as it was used in Britain, employs the original 24 letters, which the Anglo-Saxons later eked out with six to keep abreast of phonological development in their language since the Continental period. After the introduction of Christianity the runes came to be associated with heathenism and superstition and were gradually replaced by the Latin alphabet.

There are about 50 Anglo-Saxon runic inscriptions extant, the chief monuments being the Ruthwell cross, the Bancastle pillar and the Frank's casket.

The history of English orthography begins with the introduction of Christianity when the fourth system, the so-called *Insular half uncial script* spreads from the Northumbrian centres of learning to large parts of the island. It is the hand in which practically everything written in OE has come down to us. The Insular style owes its introduction to Christian missionaries from Ireland (see p. 28) and is in all essentials an Iro-Celtic adaptation of the Latin alphabet. The earliest specimen is the late-7th-century Lindisfarne Gospels.

But unlike the runes, the Insular script with its 23 letters and tailored for mediaeval Latin could afford only partial coverage of the OE phonemic system. In other words there were more sounds than letters, so four symbols, æ (from Latin ligatured *ae*), þ and ƿ (=w) (both from runic script) and ð (orig. an Irish *d* with a diacritic stroke) were later added to the system. Apart from þ, however, none of these were to survive the early ME period.

In spite of these additions, however, OE was still far from achieving a one-to-one relationship between phoneme and symbol, and many symbols therefore had to carry up to three positionally determined values (see further p. 66).

The Insular script is bold and simple and generally considered the most handsome of the many national varieties of Latin script. It is the hand in which Irish is written today (see cover illustration).

Originated by King Alfred in his royal secretariats (see p. 29), the West Saxon scribal tradition, which could also be called our first chancery writing, had by late OE come to be characterized by such consistency and regularity that it is justified to speak of a national literary standard without parallel in Europe. Writing throughout the island now for the first time conformed to a universally accepted standard.

The Insular script died out with the supersession of the West-Saxon standard by Latin and French consequent on 1066. The new rulers, now installed in all key positions in Church and administration, had no use for it.

The Normans introduced *Continental script* (or the Carolingian minuscule),[3] a script style used throughout the Western World and the basis for all national variants down to the invention of moveable type in the 15th century. It is the direct ancestor of the later angular and pointed hand known as Gothic or 'black letter', which, however, was more difficult to read because some letters resembled each other closely (see p. 58).

As we have touched upon earlier, the OE alphabet afforded only partial coverage of the sounds, but with the introduction of Continental script this inadequacy was remedied to some extent. The Norman scribes, trained in the Latin tradition that spelling was phonetic, transcribed English words as they heard them, and as they were not bound by any English spelling convention, they supplied from their own what they needed, or combined existing vowel or consonant symbols in entirely new ways. Their innovations gave the English language a totally different aspect, but they were with few exceptions advantageous. Orthography, already in late OE a standard and thus failing to convey a true picture of the actual pronunciation, became as it were more 'phonetic'.

The innovations introduced were the new consonant symbols *v, z, g, k* and *q*. Other orthographical changes, including the new digraphs *th, ch* and *sh*, represent a different application of already existing symbols.

Consonants

The symbol *v* was introduced from French to cover the voiced variant of the /f/ phoneme (see p. 66). As OE /f/ was the only possibility initially, all words with /v/ in this position must be borrowed (*very, virtue, visage*, etc.).[4] Norman scribes followed Continental practice in using the symbols *u* and *v* indiscriminately, but show a tendency to prefer *v* initially (*very, vnder, vnhappie*, etc.) and *u* medially (*loue, haue, seruise*, etc.).

This distribution was still common practice in early Mod. Eng., but the PE norm with *v* as a consonant and *u* as a vowel was in the main established in the 18th century. Dr Johnson in his 'Dictionary' (1755) still treats *u* and *v* as one symbol.

The symbol *z* was also introduced from French to mark the voiced variant of the /s/ phoneme (see p. 66), but it was not common till late ME. Since /s/ in OE occurred initially, words with /z/ in this position (*zeal, zero*, etc.) must be borrowed.

The symbol *g* originally stood for the velar fricative (see p. 66) which in OE had developed two positional variants as seen in *giernan* 'yearn', *gaderian* 'gather'. All three values, however, were written ȝ in the Insular script.

Norman scribes introduced *g* from Continental script, but were consistent in using it for the stop (*god, growen*, etc.). If, however, it occurred before *e* the only way to indicate the stop was to insert a *-u-* (*tongue, guess*, etc.) according to French practice. The old Insular ȝ they reserved for the fricatives (*ȝernen* 'yearn', *boȝe* 'bow'), which later in ME came to be represented by *y* and *w*. Further, ȝ was used for the fricative in the group *ht* (*niȝt* 'night', *kniȝt* 'knight', etc.), later in ME represented by *ght*.[5]

The symbol *k* was rarely used in OE, but was introduced by the Normans to render the stop [k] in positions where *c* in French would be pronounced [s], namely before the front vowels *i* and *e* (*ceci, citoyen, certain*). Hence PE spellings like *king* (OE *cyning*), *kiss* (OE *cyssan*), *keen* (OE *cēne*). In all other positions the original *c* could be safely maintained (*cat, curse, cock, crow, clean*, etc.).

The symbol *q* owes its adoption to Norman scribes trying to render OE *cw-*. Hence PE *queen, quake, quick*, etc. This innovation, however, was purely graphical.

The digraph *th*. The Insular *ð* fell into disuse in early ME, and throughout the remainder of the period the ancient runic *þ* came to be used along with the Continental newcomer *th*, which latter is universal by 1500. With the decreasing use of þ, however, it was written more and more carelessly and came close in shape to *y*. Hence the frequent 16th-century compendia spellings like *y^e* and *y^t* for 'the' and 'that', of which the former has survived in fake antique inn signs of the 'Ye Olde Inne' type, and quite erroneously pronounced [ji:].

The digraph *ch* was introduced by the Norman scribes to render the OE palatal *c* as in *cīld* 'child', and is reflected in spellings like *chin, chaff, church, choose*.

The digraph *sh*, in ME sometimes written *sch*, was a Norman innovation to render OE *sc* [ʃ]: *shell* (OE *scell*), *shield, shoot, shut, shy, shrink, shroud*. PE words with *sc-* (*science, scene, scribe*, etc.) must therefore be of foreign extraction.

For *sc* [sk] in Scandinavian loans, see p. 44.

Vowels
Norman scribal practice introduced no new vowel symbols, but some were applied with French values (on *ū* for OE *ȳ*, *ou* for OE *ū*, see p. 69).

OE *æ* disappeared in early ME. Norman scribes rendered it by *e* or *a*.

Spellings to indicate length
OE consonants were usually doubled to indicate length (see p. 66), but vowel length was unmarked, the macrons in textbooks being editorial. In late ME, however, vowel length began to be indicated in two ways, both of which have survived into PE, namely by doubling or by *-e* after a single consonant.[6]

Examples are *blood* or *blode* (OE *blōd*), *foot* or *foote* (OE *fōt*), *root* or *rote* (ON *rōt*), *street* or *strete* (OE *strǣt*). PE survivals of *-e* as length marker include *rope* (OE *rāp*), *write* (OE *wrītan*), *mete* (OE *mētan*), *case* (ME *caas* or *case*), *made* (OE *macode*).[7]

Spellings to increase legibility
In mediaeval script many stroke letters (minims), particularly *w*,[8] *n*, *m* and *i* (which was not dotted until late ME) were difficult to distinguish from each other. For legibility and following Continental scribal practice the Normans were apt to introduce *o* as a graphic alternative to *u* to avoid minim confusion, e.g. *note* 'nut', *sonne* 'sun', *domb* 'dumb', and early Mod. Eng. usage is still highly fluctuating (*nomber/number, wun/won, sonne/sunne*, etc.). Reflexes today are *honey, tongue, monk, wonder*, etc.

The typical ME interchange of *i* and *y* (*wyse/wise, smylyng/smiling*, etc.) should be viewed on a similar background. In OE *y* and *i* had been different phonemes, but had fallen together in ME *i*, for which sound a graphic alternative was now available, *y* being usually preferred to avoid minim confusion (*comynge, myne, synnys* 'sins', *connynge* 'cunning', etc.).

In the 17th century the PE norm was in the main established, *y* being used only finally (cp. *happy, try, holy* vs. *happily, tried, holiday*). A double *ii* was avoided by the printers by spelling *yi* (*crying, tarrying*, etc.).

Alternative *y/i* spelling survives in *gipsy/gypsy, tire/tyre* and in personal names like *Byrd, Smyth, Whyte,* etc.

The Normans are responsible for the introduction of *j*, which historically is merely a variant of *i* and used in Latin when it occurred finally (cf. *filij,* numerals like *iij, viij,* etc.). The dot over minuscule *i,* introduced in late ME to avoid minim confusion, was later to be transferred also to *j* because the two letters were used more or less as graphic variants. Capital *J* is a product of the 17th century.

The present vowel-consonant contrast between the letters *i* and *j* was not yet observed in EMnE, where spellings like *Iohn, Iewes* 'Jews', *ioye* still occur. Dr. Johnson treats them as one symbol in his 'Dictionary' (1755).[9]

Final -e

There were in late ME and EMnE no rules determining the use and non-use of final *-e,* the last vestige of OE distinctive vowels in unaccented syllables. The fact that *-e* had ceased to be pronounced in late ME but was retained in writing was bound to cause great confusion, and many writers began to add *-e* where it had no historical justification (*grasse, coole, yeare,* etc.). The height of arbitrariness was reached in the 16th century, when the early printers often used it as type-justification to achieve a straight right-hand margin. This seems the only way to explain variants like *fysh/fysshe, fairly/fairlie, most/mooste* that can be found even within the same paragraph.[10]

Gradually, however, *-e* also ceased to be written in most cases, and about 1700 the MnE norm prevailed. Final *-e* was dropped after short stem vowels: *cat* (ME *catte*), *dog* (ME *dogge*), *help* (ME *helpe*), *spit* (ME *spite*), etc.,[11] whereas it was retained after long stem vowels as a quantity marker, as shown by *nose, lose, shoe, hare* and pairs like *rode/rod, grime/grim, fate/fat.*

If, however, length was marked by digraph spelling, *-e* was felt to be superfluous and was eventually dropped: *meet, seed, leach, beat, room, fool, field, shield, boat, road, proud, cow, waist,* etc. – but spellings with double marking like *meete, beate, moone,* etc. continue to occur until well on into the 17th century.

Latinized spellings

As we have touched upon earlier (p. 36), Latin was universally admired by the Renaissance humanists for its perfection. Among its many assets was a fixed and consistent orthography. Consequently many French words adopted in ME and through the wear and tear of centuries reduced to forms deviating considerably from their Latin origins, were a source of constant annoyance to men of erudition. They looked upon such forms as degenerate and debased Latin, which should be restored to former elegance, and the unsettled spelling of the period afforded ample latitude for experiment and change.

Among the modern survivals of such learned respellings should be mentioned *debt* (ME *dette,* Lat. *debitum*), *doubt* (ME *doute,* Lat. *dubitatio*), *sal-*

mon (ME *saumon,* Lat. *salmo*), *subtle* (ME *sotil,* Lat. *subtilis*), *indict* (ME *endite*), *April* (ME *Averil*), *picture* (ME *peynture*), *victuals* (ME *vittles*), *fault* (ME *faute*), *parliament* (ME *parlement*), *verdict* (ME *verdit*), *perfect* (ME *parfit*). In many cases, it will be observed, the pronunciation has remained unaffected by the latinized spelling.

Latin models are also responsible for the insertion of *-d-* in words like *advice* (ME *avis*), *adventure* (ME *aventure*),[12] *advance* (ME *avauncen*), *advantage* (ME *avauntage*).

The Renaissance respellers were not all Classical scholars, and many of their products were regular howlers. *Admiral,* an Arabic word and originally without the *-d-*, was wrongly associated with Latin *admiratio. Island* (OE *īeglond*) was erroneously derived from Latin *insula,* but the pronunciation reflects the historical form. *Sovereign* (ME *soverain*) was wrongly linked up with *reign* (Lat. *regnum*), which also explains the spelling of *foreign* (ME *foraine*). *Scissors* would today have been without *-c-* (ME *sisoures*) if it had not been for the mistaken analogy of Latin *scindo* 'I cleave', which has also changed the native word, ME *sithe,* into *scythe.*

Modern words like *throne, theatre, catholic, thesis, anthem, apothecary* were originally introduced from French without *-h-*, which was grafted on by Renaissance humanists in imitation of Latin transliteration of Greek θ, and later came to affect also the pronunciation. In *author* there has never been an *-h-* even in the classic model (Lat. *auctor*).

Names like *Thomas, Anthony* (cp. *Tony*), *Thames* have retained the historical pronunciation, and only the spelling is artificial.[13]

Ph (the conventional Latin transliteration of Greek φ) came to be commonly used for ME *f* in the Renaissance: *philosophy, triumph, phantom,* etc. In the name *Ralph* it is trespassing upon a word of non-Greek origin.

Until the 18th century initial *h-* was frequently silent in French loans like *humble, herb, homage, hospital, heritage,* but has later been restored through the influence of the orthography. Only in *heir, honour, hour* and *honest* has the French pronunciation prevailed.

Dutch influence

Many of the early printers and compositors in England were foreigners (Pynson, de Machlinia, Wynkyn de Worde). Caxton (see p. 35) spent most of his life in the Low Countries where he learnt the craft, and on his return to England in 1476 created an English typographic tradition based on Dutch models. His Continental background is ultimately responsible for the peculiar *gh-* spellings in his prints, e.g. *ghod* 'good', *ghospel, ghess* 'guess' on the analogy of Dutch usage (cp. *Ghent*). Of such spellings, however, only *ghost, ghastly* and *gherkin* have survived into the present standard.

The development of a new standard

ME literature, as we have mentioned earlier (see p. 34), was written in a variety of dialects until late in the 14th century when the East Midland or

London speech, for reasons touched upon p. 35, began to establish its superiority over all other types of regional English. When about 1430 French and Latin had been abandoned and the central administration began to issue official documents in English, a professional rather stable orthography was gradually evolved, the so-called chancery spelling, which was soon to influence the orthographic practices of manuscript shops all over the country.

When printing was introduced late in the 15th century, the only stabilized spelling convention was that of the chancery scribes, and that was also the one adopted by Caxton and his successors and in broad outline that which is reflected by the norm of today.

But the early 16th century was far from having a fixed standard in the modern sense of the word. Individual words could still be spelled in a bewildering variety of ways. If the early printers made any contribution to the stabilizing efforts of the professional scribes, it was one prompted by economic necessity. They needed spellings that could be used routinely whenever a word recurred. Consequently we now begin to see such a phenomenon as 'house styles', i.e. consistent spellings of individual words and typical of the individual presses. But there continued to be wide scope for variant forms (doubling of consonants, final -e, etc.) throughout the century.

The ultimate rootedness of English spelling in mediaeval scribal tradition is the main reason why it is so 'unphonetic'. The 15th and early 16th centuries were a period of radical phonological change, but the prevailing orthographic convention was already too fixed and dogmatic to record it.

Already the Elizabethans were painfully aware of the inadequacy of their spelling to reflect the actual pronunciation. Attempts to make it keep pace with sound-changes are legion, but they have with few exceptions left no imprint on today's usage. The earliest proposals for spelling reform go back to the 16th century, when the desire to give English the phonetic and stable spelling which they admired in Latin had caused Renaissance scholars to be intensely preoccupied with spelling problems and the invention of new consonant and vowel symbols to achieve the desired one-to-one correspondence of phoneme and letter. Important endeavours in this field are John Hart's 'An Orthographie'(1569), William Bullokar's 'Book at Large for the Amendment of Orthographie for English Speech' (1581), and Alexander Gill's 'Logonomia Anglica' (1621).

Yet a tendency towards standardization becomes increasingly perceptible in the Elizabethan period, but it came from more traditionalist circles. Already in 1582 Richard Mulcaster had published his 'The Elementarie' with recommended spellings of some 7000 words, and in 1596 followed Edmond Coote's limited but more pragmatic 'The English Schoole-maister'.

These early surveys of rules for spelling do not recommend any disruption of tradition, but they are important in that they codify what they found were the clearest and most serviceable of existing spelling variants. Through the influence they came to exert on contemporary teachers and printers they did more than anything else to pave the way for increased uniformity.[14]

It was tradition and convention, not experiment that won the day. Attempts to make English orthography more 'phonetic' had been largely futile.

By the middle of the 17th century a set of norms had crystallized to which most writers and printers now tried to conform, and these were gradually embodied in a large number of dictionaries published in the 17th and 18th centuries, e.g. Cawdrey's 'A Table Alphabeticall of Hard Wordes' (1604), Bullokar's 'An English Expositour' (1616), Blount's 'Glossographia' (1656). The first really inclusive dictionaries were Bailey's 'Universal Etymological English Dictionary' (1721) and the most impressive lexicographical achievement of the day, Dr Samuel Johnson's authoritative 'Dictionary' (1755), which apart from a few spellings like *publick, critick, terrour, interiour* in all essentials corresponds to the norm of our present-day usage.

The general aim of these lexicographers, like that of the later prescriptive grammarians (see p. 37), was not to record usage but rather to act as arbiters of correctness, to fix, stabilize and preserve the language from 'corruption and impuritie'. And Latin was the beau ideal.

More recent attempts to reform traditional spelling and devise new alphabets for English have been equally unavailing. We may mention Pitman's 'Phonotype Alphabet' from 1837 (based on shorthand), Ellis's 'Glossic' (1871), Zachrisson's 'Anglic' (1930), Wijk's 'Regularized Inglish' (1959) and Bernard Shaw's 'Shavian' (1962).

CHAPTER VI

Phonology

The OE period

The vocalic inventory of OE[1]

OE possessed seven long and seven short vowel phonemes represented gra-phically by *i, e, æ, a, o, u* and *y.* Length was phonemic (e.g. *dæl* 'valley', but *dǣl* 'part', *god* 'God', but *gōd* 'good', etc.), but was not indicated regularly in OE script, the macrons commonly found in textbooks and grammars being editorial.

There were four normally falling diphthongs *ēa, ea, ēo, eo* and (peculiar to early WSax) *īe* and *ie,* which were later monophthongized and rounded to *ȳ* and *y.*

Pronunciation

The pronunciation of OE vowels presents no difficulties to speakers of Con-tinental Germanic languages. Their values are approximately those we know today from German or Scandinavian. The diphthongs, it should be noted, form only one syllable, e.g. *sēon* 'see', *heard* 'hard'.

Some important vowel changes

The Germanic vocalic system underwent radical modifications on its way to OE. Some of these occurred in prehistoric times, and our knowledge, there-fore, is bound to be inferential, i.e. based on reconstruction. Some import-ant vowel changes will be discussed in rough outline below. The vowels will be seen to have undergone isolative as well as combinative changes. By iso-lative change is understood a change which occurs spontaneously, i.e. with-out any influence having been exerted upon it by contiguous sounds, whereas a combinative change is one which can be attributed to the influ-ence of contiguous sounds.

I) Isolative changes

Germ. **ai* > OE *ā*   OE *hāl* 'whole' (cp. OHG *heil,* Gothic *hails,* ON *heil*); OE *stān* 'stone' (cp. OHG *stein,* Goth. *stains,* ON (runic) *stainaR*) (see p. 25).

Germ. **au* > OE *ēa*   OE *ēage* 'eye' (cp. OHG *ouga,* Goth. *augo,* ON *auga*); OE *lēaf* 'leaf' (cp. OHG *loub,* Goth. *laufs,* ON *lauf*).

Germ. **eu* > OE *ēo*   OE *þēod* 'people' (cp. OHG *diut(isc),* Goth. *þiuda*); OE *dēop* 'deep' (cp. WGerm **deupa,* Goth. *diups,* ON *djupr*).

Germ. *$\bar{a}$ > OE $\bar{æ}$ OE *slǣpan* 'sleep' (cp. OHG *slāfan*, OS *slāpan)*; OE *strǣt* 'street' (cp. OHG *strāza* OS *strāta*, Latin *(via) strata*).[2]

Germ. *a > OE $æ$ OE *dæg* 'day' (cp. OHG *tag*, OS *dag*, ON *dagr*, Goth. *dags*); OE *fæder* 'father' (cp. OHG *fater,*, ON *faðir,* Goth. *fadar*).[3].

II) Combinative changes

Breaking

Affects the front vowels $\breve{æ}$, $\breve{e}$ and $\breve{i}$ when immediately followed by *h* or *h* + consonant, *l* + consonant or *r* + consonant. The resultant diphthongs are $\breve{e}a$, $\breve{e}o$.

Examples: OE *eald* 'old' < earlier *$æld$ (cp. OHG *alt*); OE *nēah* 'nigh' (cp. OHG *nah*); OE *steorra* 'star' (cp. OHG *sterno*); OE *lēon* 'lend' (cp. OHG *līhan);* OE *seolh* 'seal' (cp. ON *selr)*, etc.[4]

It should be observed that breaking of *$æ$ > *ea* did not take place in the Anglian dialects before *l* + consonant. Instead *æ* was retracted to *a,* and we get typically Anglian forms like *haldan* 'hold', *ald* 'old', *talde* 'told'[5], ancestors of our MnE forms.

The influence of nasals

WGerm *a* + nasal developed into *o,* which sound, however, must have had an open quality, for the scribes render it inconsistently now as *o,* now as *a: mon/man, þoncian/þancian* 'thank', *hond/hand*. This vacillation continued in ME and is reflected even today by West Midland regional forms like 'hond', 'mon'.

WGerm *an* + unvoiced fricative was first rounded to *on,* which then with the loss of the nasal became $\bar{o}$ (compensatory lengthening): OE *gōs* 'goose' (cp. OHG *gans*), OE *ōðer* 'other' (cp. OHG *ander*), OE *tōþ* 'tooth' (cp. OHG *zand*), etc.

The WGerm short vowels *u* and *i,* however, were only affected quantitatively when followed by nasal + unvoiced fricative: OE *ūs* 'us' (cp. OHG *uns*), OE *mūþ* 'mouth' (cp. OHG *mund*), OE *fīf* 'five' (cp. OHG *fimf*), OE *hrīðer* 'ox' (cp. OHG *rind*).

Palatal diphthongization

After the initial palatal consonants *c, g* and *sc* the vowels $\breve{æ}$ and *e* were diphthongized to $\breve{e}a$, *ie* respectively. This sound change, it should be emphasized, is a specifically WSax development. Examples: *ceaster* 'town' (non-WSax *cæster*, Latin *castra*), *geat* 'gate' (non-WSax *gæt*), *scēap* 'sheep' (non-WSax *scǣp*), *gieldan* 'yield' (non-WSax *geldan*).

I-umlaut (or i-mutation)

This is the customary designation for the change operating on certain root-vowels or diphthongs under the influence of an *i/j* in the syllable immediately following. Through anticipation, attraction or assimilation (what actually happens is not quite clear) vowels distant in quality from *i/j*, i.e. all back vowels and certain front vowels, underwent a process of fronting, i.e. they moved articulatorily in the direction of the *i/j* sound. Examples: OE *fyllan* 'fill' < earlier **fulljan*, OE *sēcan* 'seek' < earlier **sōkjan*, OE *menn* 'men' < earlier **mænni* (WGerm **manni*), OE *strengðu* 'strength' < earlier **strangiðu*, etc.[6].

I-umlaut is shared by all Germanic languages except Gothic[7]. English *tooth-teeth, man-men, old-elder, sale-sell, full-fill*, etc. are products of the same mechanism as gave German and Danish *Zahn-Zähne, tand-tænder; Mann-Männer, mand-mænd; alt-älter; salg-sælge; fuld-fylde*, etc.

The dramatic impact of i-umlaut upon the Germanic languages derivationally and in the setting up of new grammatical contrasts will be evident from the following examples:

$\breve{u} > \breve{y}$	*fyllan* 'fill' (cp. adj. *ful* and Goth, *fuljan*[8]), *gylden* 'golden' (cp. OHG *guldin*), *mӯs* 'mice' from earlier **mūsi*.
$\bar{o} > \bar{e}$	*bēc* 'books' from earlier **bōki, dēman* (cp. *dōm* 'judgment' and Goth. *dōmjan*).
$\bar{a} > \bar{æ}$	*hǣlan* 'heal' (cp. adj. *hāl* and Goth. *hailjan), hǣþ* 'heath' (cp. Goth. *haiþi*), hwǣte 'wheat' (cp. OHG *hweiti*).
æ > *e*	*settan* 'set' from earlier **sættjan* (cp. Goth. *satjan), here* 'army' (cp. Goth. *harjis), betera* 'better' (cp. Goth. *batiza*).
$\bar{æ}$	was unaffected by i-umlaut.

The following diphthongs, whether the result of isolative or combinative changes, were affected by i-umlaut chiefly in WSax:

$\bar{ea} > \bar{ie}$	*hīeran* 'hear' (cp. Goth. *hausjan), nīehst* 'next' (superl. of *nēah* 'nigh'), *ieldre* 'elder' (comp. of *eald*, see p. 90), *ciese* 'cheese' from earlier **cēa-si* (cp. OHG *kāsi*).
$\bar{eo} > \bar{ie}$	*līehtan* 'lighten' (cp. *lēoht* and Goth. *liuhtjan), weorpan – he wierpþ* 'he throws' (cp. German *werfen – er wirft*).

Some quantitative changes
I) Lengthening before consonant clusters
Short vowels and diphthongs were lengthened in late OE before the consonant clusters *ld, rd, rn, rl, rþ, nd, ng,* and *mb* (cp. mod. German cognates): *fēld* 'field', *wōrd* 'word', *lēornian* 'learn', *eorl* 'earl', *eorðe* 'earth', *fīndan* 'find', *ēnd* 'end', *sīngan* 'sing', *þīng* 'thing', *clīmban* 'climb', etc., but not if these combinations were followed by a third consonant: *lāmb* but *lambru* 'lambs', *lāng* but *lengra* 'longer', *cīld* 'child' but *cildru* 'children'.[9]

II) Shortening before consonant clusters

Long vowels were in OE normally shortened before consonant clusters other than those listed above: *fīf* 'five' but *fifta* 'fifth', *cēpan* 'keep' but *cepte* 'kept', *lǣdan* but *lædde* 'led', *hwīt* but *hwittra* 'whiter', etc. and in words of three or more syllables: *sūþ* but *suþerne* 'southern', *hālig* but *haligdæg* 'holiday'. This type of shortening was operative at varying times, some in OE, some as late as early ME.

Now we can account for the puzzling inconsistency of MnE pairs like *five-fifth, meet-met, food-fodder, house-husband, good-gospel* (OE *gōd spel*), *broad-Bradley, deep-Deptford, street-Stratford, white-Whitaker, wild-wilderness, holy-holiday, out-utter.*

The consonant inventory

The OE consonant system comprised from 15 to 19 phonemes, depending on how we interpret them. Long consonants were indicated by doubling the symbol for the short as shown contrastively by pairs like *cwelan* 'die' – *cwellan* 'kill', *manian* 'remind' – *mannian* 'to garrison'.

The symbols *b, d, p, t, l, m, n,* and *w* had approximately the same values as in MnE.

A few consonant symbols, however, require special mention. OE *f, s,* and *þ/ð* represented different values according to their position. They were unvoiced when they occurred initially and finally, but were voiced between voiced sounds: *feðer* [f-] 'feather', *sceaf* [-f] 'sheaf',[10] but *ofer* [-v-] 'over'; *singan* [s-] 'sing', *hūs* [-s] but *cēosan* [-z-] 'choose'. The symbols *v* and *z* would have been useful here, but they were not introduced until ME (see p. 57). Further *þōht* [θ-] 'thought', *wearþ* [-θ] 'he became' but *weorðan* [-ð-] 'to become'.[11]

The symbol *c* carried two values in OE that were also determined by position. Before a consonant or a back vowel it was always pronounced [k] as in *clǣne* 'clean', *cnotta* 'knot', *cuman* 'come', *bacan* 'bake', etc. Before or immediately after a front vowel, however, its value is palatal [tʃ] as in *cīld* 'child', *ciele* 'chill', *cēosan* 'choose', *cyrice* 'church'[12], *gelīc* 'similar', etc.

The digraphs *sc* and *cg* were pronounced [ʃ] and [dʒ] respectively: *scip* 'ship', *scamu* 'shame', *wȳscan* 'wish', *ecg* 'edge', *secgan* 'say', etc.

The symbol *g* carried three positional values. Initially before back vowels or a consonant it was used for the stop [g] as in *gōd* 'good', *guma* 'man', *gān* 'go', *gram* 'angry', *glæs* 'glass', *gnæt* 'gnat'. But if the contiguous sound had front quality, *g* should be pronounced [j] as in *geard* 'yard', *gimm* 'gem', *dæg* 'day', *wīg* 'war', *mægden* 'maiden', etc.

In back environments, however, the original Germanic velar fricative [ɣ] was retained. The sound may for practical purposes be approximated by [w]; *dagas* 'days', *fugol* 'fowl'.

The symbol *h* represented three positional values. It was aspirated initially: *hors* 'horse', *hund* 'hound', *hāt* 'hot', *hring* 'ring', *hlāford* 'lord', *hnutu* 'nut', *hwīt* 'white'[13], but elsewhere it was a velar or a palatal fricative (as in German *ach* and *ich)* depending on the back or front quality of the contiguous sound: *dohtor* 'daughter', *cniht* 'knight'.

The symbol *r*, when used initially, represented a strongly trilled sound much as in modern Scots, but finally and before a consonant it may well have approximated the retroflex variety we know from American: *riht* 'right', but *sēar* 'dry', *heard* 'hard'.

Some important consonant changes

Metathesis
Metathesis denotes a change in the sequence of a consonant and a neighbouring vowel. The phenomenon was frequent in OE in connection with *r*: *bærnan* 'burn' (cp. German *brennen*)[14], *ærn* 'house' (cp. Danish *rønne*), *hors* 'horse' (cp. German *Ross*), *þerscan* 'thresh' (cp. German *dreschen*, but Danish *tærske*). Metathesis of *r* continued to be common in ME and EMnE: *fryst* 'first', *thrist* 'thirst', *Kyrstmesse* 'Christmas', and in the modern dialects we still find *gurt* 'great', *purdy* 'pretty', *girn* 'grin', etc.

Palatalization
Some stop consonants, particularly *k* and *g*, underwent palatalization when preceded or followed by an original front vowel:

k > tʃ   *ic* 'I', *cild* 'child', *stenc* 'stench'. Similarly *sk* became [ʃ]: *fisc* 'fish', *scīnan* 'shine'.

g > j   *gimm* 'gem', *bodig* 'body', *dæg* 'day', *geong* 'young'. Similarly *gg* became [dʒ]: *secgan* 'say', *hrycg* 'ridge' (< *hrugjo*).

Palatalization, however, did not take place in the North, witness MnE place-name pairs like *Greenwich* vs *Warwick*, *Winchester* vs *Lancaster* (cp. Lat. *vicus* (OE *wīc*), *castra* (OE *ceaster*)).

Loss of consonants
a) Loss of nasals before unvoiced fricatives was dealt with p. 64.

b) Loss of *h*. Intervocalic *h* is often lost in OE with subsequent lengthening of the vowels thus brought together. The verb *slēan* 'slay' has the past partc. *slegen*, and the *g*-less infinitive can be explained from earlier **sleahan* with loss of *h*, contraction and compensatory lengthening of the vowel[15]. Thus also *sēon* 'see' (< **seohan*) past partc. *segen*; *fōn* 'catch' (< **fohan*) past partc. *fangen*; *tēon* 'draw' (< **teohan*) past partc. *togen*. Cp. German *ziehen – gezogen*.

c) Loss of *g*. Subsequent upon the loss of *g* before *n* and *d*, short vowels underwent compensatory lengthening: *rīnan* 'rain' (cp. German *regnen*), *frīnan* 'ask' (cp. German *fragen*), *mǣden* 'maiden' (cp. German *Magd*), *sǣde* 'said' (cp. Danish *sagde*).

Consonant lengthening (gemination)
As we have indicated briefly p. 66, doubling was in OE a graphic device to indicate consonant length. In WGerm all consonants except *r* were lengthened after a short syllable when followed by *j* as in *settan* (cp. Gothic *satjan*), *cnyttan* 'knit' (< **knutjan*), *steppan* 'walk' (< **stapjan*), *secg* 'man' (< **sagja*). On *cg* from *gg*, see p. 67.

The ME period
ME was a period of extensive phonological change. If we compare the late OE of Ælfric and Wulfstan with early ME, it is as if the language has been transformed almost overnight, and we feel tempted to ascribe the abruptness of the change to the Norman Conquest. It is true that the impact of French is overwhelming, but, as we shall see, that was in other areas than phonology.

It is important to remember that what we customarily refer to as OE is the WSax standard as it was written down by scribes adhering to traditional spelling conventions (see p. 29), which had long ceased to give a true picture of the language actually spoken. The changes in sound (and also grammatical structure for that matter) that we find so dramatic in ME are the results of developments that were noticeable already in late OE and were on the march even earlier in spoken usage. They are now visible because they are no longer obscured by scribal convention. The chief contribution of the Normans to the phonology of English is therefore that they eliminated the written WSax standard with its conservatory influence, thereby causing phonological developments that had long been on their way to surface freely in written form and dialectal diversity.

Some important vowel changes[16]
1) OE *ā* became *ǭ* about 1200 in all dialects south of the Humber, but remained unrounded in the North as *ā* till about 1300 when it became *ę̄*, which has been preserved in the Scots dialects of today. Examples are OE *bān* 'bone' > ME *bǭn* OE *gāst* 'spirit' > ME *gǭst*, OE *ān* 'one' > ME *ǭn*.

MnE reflexes like *hale* (OE *hāl*), *raid* (OE *rād*) are due to Northern dialectal influence in the modern standard. The Southern development has given us *whole, road*.

2) OE *æ* became retracted to *a* in most dialects of ME. OE *wæs* > ME *was*, OE *þæt* > ME *that*, OE *æppel* > ME *appel*.

3) OE *ǣ* was in most ME dialects represented by *ę̄* or *ē*[17]. But unfortunately both *ę̄* and *ē*, though separate phonemes, were both written *e*, until scribal practice in late ME began to distinguish them.

This makes it very difficult for the non-expert to determine their value, but the following rule of thumb may be of some help. ME *e* generally represents the close ē sound if its modern reflex is spelt with *ee*, but the open ę̄ sound if its modern reflex is spelt with *ea*. Examples: OE *slǣpan* 'sleep' > ME *slepen*, OE *strǣt* 'street' > ME *stret*, OE *dǣd* 'deed' > ME *dēd*, but OE *hǣlan* 'heal' > ME *hę̄len*, OE *sǣ* 'sea' > ME *sę̄*, OE *dǣlan* 'deal' > ME *dę̄len*.

4) OE *ē* became ME *ē*, in late ME often written *ee*, whereas spellings with *ie* are due to the influence of French orthography. Modern reflexes are usually spelt *ee* or *ie*: OE *dēman* 'deem' > ME *dēmen*, OE *fēt* 'feet' > ME *fēt*, OE *fēld* 'field' > ME *fēld*.

5) OE ĭ were preserved in ME. OE *biddan* 'bid' > ME *bidden*, OE *þing* 'thing' > ME *þing;* OE *fīf* 'five' > ME *fīve*. On *i* and *y* as purely graphic variants, see p. 59.

6) OE *ō* became ME *ō*: OE *bōc* 'book' > ME *bōke*, OE *blōd* 'blood' > *blōde*, OE *mōna* 'moon' > ME *mōne*.[18]

7) OE *u* was preserved in ME: OE *ful* 'full' > ME *ful*, OE *lufu* 'love' > ME *luve*, OE *hnutu* 'nut' > ME *nute*.

In minim surroundings *u* was often written *o* for legibility: *note* 'nut', *sonne* 'sun', etc. (see further p. 58).

8) OE *ū* was retained in ME: OE *cū* 'cow' > ME *cū*, OE *mūþ* 'mouth' > ME *mūth*. From the 13th century, however, ME *ū* began to be rendered *ou/ow* by Anglo-Norman scribes in whose native speech *u* was [ü]. MnE reflects both spellings: *cow, down, house.*

9) OE ȳ were both unrounded to *i* in early ME: OE *brycg* 'bridge' > ME *brigge*, OE *fȳr* 'fire' to ME *fīr*, ON *skȳ* 'sky' > ME *skī.*

Some dialectal developments are important for their bearing upon MnE. In Kentish OE y̆ became ĕ, and a few MnE words are of this dialectal origin, e.g. *merry* (OE *myrige*), *knell* (OE *cnyllan*), *kernel* (OE *cyrnel*), *left* (OE *lyft*), *hemlock* (OE *hymlic*). With West Midland or South Western spelling: *bury* (OE *byrgan*), *(Canter)bury* (OE *byrig* 'town'). MnE *busy* shows the same spelling, but has East Midland pronunciation.

10) OE ĕo both became monophthongized and were pronounced [ö:] or [ö] in late OE, although the spelling was retained in some dialects till as late as about 1200. Then they were unrounded to *e* or *ē* with *ee, ie* as the typical MnE spelling reflexes of the long vowel: OE *heorte* 'heart' > ME *herte*, OE *ceorfan* 'carve, cut' > ME *kerven;* OE *þēof* 'thief' > ME *þēf*, OE *dēop* 'deep' > ME *dēp.*

11) OE *ea* became monophthongized to *æ* in late OE though the spelling was retained considerably longer. Examples are OE *feallan* 'fall' > ME *fallen*, OE *geaf* 'he gave' > ME *gaf*, OE *healp* 'he helped' > ME *halp*, OE *eall* 'all' > ME *all*, OE *sceal* 'shall' > ME *schall.*

12) OE *ēa* became *ǣ* in late OE, fell together with *ǣ²* (see p. 146, note 17), and came to be represented by *ē* through Anglo-Norman scribal practice: OE *hlēapan* 'leap' > ME *lēpen*, OE *dēad* 'dead' > ME *dēd*, OE *hēafod* 'head' > ME *hēved*. MnE spelling reflexes are, as of *ǣ²*, normally *ea.*

13) OE ĭe, it will be remembered, was a specifically WSax development. It

69

was monophthongized to $\bar{\imath}/\bar{y}$ in late WSax, and its development in ME thus concerns the South Western and West Midland dialects alone. Here the spelling was normally *u* according to Anglo-Norman practice. The non-WSax dialects had $\bar{e}$, giving *e* and $\bar{e}$ respectively as the typical ME forms: OE *giest* 'guest' > ME *gest*, OE *híeran* 'hear' > ME *hēren*, OE *cíese* 'cheese' > ME *chēse*.

e + r > ar

ME short *e* + *r* became *ar* by the end of the period. In most cases MnE spelling reflects the change: *star* (ME *sterre*), *dark* (ME *derk*), *darling* (ME *derling*), *far* (ME *ferre*), *starve* (ME *sterven*), *start* (ON *sterta*), and the name of the letter *R*.

The change also involved French borrowings: *farm* (OF *ferme*), *war* (AN *werre*, see also p. 49), *marvel* (OF *merveil*), *parsley* (OF *persil*).

In a number of words, including also some place-names, the original spelling has been retained: *clerk* (but cp. the personal name *Clark*), *sergeant* (but cp. the personal name *Sargeant*), *Derby, Hertford, Cherwell*. Both types have survived with semantic shift in *person – parson* (< *persona ecclesiastica*)[19].

French or Latin loans introduced after the change was operative retain *er*: *deter, aver, alert, inert*.

French vowels usually fell into the ME phonemic pattern. French [ö], however, was usually rendered $\bar{e}$ as in *bēf* 'beef', except in the West Midlands where it was retained and spelt *eo*. Hence MnE spellings like *people, jeopardy* (< *jeu parti*).

French nasal vowels were denasalized in ME, $\bar{a}$ becoming *aun* or *an* as in *chaunce, chance*.

French *y* was probably different from OE *y* since it did not undergo the same development in time and dialect, but ultimately became *ju* in open syllables (e.g. *pursuen, sure, creature*) and *u* in closed syllables (e.g. *just, sepulchre*).

On Anglo-Norman and Parisian French vowels, see p. 50.

Scandinavian vowels are dealt with p. 43.

New diphthongs

All OE diphthongs, as we have seen, were monophthongized in passing into ME, but new diphthongs were created from the development of an *i*-glide between front vowels and *g* and later also of an *u*-glide between back vowels and *g*: OE *sægde* 'said' > ME *seide*, OE *weg* 'way' > ME *wei*, OE *flēogan* 'fly' > ME *flīen*, OE *āgan* 'own' > ME *ouen*, OE *boga* 'bow' > ME *boue*, OE *fugol* 'fowl' (:bird) > ME *foul*.

Similar glides were developed before *h*, which, however, was not lost like the *g*: OE *eahta* 'eight' > late OE *ehta* > ME *eihte*, OE *feohtan* 'fight' > late OE *fehten* > ME *feihten*.

OE *hagu* 'haw' > ME *hau*, OE *āht* 'ought' > ME *aught*.

French diphthongs

Important is *oi* as in *joie* 'joy', *cloistre* 'cloister', *chois* 'choice' – an almost infallible criterion of a French loan in English. Another diphthong of French origin is *ui*, usually spelt *oi*, as in *builen* 'boil', *puisen* 'poison', *juin* 'join'.

Rising diphthongs

Through shift of accent some OE falling diphthongs may become rising diphthongs and lose the first element. OE *cēosan* could thus develop in two ways, either become ME *chēsen* or through *ceósen*, become ME *chōsen*. Similarly OE *scēotan* > ME *schēten/schōten*, OE *scēawian* 'behold' > ME *schēwen/schōwen*. MnE still reflects this development in *show/shew*. MnE *sew* (OE *sēowian*) represents one development in form, the other in sound.

Some important quantitative changes

Lengthenings

The lengthening (and shortening again in ME) of short OE vowels before certain consonant sequences was dealt with p. 65.

Important is the early ME lengthening of vowels in open syllables of dissyllabic words. This change affects the short vowels *a, e* and *o*: OE *faran* 'fare' > ME *fāren*, ON *taka* 'take' > ME *tāken*, OE *stelan* 'steal' > ME *stēlen*, OE *flotian* 'float' > ME *flōten*, OE *þrote* 'throat' > ME *þrōte*.

Under similar conditions *i* and *u* became *ē* and *ō* respectively in late ME: OE *sicor* 'secure' > ME *sēker*, OE *wicu* 'week' > ME *wēke*, OE *wudu* 'wood' > ME *wōde*.

Monosyllabic words, however, might through inflexion acquire that extra syllable that made them susceptible to lengthening. Thus MnE *gate* cannot be explained from OE *geat*, but reflects the plural OE *gatu*, MnE *black* goes back to OE *blæc*, but the personal name *Blake* must derive from some inflected dissyllabic form.

Syllable and inflection

Some words might acquire trisyllabic form through inflection and hence remain immune from lengthening (see p. 65). MnE words like *saddle* (OE *sadol*), *heavy* (OE *hefig*), *heaven* (OE *heofon*), *weather* (OE *weder*), *body* (OE *bodig*) have retained short vowels although all conditions were present for lengthening, and can only be explained as reflexes of some trisyllabic form acquired through inflexion (e.g. *wederes, heofonum*). Both long and short form survive in MnE *shade* (OE *sceadu*) and *shadow* from the inflected form. Similarly *mead-meadow*.

Conversely many words with originally long vowel were shortened if inflexion made them add extra syllables: OE *ǣnig* 'any' > ME *ani, eni* (through plur. *ænige*), OE *cīcen* 'chicken' > ME *cicen* (through plur. *cicenu*), OE *hēafod* 'head' > ME *heued* (through plur. *heafdu*).[20]

Vowels in unaccented syllables

Of far-reaching importance for the grammatical structure of English is the levelling under [ə] of the OE distinctive vowels *a, o,* and *u* in unaccented position. ME usually had *e* for these OE vowels when unaccented: OE *cuman* 'come' > ME *cumen,* OE *wē þolodon* 'we suffered' > ME *we þoleden,* OE *hara* 'hare' > ME *hare,* OE *nosu* 'nose' > ME *nose,* OE *mid handum* 'with hands' > ME *mid handen,* OE *nacod* 'naked' > ME *naked.*

Some important consonant changes

The OE consonant system has proved remarkably stable, there being only two sounds that have not survived to the present day, namely OE [ɣ] and [χ/ç] (see p. 66), which latter, however, lived on till late ME and is still heard in Scots dialects.

Fricatives

Southern voicing

A characteristic of the Kentish and South Western dialects of ME is the voicing of the initial fricatives *s* and *f*. This change took place early, probably about 1100, since no French loans participate in it. Examples are: *zome* 'some', *zeluer* 'silver', *zuo* 'so'; *vor* 'for' *uol* 'full', *vyf* 'five'.[21] A few words like *vat* (OE *fæt*), *vane* (OE *fana*), *vixen* (OE *fyxen*) in the modern standard must therefore have been introduced via Southern dialect. Today the feature is typical only of some Southwestern dialects, particularly Dorset and Somerset, e.g. *varmer* 'farmer', *vace* 'face', *zun* 'sun', *zez* 'says'[22].

New phonemes

As we have already noted p. 65, [f] – [v], [θ] – [ð] and [s] – [z] were in OE positional variants of three phonemes. In ME, however, they achieved phonemic status as a result of the introduction of foreign words with *v-* (*vine, veal, visit*), with *z-* (*zeal, zephyr*), and as a result of the voicing about 1400 of initial [θ] in monosyllabic words like *this, thou, they,* etc. (see p. 78).

The f – v pattern

The OE rule according to which *f* was pronounced [f] finally and [v] medially in voiced surroundings, and which we see reflected in the MnE plural type *loaf – loaves* (OE *hlāf-hlāfas*), *wife – wives, knife – knives,* etc. came to generate a regular *f*-singular and *v*-plural pattern, on the analogy of which many words were remodelled in ME, so that they acquired, etymologically unwarranted, an unvoiced spirant in the singular: *sheriff* (OE *scīr gerēfa*),[23] *belief* (OE *gelēafa*).

French words with the exception of the semantically differentiated *beef-beeves,* however, have successfully resisted the pull of the *f-v* pattern (*brief-briefs, proof-proofs,* etc.).

Loss of fricatives

v was lost before a consonant in ME: OE *hlāford* 'lord' > ME *lāvrd* > *lord,*
OE *hēafod* 'head' > *hevd* > *hed,* OE *hæfst* 'thou hast', *hæfþ* 'he hath',
hæfde 'he had' > ME *hast, hath, had.* Similarly OF *povre* > *poor,* OF *couvre
feu* > *curfew* and poetical archaisms like *e'er, ne'er, e'en, o'er.* The old-fash-
ioned local pronunciation of the place-names *Daventry* and *Cavendish* was
[deintri] and [kændiʃ].

-*tʃ* was lost in unaccented syllables: OE *ǣfre ǣlc* 'every' > ME *everiche,*
OE *ic* 'I' > ME *ich* > *i/ī* (according to emphasis), the OE suffix -*līc* became
ME -*li* (*frelie* 'freely', *lyghtlie* 'lightly').

h was lost in the sequences *hl, hr, hn* and to some extent in *hw*[24]: OE *hlūde*
'loud' > ME *loude,* OE *hring* 'ring' > ME *ring,* OE *hnutu* 'nut' > ME *nute,*
OE *hwæt* 'what' > ME *what.*

The OE palatal fricative [ç] (see p. 66) which in ME occurred before *t* or
finally *(night, light, bright, fight, thigh, high)* was gradually lost in ME and
EMnE with compensatory lengthening of the preceding vowel, but is still
preserved in Scots before *t* [breçt, neçt]. In *delight* (ME *delite*) we have unetymological *gh,* which, however, indicates that *gh* must have been silent
when it was added.

The velar positional variant [χ] was retained in the north and written *ch,*
but was lost finally, or in the sequence *ht* in the other ME dialects *(plough,
daughter),* or became *f (laugh, rough, draught).*

Nasals

Loss of -n

Final unstressed -*n* was lost in a vast variety of words, exerting a far-reaching influence upon the morphological structure of English. Final -*n* was lost
in infinitives (OE *lufian* > ME *lufe(n)*), in past participles (OE *druncen* >
ME *drunke*), in possessive pronouns before consonants (OE *mīn, þīn* > ME
mī, þī), in the indefinite article before consonants (OE *ān* > ME *a*), in the
plural of verbs (ME *we comen* > *we come*), and in uninflected words like
about, without, before above, but (cp. OE *ābūtan, wiþūtan, beforan, ābūfan,
būtan*). Similarly the preposition *on* + consonant became *a: alive* (OE *on
līfe*), *abed, afoot, aboard, ashore, a hunting* (OE *on huntunge*).

The loss of -*n* began in the Northern dialects of late OE, and extended
southwards and was operative in the South towards the close of ME.

Since -*n* was lost only when it was strictly final, it might in several cases be
retained if the word in which it occurred was frequently used in some inflected form. Such inflected forms account for MnE *maiden* (OE *mǣden*) vs.
maid (but non-final position has preserved the otherwise archaic -*n* form in
maidenhood, maidenlike), *even* (as in *Hallowe'en* (OE *ǣfen*) vs. *eve, lenten*
(OE *lencten*) vs. *Lent.*

In many cases, however, only the reflex of the inflected form has survived
into MnE: *burden, heaven, weapon, oven, open, nine* (OE *byrðen, heofon, wǣ-*

pen, ofen, open, nigon). Final *-n* was lost in the sequence *-mn: column, damn, autumn, solemn* (but *damnation, solemnity*).

Metanalysis

In the absence of a fixed spelling convention in ME, many writers, guided by their pronunciation, were apt to make misdivisions like *a noke* 'an oak', *a nuncle* 'an uncle', *a nox* 'an ox', *a nodyr* 'another'. A few of these metanalyzed forms have crept into MnE: *nickname* (ME *ēkename*), *newt* (OE *efeta*).

The reverse process is seen in MnE *apron* (OF *naperon*), *umpire* (OF *nompere*), *adder* (OE *nǣdre*). MnE petnames like *Nan, Ned, Noll, Nell* have probably originated from metanalysis involving the possessive *mine: (mi)ne Ann, Ed(ward), Ol(iver), Ell(en).*

Stops

-mb > m. Final *-b* was lost in late ME after *m*, but has been retained in spelling: *womb* (OE *wamba*), *climb* (OE *climban*), *comb* (OE *camb*), *lamb* (OE *lamb*), *dumb* (OE *dumb*), *tomb* (OF *tombe*).

Inverse spellings are seen in *thumb* (OE *þūma*), *limb* (OE *lim*), *numb* (with cold) (OE *numen*), *crumb* (OE *cruma*).

Some later loans have fallen into this pattern: *succumb, rhomb. Iamb* is still pronounced with [b].

Medially, however, [b] was retained: *chamber, humble, bramble, shambles, slumber.* In the last three, it should be noted, *b* is excrescent and inserted after *m* (OE *brǣmel, scamol, slūma*).

Excrescent d

The adding of *-d* after *n* in many words both of French and Germanic origin took place in late ME, but is continuous into EMnE: *sound* (OF *son*), *expound* (ME *expounen*), *astound* (OF *estoner*), *bound* (for) (ON *buin*), *pound* 'beat, batter' (OE *pūnian*), *thunder* (OE *þunor*).

Many other ME and EMnE *-nd* forms have survived to the present day in dialectal speech, e.g. *drownd* (pret. *drownded*).

Liquids

Loss of l. Before [tʃ] *l* was dropped in early ME: *which* (OE *hwylc*), *each* (OE *ǣlc*), *such* (OE *swylc*), *much* (OE *mycel*). It was lost also in the unstressed forms of OE *ealswā* 'also' > ME *alse, ase* > MnE *as*, the stressed form surviving in *also.*

R- metathesis was dealt with p. 67.

The Modern English period

The Great Vowel Shift

This is the most thoroughgoing change that has ever taken place in the history of English sounds. At the time of Chaucer English vowels still retained their so-called Continental values, but between roughly 1400 and 1700 all long vowels, however they originated, were raised in their articulation. The two highest vowels $\bar{\imath}$ and $\bar{u}$, which could not be raised without becoming consonantal, became diphthongs. The change may be provisionally diagrammed like this:

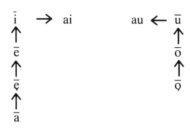

Further illustration may be given in the following slightly oversimplified diagram of ME, EMnE and MnE pronunciations. The individual developments will be discussed in more detail below:

ME	EMnE	MnE	
ī — ij — ei ————		ai	as in *life, bite, wise*
ẹ̄ ———— ī ————		ī	as in *see, meet, beet*
ę̄ ———— ẹ̄ — ī —		ī	as in *sea, meat, beat*
ā ———— ę̄ — ẹ̄ —		ei	as in *hate, lady, name*
ū —uw— ou————		au	as in *house, cow, down*
ō ———— ū ————		ū	as in *fool, goose, moon*
ǭ ———— ō ————		ou	as in *coast, rode, boat*

What took place was probably this. When the two highest vowels shifted to diphthongs, the pair below moved up to fill the gap, leaving room for the next pair below to move, etc. We shall not here be concerned with whether the whole process actually started from the top (the pull theory) or whether it could also have started from the bottom (the push theory). It is more important to note that the transition was gradual and that phonemic distance was always maintained so as to avoid homophony.

Evidence that permits us to follow the shift in some detail is chiefly the rhymes and puns of poets, foreign phrase books describing English pronunciation,[25] early spelling reformers like Hart (see p. 61), spellings in diaries, memoirs and private correspondence,[26] and developments in modern English dialects.

Vowel shift and spelling

As will appear from the MnE illustrations, the Vowel Shift played havoc with spelling, since most changes occurred after a spelling standard had begun to solidify. MnE spelling will therefore be seen to reflect mediaeval pronunciation in many cases. Even forms like *house* and *cow* are only seemingly phonetic, for *ou/ow* as we have noticed p. 69 originally denoted [ū].

Further, the Vowel Shift caused original differences in quantity to emerge in MnE as differences in quality, but often disguised by the spelling:[27] *child-children, wise-wisdom, hide-hid, sheep-shepherd, mean-meant, read-read, shade-shadow, pale-pallor, south-southern, flower-flourish, goose-gosling, fool-folly, nose-nostril, holy-holiday.*

Some important vowel changes

1) ME *a* was raised to [æ] about 1600 (Shakespeare rhymes *scratch-wretch, back-neck*), but the old back quality of ME *a* has remained unchanged in many chiefly Northern dialects of today. If followed by an unvoiced fricative, however, [æ] was lengthened in the 17th century and later retracted to *ā* (*ask, castle, bath, laugh, chaff,* etc.), but modern American and many English dialects still reflect the old *ǣ*-stage. Before *r* ME *a* was first lengthened to *ǣ*, and then became *ā* about 1800 *(artist, bar, hard, sharp).*

When followed by dark *l*, an *au*-glide developed, which was later monophthongized to *ǭ*, *(hall, call, also, altar)*. MnE *shall* reflects an unaccented form, the accented variant 'shaul' being now dialectal.

2) ME *i* remained unchanged *(bid, ship, winter)*. If followed by *r* it became [ə̄] *(fir, stir, mirth,* etc.).

3) ME *o* became *ǫ* in EMnE *(body, rotten, gosling, common)*. An EMnE unrounded variant (Spenser rhymes *plot-that,* Shakespeare *dally-folly*) is still reflected in modern American pronunciation and by MnE doublets: *strop/strap, God/Gad (by Gad!)*.

When followed by *l* an *ou*-glide developed *(roll, molten, soldier)*, which is still registered in the spelling of *bowl* (ME *bolle*), *mould* (ME *molde*). Before an unvoiced fricative ME *o* appeared as *ǭ*, later shortened to *ǫ (loss, cross, cloth, coffee)*. If followed by *r*, it became *ǭ* in the 17th century *(morning, horn, horse, absorb)*.

4) ME *u* became [ʌ] about 1700[28] as in *thunder, much, mud, number,* but the original sound was retained in many cases after a labial *(push, bush, full)*. The *u* > [ʌ] change, however, did not affect the North and a good deal of the Midlands, where *rush* still rhymes with *bush*. Note minim spellings like *come, won, monk, tongue, honey,* etc. (see p. 58).

5) ME *ā* became EMnE *ę̄* and, through a 17th century *ę̄*-stage, became the

MnE diphthong *ei* about 1800 (*lady, name, blame, tale*). The early *ę̄*-stage is reflected by Spenserian rhymes like *feature-nature, speake-make, states-seates*. Shakespeare puns on *abased – a beast, grace-grease-grass*. The *ē*-stage has survived in *Jem/Jim* for *James*. Pronunciations reflecting the former *ę̄* and *ē*-stages are still typical of many chiefly Northern dialects.

6) ME *ē* became EMnE *ī*, from the 16th century usually spelt *ee* or *ie* (*meet, street, wheel, thief, achieve*). 'Private' spellings like *shype* 'sheep', *besyche* 'beseech' in late ME suggest an early transition to *ī*.

7) ME *ę̄* began to be written *ea* in the early 16th century (*heat, beat, sea, dream, treat*) to indicate the open sound. Note also Elizabethan rhymes like *uncleane-maintaine, dreams-Thames, maids-beads, sea-way, snake-speake*.

Words like *dead, threaten, breath, sweat, bread, heaven* still preserved their original long vowel in EMnE, witness rhymes like *eaten-threaten, breath-beneath*, and their present form must be due to later shortening.

About 1600, however, *ę̄* was raised to *ē*, and about 1800 an additional raising gave *ī*, which caused it to join the development of ME *ē*. The result was extensive homophony (*meat-meet, beat-beet, leak-leek*, etc.). The two sounds are still kept apart in Northern and Irish dialect, cp also Irish proper names like *Yeats, Reagan, O'Shea* with *ę̄*.

MnE *break, great, steak, yea* were in the 18th century and are still dialectally pronounced with *ī*. Our present pronunciation is hard to account for, but could be due to South Western dialectal influence, or they could be survivals of a group of words that did not follow the prevalent development *ę̄ > ī*, but remained at the *ę̄* stage and became *ei*.

8) ME *ī* became *ai* in the 18th century through the EMnE stages *ij > ei*, witness 16th-century 'private' spellings like *feyr* 'fire', *bleynd* 'blind'.

9) ME *ō* developed into EMnE *ū* and was from the 16th century usually spelt *oo* (*goose, moon, choose, prove*). MnE forms like *book, foot, stood, took, hook, shook*, etc. testify to the vowel having been shortened some time after 1700, otherwise it would have joined the *u > ʌ* development. MnE *roof, room, broom* still vacillate as to quantity[29]. In *blood, flood, other, brother, done, month*, on the other hand, shortening occurred early enough for the resulting *u* to become *ʌ*. *Soot* was pronounced [s ʌ t] till about 1900.

10) ME *ǭ* became MnE *ou* (*oak, road, coast, toe, holy*) through an EMnE *ō* stage. The *ou*-stage is late, and many dialects of today still reflect both *ǭ* and *ǭ* stages. The *oa*-spelling represents 16th-century attempts to separate the open *ǭ* from the close *ō*-variety, which had come to be written *oo*. The *oa*-spelling thus constitutes a parallel to the *ea*-spelling of the open *ę̄*-sound[30].

11) ME *ū* became MnE *au* (*house, mouth, cow, power*) via the EMnE stages *uw > ou*. It did not diphthongize in the North, however, and a word like *uncouth* can be explained as a dialect loan in the standard.

Before labials, however, ME *ū* remained (*stoop, droop, room, tomb, loop, Cowper* (note variant *Cooper*). The combination *wū-* also remained unchanged as in the verb *to wound*, but the preterite of *wind* is [au] because of the analogy of *found, bound*.

12) ME *ü* in French loans became *jū* about 1600 in open syllables *(duke, use, accuse, human)*, and *ju* in closed *(just, judge)*.

13) ME *ai* became EMnE *ẹ̄*, which then joined ME *ẹ̄* and the *ẹ̄* > *ẹ̄* > *ei* development of ME *ā* (see p. 76), witness 16th-century 'private' spellings like *panes* 'pains', *agane* 'again', *wate* 'wait' and rhymes like *despair-fear, please-days, staid-made-shade-displaide.*

14) ME *oi* became MnE *oi (cloister, choice, employ, joy)*. With the sole exception of *boy* (which is probably from Dutch), this diphthong indicates loans of French origin.

ME *ui* (< Anglo-Norman *ui)* was also written *oi*, but words of this origin were pronounced [ui] till about 1600 when they became *ai* as evidenced by rhymes like *toyle-awhile-assoile* (Spenser), *refines-joins* (Dryden), *join-divine* (Pope). 'Private' spellings like *pyson* 'poison', *gine* 'join' tell the same story[31]. Our pronunciation today is due to the influence of the spelling with *oi*. Some dialects still widely retain the *ai*-pronunciation for historical *ui*, having thus *oil* and *isle* and *toil* and *tile* as homophones.

15) ME *au* regularly developed into MnE *ǭ (taught, daughter, law, fault, cause)*. Some Anglo-Norman words with *au* before nasals, e.g. *haunt, launch, laundry, taunt* also take part in the development.

Others like *grant, chant, dance, advance, command, chance, branch* had in ME the typical Anglo-Norman *au*-forms *(graunt, chaunt, daunce, etc.)*, which would have developed regularly into MnE *ǭ*, but their present spelling and pronunciation with *ā* are probably due to the influence of Parisian French in late ME. MnE *aunt* has Parisian-French pronunciation, but has retained the Anglo-Norman spelling, and also *launch, laundry, staunch* had until recently an alternative pronunciation with *ā*. MnE *chamber, angel, ancient, change*, etc. show the Parisian-French forms to have developed early enough to join the *ā* > *ei* change.

16) ME *ou* remained diphthongal in MnE *(flow, grow, own)*, joining the development of ME *ǭ*. Before *ht* it became monophthongized to *ǭ* in the 17th century *(brought, nought, thought)*.

Some important consonant changes

Voicing of fricatives (Jespersen's Law)
Starting in late ME, but extending till well on into EMnE, the unvoiced fricatives *f, s, þ* and the combinations *tʃ, ks* became voiced to *v, z, ð, dʒ* and *gz* under conditions strongly recalling Verner's Law (see p. 24), namely if the syllable or vocalic element immediately preceding was unaccented. This voicing was first accounted for by the Danish linguist Otto Jespersen, and is sometimes referred to as Jespersen's Law.

The *f* > *v* change is seen in MnE *of*, but an unvoiced accented variant of the same word survives in *off*. Marlowe illustrates the principle in: *Which of my shippes art thou master off? – Of the Speranza.* Only the accented form of *if* has survived into MnE, but in EMnE the now dialectal unaccented variant [iv] was common.

The *s* > *z* change has influenced MnE pronunciation considerably, being reflected in the genitive and plural of nouns, and in the present tense third person of verbs where *s* underwent voicing after unaccented *e*: ME *wordes* > *words* [z], *he runnes* > *runs* [z].

In a number of words like *hence, pence, since, invoice, dice, trace, once, twice,* the unvoiced fricative has been indicated by the spelling, thus presupposing an earlier form which either never had an *e*, or where it had been lost: *hens* (but cp. *hennes* > MnE *hens*), *pens* (but cp. *pennes* > MnE *pens*), *sins* (but cp. *sinnes* > MnE *sins*), etc.

MnE *is, was, has, as, his,* with [-z] presuppose earlier unaccented forms, but in *thus, us* the accented variety has become the standard. Note also pairs like *re'sign* [z] but *'re-sign* [s].

The *þ* > *ð* change may have begun early if a Chaucerian rhyme like *sothe – to thee* is anything to go by. To understand the voicing of the initial fricative in monosyllabic words like *this, thou, thee, thy, them, their, than, thence, thus,* etc. it is necessary to presuppose that they must have occurred frequently in connected speech with an unaccented element of some kind preceding (e.g. *to that, on those, in them*). Similarly the voicing of the initial consonant in *though* must have started in forms like *although*. In *with* it must have begun in *within, without*.

The *tʃ* > *dȝ* change is seen in MnE *knowledge* (ME *knowleche*), *partridge* (ME *partriche*). The old spelling has been retained in *spinach* [-dȝ], *ostrich* [-dȝ], or with spelling pronunciation [-tʃ]. Place-names in *-wich* (*Harwich, Woolwich, Norwich*) usually have [-dȝ], but spelling pronunciation accounts for the return to [tʃ] in *Ipswich*.

The *ks* > *gz* change operates is pairs like *exhibition* [ks], but *exhibit* [gz], *anxious – anxiety, exercise – exert,* etc.

Loss of *h* in unaccented position was a frequent feature in late ME and EMnE: *lyvelod* 'livelihood', *lykeluod* 'likelihood'. But *h* could also be dropped in accented position: *oost* 'host', *beold* 'behold', *orse* 'horse', a feature which has remained typical, socially conditioned, of many regional accents of today[32]. Inverted spellings are also common: *howld* 'old', *harm* 'arm', *hoxen* 'oxen'. The modern standard only drops *h* in words with unaccented first syllable: *Hungarian, historical, hotel,* etc., and in connected speech in small unaccented words like *his, him, have, had*. For the loss of *h* in *'em* (e.g. take *'em*), see p. 107. For the loss of *gh* (*bright, night, light*) and its retention in dialects, see p. 73.

Stops

Loss of *t* and *d* between consonants took place in EMnE, and is reflected by pairs like *Christ-Christmas, apostle-apostolic, hand-handsome*. Further in *listen, castle, ostler, bustle, thistle, pounds, landscape* and place-names like *Hertfordshire, Windsor, Guildford*. Often, *waistcoat* can have a -*t*- through spelling pronunciation.

Loss of *k* and *g* in the sequence *kn-* and *gn-* probably began already in the 16th century as suggested by Shakespearean puns on *knack-neck, knight-night,* but the process was not completed till about 1700. MnE examples are *know, knead, gnaw, gnat.*

d + r > ðr began to appear shortly before 1500: OE *mōdor* > *mother,* OE *fæder* > *father,* OE *gaderian* > *gather,* OE *hider* > *hither.* Already Shakespeare had *th* throughout in these word, but Caxton had now *th,* now *d.*

Frequent EMnE inverted spellings are *odyr* 'other' (OE *ōðer*), *wordy* 'worthy', *broder* 'brother'.

An inverse change, namely from fricative to stop, is found in MnE *murder* (OE *morðor*), *burden* (OE *byrðen*), where the old pronunciation (and spelling with *-th-*) was usual down to the 19th century.

Liquids
The loss of r. The historical *r* in English – the rolled or trilled point *r* – is still preserved in Northern and Scots dialects. In the other dialects it began to be dropped after vowels in the 17th century, reflected by rhymes like *aunt-aren't, farce-grass, fawn-morn.* The loss of *r* was gradual and probably took place via a retroflex stage, still heard dialectally in the South West (particularly Dorset and Somerset) and in current American speech. The loss of *r* was often followed by compensatory lengthening of the preceding vowel, as we have seen above (e.g. p. 76).

In the modern Standard *r* is now pronounced only before a vowel (*rich, write, arraign, far away*).

The loss of l. In EMnE *l* began to be dropped in unaccented position in the preterites *should* and *would* (OE *sceolde, wolde*), but it was probably pronounced till about 1700 in accented position (17th-century grammarians give *could-cooled* as homophones). The *-l-* in *could* is unetymological (OE *cūðe*) and has been inserted on the analogy of its two fellow auxiliaries.

The loss of w took place in EMnE in a number of cases, primarily before a rounded back vowel: *two, sword, who.* Cp. also *sultry,* but *swelter.* On the authority of rhymes and the statements of contemporary grammarians words like *swore, swung, swum, swoon, swoop* were frequently pronounced without [*w*] in the 18th century. Our modern pronunciation is due to the influence of the spelling or to the analogy of other forms of the verb *(swim, swing, swear).*

In unaccented position *w* was lost between a consonant and a vowel: *liquor, conquer, boatswain, gunwale* and place-names like *Greenwich, Harwich, Southwark.* Similarly *I will/would > I'll/I'd.*

CHAPTER VII

Nouns

The Old English period

The IE inflexional system (see p. 13) had by OE times been reduced to two numbers (sing. and plur.) and four cases (N-A-G-D) – a system closely resembling that of modern German.

Nouns are grouped into stems according to the sound in which these stems ended in Germanic. This criterion divides them into two major classes, the vocalic (or strong), and the consonant (or weak) declension.

The most important OE declensions (of a total of ten) are the masculine *a*-stems, the neuter *a*-stems, the so-called root-stems (with umlaut), the feminine *ō*-stems, and the consonant *n*- (or weak) stems. In spite of this multiplicity of declensions well over 75% of the OE nominal inventory follow the three strong paradigms for masculine, feminine and neuter. The most important declensions are here presented with their appropriate article forms:

singular

N	(se)	fisc	(þæt)	swīn	(se)	fōt	(seo)	lufu	(se)	hunta
A	(þone)	fisc	(þæt)	swīn	(þone)	fōt	(þā)	lufe	(þone)	huntan
G	(þæs)	fisces	(þæs)	swīnes	(þæs)	fōtes	(þære)	lufe[1]	(þæs)	huntan
D	(þǣm)	fisce	(þæm)	swīne	(þæm)	fēt	(þære)	lufe	(þæm)	huntan

plural

N	(þā)	fiscas		swīn		fēt		lufa		huntan
A	(þā)	fiscas		swīn		fēt		lufa		huntan
G	(þara)	fisca		swīna		fōta		lufa		huntena
D	(þǣm)	fiscum		swīnum		fōtum		lufum		huntum

The MnE reflexes should be carefully noted. The masc. *a*-stems are most important in having supplied the plural and genitive suffixes of practically all MnE nouns. The neuter *a*-stems have supplied a few Ø-plurals like *deer, swine, sheep*, the *n*-stems MnE plurals like *oxen, children, brethren* and the root-stems umlaut plurals like *feet, teeth, geese, mice, men*. The umlaut plurals, of which there were 25 in OE (including *bōc-bēc* 'books', *cū-cȳ* 'cows', *hnutu-hnyte* 'nuts', *āc-ēc* 'oaks') were early reduced to the seven we know today. All these modern reflexes will be dealt with in more detail below.

The use of case forms

Modern German may give us a relatively faithful picture of OE case-syntax. The nominative is the case of the subject of the verb: *se cyning wæs dēad* 'the king was dead', and the accusative the case of the direct object: *hīe grētton þone cyning* 'they greeted the king', and the one governed – though not with German consistency – by certain prepositions like *geond* 'through', *ofer* 'beyond', *wiþ* 'against', *in* 'into', especially when they carry a notion of directedness. The adverbial accusative denotes extent of time and space: *ealne þone dæg* 'the whole day' (cp. German *den ganzen Tag*), *ealne weg* 'the whole way'.

The dative is the case of the indirect object: *hē sealde þæm cyninge þone fisc* 'he gave the king the fish', and the one governed by prepositions like *for* 'for', *mid* 'with', *æfter* 'after', *tō* 'to', *on* 'on'. As in modern German certain verbs occur with a dative as sole object. They include *fylgan* 'follow', *hȳrsumian* 'obey', *þēowian* 'serve', *þancian* 'thank', *helpan* 'help'.

The so-called dative absolute is a calque on the Latin ablative construction: *fultumiendum Gode (:deo favente)* 'if God wills it', *þissum eallum þus gedōnum (:his rebus gestis)* 'when these things were done'. The OE possessive dative closely resembles the modern German variety: *hē sticode þæm cyninge þā ēagan ūt* 'he pricked 'dem König die Augen' out'.

Further, the dative is used to express the functions of the ancient instrumental, of which distinctive forms have survived only in the strong adjective and the pronouns (see p. 89). The dative with instrumental function usually expressed means and manner: *he wæs wundum wērig* 'he was exhausted through wounds'.

The genitive displays an even greater multiplicity of uses. It is used in possessive, subjective and objective relations: *þæs cyninges heall* 'the king's hall', *ealdra manna dǣda* 'old men's deeds', *in leornunge hāligra gewrita* 'in learning (of) holy scriptures'. The partitive genitive: *hwilc þara manna is blind?* 'which of the men is blind' is closely related to its use after numeral or quantitative words: *hē cōm mid fīf scipa* 'he came with five (of) ships', *twā hund punda goldes* 'two hundred pounds of gold'. The genitive of measure: *þrēora daga færeld* 'three days' journey', *ānes gēares fyrst* 'the space of one year'.

As in modern German the genitive may be governed by certain verbs, e.g. *wilnian* 'desire', *bīdan* 'wait for', *benǣman* 'deprive', *blissian* 'rejoice' etc. *He wilnode þæs cynerīces* 'he desired the kingdom'.

Case-form as·adverbs

More or less fossilized case-forms may be used as adverbs: *dæges ond nihtes* 'by day and by night', *winteres* 'in the winter', *gēara* 'of yore', *nīedes* 'needs', *stundum* 'at times', *hwīlum* 'once', *wundrum* 'strangely', *sāre* 'sore' (cp. German *sehr,* Danish *såre*).

The category of gender

Gender, like case, applies not only to nouns, but also to pronouns and adjectives. The three genders inherited from IE – masculine/feminine/neuter –

were still alive in OE. The system observed is that usually referred to as grammatical gender, which was originally determined by form and had nothing to do with sex, but was a grammatical category useful to indicate the grammatical relationship between the words in a sentence. It is the gender system we find in all other Germanic languages, but most undisturbed in German with its many clashes between the grammatical gender of a noun and its notional content (*das Mädchen, das Fräulein, die Schildwache*).

OE *mǣden* 'maiden', thus, is neuter, *wīfman* 'woman' is masculine (because of its second component), but *wīf* alone is neuter. *Cīld* 'child' is neuter.

In the majority of cases OE gender corresponds with that of modern German: *stān* 'stone', *fish* 'fish' (masc.), *bedd* 'bed', *ēage* 'eye' (neut.), *wicu* 'week', *lufu* 'love'(fem.) – which may often be a useful guide.

The OE system of grammatical gender, as in modern German rigidly observed by concord of nouns, adjectives, and pronouns, begins to crumble early. Human beings are thus nearly always referred to by a personal pronoun indicating natural gender: *þā þæt mǣden gehīerde þæt, þā cwæþ hēo.* 'when the girl heard that, then she said'. Various other approaches to natural gender are observable in late OE. Neuter pronouns, particularly demonstratives and relatives, are thus often found to refer back to other than neuter antecedents.

The ME period

The loss of case forms
The OE noun, it will be remembered, had rarely more than three, often only two distinctive case forms in each of its singular and plural paradigms. A typical example is the strong masculine *stān* 'stone' (N+A), *stānes* (G), *stāne* (D), and in the plural *stānas* (N+A), *stāna* (G), *stānum* (D).

In the course of ME this system was to undergo further reduction and became roughly identical with that of MnE: *ston* (common case) and *stones* (common case + genitive) representing the only plural forms.[2]

Vestiges of other case-forms, however, straggled into early ME, and were found sporadically in the conservative South (at least in writing) as late as the 14th century: *fiue wintre* (OE *wintra,* gen. plur.) 'five winters', *to pouren* (dat. plur.) 'to the poor', *mid hunden* (dat. plur.) 'with hounds', *from dēaþe to līue* 'from death to life', *ine heovene* 'in heaven'.

It has been traditionally maintained that the loss of case-forms is due to the inherent Germanic initial accent having caused the vowels of distinctive suffixes to be levelled under -*e* and subsequently lost. With the failure of the case-forms to express case-relations unambiguously, the language then had to seek other means of signalling grammatical relationships, and these were primarily fixed word-order (the SVO pattern) and analytical constructions, primarily prepositional phrases. The fact, however, that trends towards fixity of word-order and towards analytic structure are shared in varying measure also by non-Germanic languages and that they were well under way already at a time when the OE inflexional system was still in full force, has caused recent authority to assume a reverse order of cause and effect. It is a well-known fact that OE prepositions were often seen to duplicate or even go beyond the notion conveyed by inflexion alone (*hē hit geaf þǣm cynge* / *hē hit geaf tō þǣm cynge* 'he gave it to the king'.[3] In the first example the datival notion is expressed by case alone, in the second twice over, as it were, by case + preposition. With the gradual shifting to the preposition of the notion formerly carried by case alone – probably a popular emphatic device originating in spoken idiom – the latter came to gradually perform a minimum of function resulting in its reduction and eventual disappearance.

The genitive

The decay of case-endings reduced most English nouns already in ME to only two distinctive forms: a so-called common-case form *stone*, *stones* and a genitive *stones*, which could be both singular and plural (see p. 83). Other genitive suffixes were in process of being crowded out by the suffix -*s* of the strong masculines and neuters which, supported by the analogy of 'his', had been extended to the rest of the declensions.

Remnants of *s*-less genitives, therefore, are a regular feature only in early ME: *min moder luue* 'my mother's love', *þes draken mouthe* 'the dragon's mouth', *deoflene fere* 'the devils' companion'.

The *of*-phrase probably has roots in OE, but its vigorous intrusion as an alternative to the native genitive construction in early ME seems to point to the influence of the structurally similar French *de*-phrase.

The functions mentioned under OE (see p. 82) now all begin to appear with increasingly common *of*-alternatives: *ine þo herte of þo gode monne* 'in the good man's heart', *þe vprising of flesch* 'the resurrection of the body', *þe monglunge of unþeawes* 'the mingling of vices', *a soiourn of fourtene niht* 'a sojourn of fourteen nights'.

The partitive genitive and the related use after quantitative or numeral words died out in early ME: *nam ic monne hendest?* 'am I not the politest of men?', *þat lastede xix wintre* 'that lasted nineteen winters' and was replaced by the *of*-phrase, later also by a simple appositional construction: *an of þes twa ententes* 'one of these two intentions', *a dozein of knyves* 'a dozen knives', *a pound of garlek* 'a pound of garlic', *a sop of wyn* 'a drop of wine'; *a barel ale* 'a barrel of ale'.

The genitive with verbs was obsolescent in early ME; *he wilnede þeos mǣidenes* 'he desired the maiden', *we ne scullen yemen þes fihtes* 'we should not care about the fight' and many verbs began to appear with a direct object or an *of*-phrase: *thou forgetist of oure myseise* 'thou forgetst our discomfort'. French verbs with *de*-objects were often construed with *of*-phrases in ME (*cease, despair, complain, repent,* etc.) and have in some cases retained this construction to the present day.

Adverbial genitives are common in ME: *þu flihst nihtes* 'thou fliest by night'. Mandeville has *as men mosten nedes* 'as men must necessarily'; more examples will be given p. 87.

The plural endings

OE possessed an inventory of about half a dozen current plural suffixes, but already late in the period there were signs of incipient simplification in that many nouns from the minor declensions began to be absorbed by major ones by force of analogy. In ME this tendency was carried even further, resulting in two major nominal declensions, one with its plural in -*s* (historically the -*as* of the OE strong masculines) which was felt to be so usefully distinctive that it was gradually extended to nouns where it did not formerly belong (*shippes* 'ships' (OE *scipu*), *deedes* 'deeds' (OE *dǣda*), *snakes* (OE *snacan*), *bokes* 'books' (OE *bēc*) – and one forming its plural in -*en* (from the OE weak declension).

In the South the -*en* plural held a strong position, and was also extended to a great many nouns originally with other suffixes: *eyren* 'eggs' (OE *ǣgru*), *children* (OE *cildru*), *worden* 'words' (OE *word*), *sunen* 'sons' (OE *suna*).[4] Many texts use -*s* and -*en* indiscriminately, sometimes with rhyme as the decisive factor. Chaucer has *bees/been* 'bees', *shoos/shoon* 'shoes', *doghtres/doghtren* 'daughters'.

In early ME the two rival plural suffixes seemed to have equal chances of becoming the universal sign of the plural. The eventual victory of -*s*, however, is due to the interaction of several factors, primarily the prevailing tendency in ME to weaken and eventually drop final unstressed -*n* (see p. 73), which made the old weak plural the less distinctive alternative. Contributory causes could be the supporting parallel of French plural -*s* (which was pronounced at that time). By about 1300 -*s* prevailed in the North, but in the South it was not the dominant form until nearly two centuries later.

For survivals of some non-*s* plurals, see p. 87.

The loss of grammatical gender

With the decay and levelling under -*e* of distinctive vowel sounds, the extension of -*s* to nearly all plurals, the reduction of the article system to invariable *the* (see p. 96), and the demonstrative system to *this-that* (see p. 96), the groundwork of grammatical gender was bound to break down in early ME.

Preserved grammatical gender, therefore, is essentially an early ME phenomenon (*in are healle* (fem.) 'in a hall', *sigge ... þesne vreisun* (masc.) 'say this prayer', *mid muchelre ferde* (fem.) 'with a big army'). In the North its last traces disappeared as early as the 11th century, whereas in the conservative South it lingered on sporadically – at least in writing – till the 14th century. Ayenbite has *uor þane day* (masc.) 'for that day'. After that time the notion of sex is the only factor determining the gender of nouns. All nouns except those denoting masculine and feminine creatures are neuter and referred to by *it*. The system is commonly referred to as natural gender, and is peculiar to English in the Germanic group.

The Modern English period

Case-forms

By late ME the noun had in all dialects been reduced to the two different forms (common case and genitive) we know today.

The genitive suffix *-es* had become *-s* by the 17th century *(dogges > dogs)*. The *apostrophe*, which is merely a graphic convention to distinguish plural from genitive forms *(dogs, dog's, dogs')* is of late growth. It was introduced by the printers, but was not a regular feature in the singular till the end of the 17th century, in the plural not until about a hundred years later. Shakespeare's *a mad tale ... of his owne doores being shut against him* could be a singular as well as a plural genitive.

The old kind of genitive without apostrophe, however, survives in *hers, yours, ours, its,* etc.

The genitive has maintained itself best in the broad category usually referred to as the possessive relation, where it is still frequent with human beings and with animals *(his master's voice, a bird's nest)* and also the genitive of measure has remained relatively stable, e.g. *a boat's length, a day's journey, a hand's breadth*.

In the subjective and objective relations we find both genitive and *of*-equivalents in EMnE, but the latter becomes an increasingly common alternative, so that today there are few cases where it cannot replace the genitive. In EMnE examples like *the brooks sweete murmur, wealthes decaye, his kingdomes great defence, the tyrants overthrow* the *of*-possibility would now be anything from obligatory to preferable.

The partitive genitive survives in Shakespeare's *alderliefest* 'dearest of all', already then a conscious archaism. Its ME equivalents, the *of*-phrase and the appositional phrase after numeral words used as adjectives *(a hundred horses,* but *hundreds of horses),* are both the rule in EMnE.

In EMnE an *of*-phrase was still frequent with a good number of verbs that now construe with a direct object or some other preposition, e.g. *feel, smell, miss, beseech, forget, like, hope.* Skelton has *of my servyce you shall not mysse,* Defoe has *she went to it, smelled of it, and ate it.*

The adverbial genitive has survived as a fairly intact category in expressions like *once, twice, nowadays, always, sideways, thereabouts, unawares, needs,* etc. Adverbial genitives of time like *nights, winters, mornings, Sundays* (e.g. *my wife works nights* (cp. German *sie arbeitet nachts, morgens,* etc.)) are still very common in American idiom.[5]

Fossilized survivals

Disused case-forms may have survived into MnE as fossils. Original weak *s*-less genitives are still seen in *Lady Day* (OE *hlǣfdigan dæg*), *Lady Chapel, ladybird,* and from the place-names we may adduce *Tottenham* (OE *Tottan-hām*) 'Totta's homestead', *Bardney* (OE *Beardan-ēg*) 'Bearda's island'. *Mon-*

day goes back to OE *Mōnandæg* (OE *mōna*, weak masc.), whereas an old feminine genitive is embedded in *Friday* (OE *Frīgedæg*).

Place-names, occurring as they do mostly after a preposition, show many instances of old datives preserved. *Cleeve* in Somerset presupposes OE *(æt þæm) clife* 'by the cliff'. Similarly *-borough* (Scots *-burgh*) reflects OE nominative *burh*, but *-bury*, the dative form, is from *byrig* (e.g. *Scarborough*, *Roxburgh*, but *Canterbury*). The OE dative in *-um* survives in numerous place-names, very often as *-ham*, e.g. *Downham* ((*æt þæm*) *dūnum* 'by the hills'), *Laneham*, *Cotham*.

Whilom, now archaic and poetic, stems from an OE dative plural *hwīlum*, on the analogy of which also *seldom* was formed. Another adverb *sore* (as in *John Barleycorn got up again and sore surpris'd them all*) reflects an old instrumental (cp. Danish *såre*, German *sehr*) and has survived now only in dialect or as an archaism.

The plural endings

By EMnE the *-s* plural had become extended to the vast majority of nouns, though *-n* forms like *eyen*, *shoon*, *housen*, *treen* were met with as late as the 17th century and can still be heard in the dialects. The only *-n* plural in regular use now is *oxen*. *Children* is a double plural, the regularly formed *childer* (OE *cildru*), to which the weak *-en* was analogically added, is now dialectal. Also *brethren* (OE *brēþer*) and the Biblical or poetic *kine* (OE *cȳ* 'cows') are double plurals, the latter probably through association with *swine*.

From the OE neuters with Ø-plural have survived *sheep*, *deer*, *swine*, *kind* (as in *these kind of...*), in EMnE also extended to *sort* (*these sort of...*). After the analogy of *sheep*, *deer* the names of many animals like *pike*, *trout*, *duck*, *pigeon*, *grouse* have come to acquire Ø-plural in the 18th and 19th centuries, particularly when regarded as game (we feed the ducks but shoot duck). Later this usage came to be extended also to more exotic species such as *bison*, *buffalo*, *rhino*, *antelope*, etc. probably through the jargon of hunters.

The seven umlaut plurals (*mice*, *feet*, *geese*, *teeth*, etc.) have proved an extremely stable category also in other Germanic languages, probably because they were words that were used with great frequency in the plural and were therefore less susceptible to the forces of analogy. It is only in the dialects that the regularized *-s* plural has gained access (*foots*, *mices*, etc.) The only plural of this type in the modern standard is *breeches* (OE *brōc – brēc*).

Foreign plurals

The Renaissance started a wholesale import of learned and technical words with Latin and Greek plurals in *-ae, -a, -i, -es*: *algae, formulae, antennae, desiderata, strata, phenomena, criteria* (the last two with sing. in *-on*), *stimuli, radii, alumni, fungi, ellipses, bases, oases, theses, appendices, matrices* (the last two with sing. in *-ix*). Later in the period, however, there is a marked tendency to extend the plural *-s* to many words if they have been assimilated into everyday-speech: *formulas, aquariums, funguses.* Note with differentiated meaning: *genii* (= tutelary spirits), *geniuses* (= brilliant persons).

Gender

The three grammatical genders died out in early ME as a living category and were supplanted by our modern system of natural gender based chiefly on the polarity animate *(he-she-who)* vs. inanimate *(it-which).* The primary bearers of gender have since early ME been these pronouns.

In late ME and EMnE we often come across cases which look suspiciously like preserved grammatical gender but which admit of other explanations. Dramatists frequently personified abstract nouns. Thus the names of vices and virtues were often masculine as an echo of mediaeval allegorical tradition when they were personified by male actors. Shakespeare has *Drunken desire must vomit his receipt, ere he can see his owne abomination.* Similarly *death* is often masculine because of the allegorical concept of the scythe man.

In Renaissance writers of erudition loanwords with etymologically feminine suffixes (*-ess, -ance, -ence, -ion, -ity*) were often seen to have carried their ancestral gender over into English. Similarly the feminine personification of abstracts like *Nature, Justice, Peace, Science, Liberty, Wisdom,* etc. is due to the influence of Renaissance Latin (*justitia, sapientia, scientia,* etc.). Shakespeare has *Peace puts forth her olive everywhere,* Pope has *Justice with her lifted scale.*

Moon and *sun* are still poetically referred to as *she* and *he* respectively after Latin usage.[6] Names of countries in non-geographical contexts have correlated with *she* since EMnE, probably under the influence of Latin, where such words were feminine.

CHAPTER VIII

Adjectives and Adverbs

Adjectives in the OE period

As we have touched upon earlier (see p. 20), the twofold adjective declension constitutes a special Germanic innovation, which with the sole exception of English has been preserved in more or less reduced form in all the descendant languages of today.

The OE so-called *strong adjective* is declined on the following model:

	masculine	*feminine*	*neuter*
N	gōd fisc	gōd dæd	gōd hors
A	gōdne fisc	gōde dæd	gōd hors
G	gōdes fisces	gōdre dæde	gōdes horses
D	gōdum fisce	gōdre dæde	gōdum horse
I	gōde fisce[1]		gōde horse

In the plural the nominative-accusative suffixes were *-e* (masc.), Ø (neuter), and *-a* (fem.). The genitive and dative had the suffixes *-ra, -um* respectively in all genders. Short-stemmed adjectives, it should be noted, had *-u* in the nominative singular of the feminine and in the nominative and accusative plural of the neuter (e.g. *gramu* 'fierce', *gladu* 'glad').

The Germanic specialty called *the weak declension* presents the following paradigm:

	masculine singular	*plural (common gender)*
N	se gōda fisc	þā gōdan fiscas
A	þone gōdan fisc	þā gōdan fiscas
G	þæs gōdan fisces	þara gōdra fisca[2]
D	þæm gōdan fisce	þæm gōdum fiscum

The feminine and neuter declensions differ from the masculine declension only in the former taking *-e* in the nominative (*sēo gōde dæd*), and the latter *-e* in both nominative and accusative (*þæt gōde hors*).

The weak declension is used as in modern German after the definite article or the demonstrative pronoun *(mit dem guten Mann, in dieser alten Stadt),* but also frequently after a possessive pronoun *(mīn gōda fisc).*

The strong form is used predicatively *(þā fiscas sindon gōde),* and when no article, demonstrative (or possessive) pronoun precedes.

Substantivization

It is a feature common to all Germanic languages that adjectives may freely assume nominal function. In English, however, this usage is limited to an early period of its history. The adjective in OE allows of substantivization much as in German and Danish: *þæs geongan snælnesse* 'the young man's speed', *se blinda gif hē blindne lǣt* 'the blind man, if he leads (another) blind man', *þā ymbsittendan* 'those sitting around'.

Comparison

The comparative and superlative are formed by suffixing *-ra* (*heardra* 'harder') and *-ost* (*heardost* 'hardest'). A small number of adjectives, however, originally took a variant suffix containing *-i* (**-ira, *-ist*) and underwent i-umlaut (*eald* 'old' – *ieldra* – *ieldest, lang* 'long' – *lengra* – *lengest, strang* 'strong' – *strengra* – *strengest*).

A few adjectives have different stems in comparison: *gōd* – *betra* - *betst, yfel* – *wyrsa* – *wyrst, lȳtel* – *lǣssa* – *lǣst, micel* – *māra* - *mǣst*.

Synthetic (suffixal) comparison was in OE – and is still in modern German – the regular mode of comparison. It was not as in MnE determined by the length of the adjective: *se wælhrēowesta cyning* 'the most ferocious king', *mid þǣm dēorwierðestan gimmum* 'with the most precious gems'.

The ME period

The adjective, in OE even more heavily inflected than the noun, came to be so drastically simplified that by early ME only two forms remained in most dialects, one in Ø for the singular of the strong declension (*god man*), and one in *-e*[3] for all other uses (*þe gode man, gode men, þe gode men),* thus strikingly parallel to the adjective in modern Danish, which has suffered similar reduction.

In the North, however, this remaining distinction was lost early, and the use of the adjective there was close to the flexionless MnE norm.

Survivals of inflexion are chiefly an early ME phenomenon; *summes weis* 'in some way', *to þe oþren* 'to the others', *for muchelre nede* 'because of great need', *to pouren* 'to the poor'. In Kentish traces of inflexion may occur as late as the 14th century.

Some fossilized case forms may occur throughout ME: *allerliefest* (OE *ealra liefost*) 'dearest of all', *halvendel* (OE *þone healfan dæl*) 'one half', *nones cunnes* 'of no kind'.

Substantivization

Owing to its levelled inflexions ME was bound to show considerably more restraint than OE with regard to substantivization of adjectives. Since *the blind* could now stand both for OE *se blinda* 'the blind man' and for *þā blindan* 'the blind men', there was an increasing tendency already in ME to use a substantivized adjective only with plural meaning, and to express the singular by means of some noun (e.g. *man, woman, person*) acting as a propword.

French adjectives
– were used along the same lines as those of native stock, taking typically Ø
or *-e (cleer* 'clear' – *cleere)* for as long as strong/weak or plural distinctions
were called for.

After the French fashion they sometimes occurred in post-position and
not infrequently even with plural *-s* (*godes temporeles* 'temporal goods',
þinges spirituels 'spiritual things').

Comparison
The normal suffixes in the comparative and superlative are *-er(e), -est(e)* for
OE *-ra, -ost* (*herder – herdest* 'hardest').

Umlaut comparison continues in ME, though only with a limited number
of adjectives (*strengre – strengest* 'strongest', *lengre – lengest* 'longest').

Periphrastic comparison
This is the usual term for comparison achieved analytically by means of the
adverbs *more* and *most.* We are here dealing with an early ME innovation,
synthetic comparison, it will be remembered, being indigenous to all Germanic languages. Since the emergence of this mode of comparison in English is
simultaneous with the impact of French, it has been traditional to ascribe it
to that source (*plus prudent > more prudent, le plus prudent > most prudent).*
But there is no consensus about the problem. It has been objected that the
two constructions are structurally too dissimilar, and that the periphrasis occurs equally early with French and native adjectives, which leaves two other
possibilities open, namely a possible influence from the Latin *magis – maxi-
me* periphrasis or an extension of a native periphrasis which in OE was confined to participial adjectives (e.g. *mā gelǣred* 'more learned' – *betst gelǣred*
'most learned').

The use and the non-use of periphrastic comparison in ME did not always follow the norm of MnE usage (*more gret* 'greater', *more strong*
'stronger' but *the merveillouseste metals* 'the most wonderful metals'). In
many cases the preference for the periphrastic alternative seems to be merely a desire for emphasis.

Another emphatic device is the so-called double comparison with *more* or
most added to a synthetic form: *þei dwellen with the most fayrest damyselles*
'they live with the fairest (of all) damsels'.

The modern English period
Already in ME the adjective had become an invariable word, incapable of
change except when compared. This feature is not found in any other Germanic language.

Substantivization
Already in late ME there was a perceptible trend for substantivized adjectives to assume plural meaning, and to express the singular by addition of

some propword like *one, man, person,* etc. The norm of today's usage, how-ever, was not fully established in EMnE: *the younger rises when the old doth fall* (Shakespeare).

Only a few adjectives, usually substantivized participles, continue to be used with singular meaning, e.g. *the accused, the deceased.* In liturgical parlance we still find *the Almighty, the Eternal.*

The spread in the 18th and 19th centuries of singular abstract neuters like *the beautiful, the sublime, the unknown, the impossible,* etc. is due directly or indirectly to the influence of German philosophy *(das Schöne, das Erhabene).*

French adjectives

These, notably those that go back to Norman legal and ecclesiastical parlance, are still frequently postposed: *Lords Spiritual and temporal, fee simple, court martial, secretary general, devil incarnate, bride elect.*

Plural concord was still usual in EMnE: *letters patents, Lords appealants. By these presents* is still a current legal term.

Comparison

From OE umlaut comparison only *old-elder-eldest* has survived to the present day, but the type *strong-strenger, long-lenger* could still be found in EMnE, e.g. in Spenser and Shakespeare.

Periphrastic comparison

This showed fairly regulated usage already by EMnE though ME practices were occasionally continued, e.g. in suffixing *-er, est* to polysyllabic adjectives as in Shakespeare's *a few of the unpleasant'st words that ever blotted paper,* and, conversely, in comparing monosyllables periphrastically: *Hath not old custom made this life more sweet than that of painted pomp?* (id.). A feature that seems to point to the periphrasis being largely a foreign intrusion is that it has never been at home in popular speech. Many modern dialects seem to prefer suffixal comparison where the periphrasis would be obligatory in the standard *(usefuller, beautifuller).*

Double comparison

This was still frequent in EMnE: *the most unkindest cut of all* (Shakespeare), *a more sounder instance* (id.) and is now a regular feature in many dialects *(more commoner, more safer, worser, worstest). Lesser,* however, has won recognition, as an adjective with reference to value or importance *(the lesser poets, the Lesser Bear,* etc.)

Adverbs in the OE period

In OE adverbs were formed from adjectives regularly by suffixing *-e* (historically identical with the instrumental *-e* of the adjectives). To *hlūd* thus corresponds *hlūde* 'loudly', to *dēop – dēope,* to *luflic – luflice* 'lovingly', etc. Adjectives already ending in -e became adverbs without any change of form, e.g. *clǣne* 'clean, cleanly'.

The MnE adverbial suffix -*ly* goes back to OE -*līce*, originally the adjectival suffix -*līc* + adverbial -*e*. Already in late OE there were signs that the whole combination, rather than -*e* alone, must have begun to be felt as an adverbial sign: *hold* (adj.) 'gracious' > *holdlīce* 'graciously', *earnost* 'earnest' > *earnostlīce* 'earnestly'.

Adverbs could be formed in other ways, and primarily, as we have seen above (p. 82), from nominal case forms where particularly genitive -*s* has been prolific in deriving adverbs from other parts of speech, witness MnE reflexes like *always, needs, homewards, onwards, once* (OE *ānes*), *twice* (OE *twĭges*), etc.

Negation
The regular negative adverb in OE is *ne*, which was placed before the verb: *wē ne cumaþ* 'we come not'. For extra emphasis negations were often doubled as in *þæt þū þæt nǣnigum menn ne secge* 'that thou sayest it not to no man' – in rare cases even trebled.

The negative force of *ne* could be reinforced by means of *nāht*, a contraction of *ne* + *ā* + *wiht*[4], the ancestor of MnE *not*: *ic ne cume nāht* 'I come not by no means'.

The ME period
In ME the -*e* suffix marking adverbs was dropped, and there was no means any longer of distinguishing formally between adjectives and adverbs. As a result the practice of regarding the suffix -*līce* as an adverbial sign in its own right was established in ME when it was analogically extended to an increasing number of words where it did not originally belong, and also to foreign adjectives (*comounlye* 'commonly', *pitouslie* 'pitifully').

For survivals of the old -*e* adverbs (*dig deep, run fast*, etc.), see below. Adverbs formed from case-forms of various parts of speech are dealt with p. 82.

Negation
Ne continued to be used as in OE in pre-verbal position: *we ne cumen* 'we come not', sometimes reinforced by *noght* (OE *nāht*): *ne doute ye not*, lit. 'doubt ye by no means not'. From about 1300, however, *ne* began to be dropped, and *noght* >*not* gradually assumed the role as the standard negative: *faileþ him nought at þis nede* 'fail him not in this (hour of) need'.

The OE practice of using multiple negation for emphasis was continuous throughout ME. Here is a famous Chaucerian case of four negatives: *he nevere yet no vileyneye ne seyde, in al his lyf unto no maner wight* 'he never did not say no evil thing in all his life to no kind of creature'.

The modern English period
The practice of distinguishing adverbs from adjectives by means of the -*ly*

suffix had gained ever increasing momentum down through the ME period, but in EMnE we still come across instances where the adverb is identical in form with the adjective: *'Tis noble spoken* (Shakespeare), *a lover that kills himselfe most gallant for love* (id.).

Only a few adverbs have resisted the pull of the *-ly* analogy. They include *(hit) hard, (run) fast, (dig) deep, (open) wide.* Some have also an *-ly* possibility, but with differentiation of meaning *(dig deep,* but *deeply moved).*

Negation

The current ME negative *ne* was still occasionally used by Spenser and Shakespeare, but was already then strongly archaic[5]. Phrases like *will he – nill he* (< *ne will he*), *will you – nill you* were stereotyped already in the 16th century, but have managed to survive into MnE in the contracted locution *willy-nilly* 'whether he will or not'.

Not, originally an emphatic intensifier of *ne,* has been the standard negative since late ME.

The former practice of doubling negatives for emphasis, although it is as old as the language, came to be frowned on by 18th-century prescriptive grammarians, who denounced it as illogical (because two negatives cancel out one another and make an affirmative). Although social judgement has since been passed on it, multiple negation (*I don't see no dog, don't give me no excuses,* etc.) has survived as one of the commonest features of nonstandard speech. Doctor: 'Now, what did your wife die of?'. Patient: 'Well, sir, I can't say as I do 'xactly remember, but 'twarn't nothing serious!' (Punch).

CHAPTER IX

Pronouns, *a/an* and Numerals

Demonstrative pronouns in the OE period
The OE demonstrative pronoun is declined on the following model:

	masculine	*feminine*	*neuter*	*plural (common gender)*
N	se	sēo	þæt	þā
A	þone	þā	þæt	þā
G	þæs	þǣre	þæs	þǣra
D	þǣm	þǣre	þǣm	þǣm
I	þȳ		þȳ	

It should be observed that, as in the strong adjective, we have a distinctive instrumental form *þȳ,* e.g. *þā wǣron hīe þȳ bealdran gewordene* 'they had become so much bolder', which has survived functionally as MnE *the* in phrases like *the sooner the better.*

Se-sēo-þæt performed a threefold function in OE, being used a) as a demonstrative (whence MnE *that*) b) as a definite article (whence MnE *the*), and c) as a relative pronoun (whence MnE *that*).

Besides, there existed a more emphatic demonstrative with undivided function, namely *þes* 'this', which declines:

	masculine	*feminine*	*neuter*	*plural (common gender)*
N	þes	þēos	þis	þās
A	þisne	þās	þis	þās
G	þisses	þisse	þisses	þissa
D	þissum	þisse	þissum	þissum
I	þȳs		þȳs	

The neuter form *þis* is the ancestor of MnE *this,* and the plural *þās* is traditionally believed to have given MnE *those* (but see p. 96).

MnE *these* is a ME innovation, see p. 96.

Demonstrative or article?
It is a question whether OE possessed a definite article of the type we know today, in other words it is difficult to decide when *se man, sēo dǣd, þæt hors* stand for *the/that man, deed, horse,* and we must often resort to the context to translate meaningfully, e.g. *He ēode tō þǣm mǣran cynge* 'he went to the/ that famous king'. Some cases are more obvious, e.g. when the pronoun precedes designations for the known and familiar: *nū scīneþ sēo sunne* 'now

shines the sun', *se bæþstede is open* 'the bath is open', where article function seems to be the only possible interpretation.

In early OE and in the conservative language of poetry the definite article was used much more sparingly than today: *strǣt wæs stānfāh, stīg wīsode gumum ǣtgǣdere ...* '(the) road was stonepaved, (the) path led (the) men on.' (Beowulf), but by late OE its uses begin to approach the norm of today.

The ME period

The OE demonstratives were *se* and *þes* with a heavy machinery of positional variants elaborately declined for gender, number and case.

In ME originally neuter *that* (OE *þæt*) remained as the only demonstrative function of *se*, the rest of the paradigm having become levelled under uniform *the*, and continuing only with article function. Already Chaucer, Wiclyffe and Gower had *the* without any distinction of gender, case or number. Mandeville (14th century) has sporadic cases of *þo* as the plural article.

ME *this*, originally the neuter form of *þes*, continued as the only emphatic demonstrative. Both *this* and *that* were now capable of referring to all cases and genders.

Remnants of inflexion straggle into early ME and may be found more or less fossilized in Kentish as late as the 14th century: *þeos hond* 'this hand', *sigge þesne vreisun* 'say this prayer', *biuoren þissere dugeðe* 'before this company of nobles', *on þære kuneriche* 'in that/the kingdom', *uor þane day* 'for that day'.

The plural forms are more complicated. *Those* (ME *þōs*), (though plural of *this*!) has traditionally been identified with OE *þās*, but could also be explained as a reflex of the regularly developed *þā* + plural *-s* added after the analogy of the nouns. Chaucer has still *thō* for 'those'.

These cannot be derived from OE *þās*, but should probably be explained as *þes* + adjectival plural *-e* > *þese, þise*.

Demonstrative or article?

The levelling in ME of demonstrative and article function under *that* and *the* respectively now enables us to distinguish the two by form alone. Only in early ME – if case and gender distinctions are still preserved – must we, as in OE, resort to context: *on þære kuneriche* 'in the/that kingdom', *on þan huse* 'in the/that house'.

This – that

This (OE *þes-þēos-þis*) was originally used primarily as the more emphatic demonstrative, and this usage continues in early ME. Later, however, through its dissociation from the article, *that* began to assume a more distinctly demonstrative character.

The MnE rule, according to which *that* denotes objects remote in time and space from the attention of the speaker, and *this* what is closer, is essentially a product of ME – at least when the opposition is explicit; *he fint somewhat that pleaseth him in this or that.*

The modern English period

By late ME the functions and forms of the demonstratives had come to conform fairly closely to the norm of present-day usage. The earlier *tho* (=*those*) was obsolescent in late ME, but survived sporadically to Elizabethan times when *those* finally took over. The northern form *thae* is still alive in Scots dialect.[1] It is worthy of note, however, that the new plural *those* seems to be current only in standard speech. In popular speech and in dialect it has never been at home. Here the plural personal pronoun *them* seems to be preferred (*He come right in when we was eatin' breakfast an' says, 'Where the hell's them new men?'*)

That, apart from dialectal or archaic survivals like *t'one, t'other* 'the one, the other' (OE *þæt ān, þæt ōðer*) has been without contact with the definite article since ME.

In the modern place-name *Atterbury* are embedded traces of the old dative form (OE *æt þǣre byrig*), which also survives in personal names of the type *Nash, Noakes, Nalder* (ME *at þen asche* 'by the ash', *at þen oke* 'by the oak-tree', *at þen aldre* 'by the alder-tree').

Relatives in the OE period

As we have already noted, the demonstrative performed the function of a relative connective, but this is a secondary development, for by heritage OE possessed no relative pronoun proper. In many cases, therefore, the pronoun allows of two interpretations. It may be taken as a demonstrative (parataxis) or a relative (hypotaxis): *þā wæs here hider send, se wæs cumende on hærfeste* 'then was an army sent hither, which (or: that (army)) came in the harvest season'.

The relative, as in modern German, shows concord in gender and number with its antecedent, but case is determined by its function in the relative clause: *se stan þone hē mē geaf* 'the stone (that)[2] he gave me', *þā hundas þā mē hulpon* 'the dogs that helped me'.

An indeclinable particle *þe,* however, could also perform relative function: *he ēode on þone weg þe him getǣht wæs* 'he walked the way that was shown him'. Whenever gender-number-case contrasts were felt necessary, this invariable particle could be coupled with *se-sēo-þæt* (*se þe, þone þe*, etc.).

It should be noted that relative *who, which* and *what* are largely ME innovations. In OE they were used exclusively as interrogatives.

The ME period

In ME the demonstrative-derived *se-sēo-þæt* relative with all its rigid concord of gender, number and case was reduced to invariable *that,* originally the neuter form. It grew to be by far the most popular ME relative, capable of referring to all kinds of antecedents and was not, as in MnE, confined to defining relative clauses.

With the disappearance of case, however, indeclinable *that* now refused to be governed by a preposition: *þatt nahht þatt Christ wass borenn onne* 'the night that Christ was born'.

The relative particle *þe* did not outlive early ME.

Interrogative-derived relatives

These are *who, which* and *what,* which in early ME came to perform relative function. Of these *which* and *what* differ from the norm of today on a few important points.

Which was currently found with personal antecedents: *Iason, which sih his fader old* 'Jason, who saw his old father', and *what* may be used with expressed antecedent: *after it what is write* 'according to that which is written'.

It is a peculiarity that the subject form of *who* – apart from indefinite uses corresponding to MnE *whoever* – does not occur regularly with relative function until EMnE. Only the oblique forms *whom* and *whose* seem to be used.

The compound relative *the which* is a ME departure. Mandeville has *the queen of Amazoine, the which maketh hem to be kept in cloos* 'the Amazon queen who causes them to be narrowly confined'. The construction has been traditionally explained as a calque on French *lequel,* but may also reflect OE *se þe* (see p. 97), where the particle *þe* has been replaced by *which.*

Ø-relatives

These began to be common in late ME. In subject function, however, most examples occur, as in colloquial MnE, after introductory 'there is': *there is no knyght wolde fyghte for him* 'there is no knight (who) would fight for him'.

Ø as object: *þe treuþe ych ou to þe* 'the loyalty I owe thee'. This relative type, originally unknown to WGerm languages and still impossible in German, has by some authorities been attributed to Scandinavian influence.

The modern English period

That had throughout ME been far and away the most common relative, capable of referring to all kinds of antecedents. Between late ME and 1700, however, it began to be exposed to the vigorous competition of the *wh-* pronouns, which, because they had so many features in common with the Latin relative (inflexion, gender, government by preposition), came to be greatly favoured by many EMnE writers[3].

The type *those who,* with demonstrative antecedent, is a product of the late 16th century, superseding earlier *they who/which/that.* The Prayer Book of Edward VI.has *malediccion shall lyght upon them that shalbee set on the left hand.*

The rules which confine *that* to defining relative clauses began to crystallize in EMnE, but our present norm was not established till the 19th century. Shakespeare has *Fleance, his son, that keeps him company.*[4]

The wh- pronoun

Who, apart from indefinite uses (= *whoever*), was recorded in ME only in the object form *whom* and in the possessive form *whose*. The subject form *who* began to be common in the 16th century, competing now with *which* and *that* in referring to personal antecedents.

The form *whose*, in spite of the fact that it is historically the possessive of all three genders (see paradigm below), had to fight hard to retrieve the indifference to gender it was born with. Grammarians even as recently as the 19th century condemned the use of *whose* referring to inanimate objects and recommended *of which*.

The gradual replacement of *whom* by *who* in present-day usage takes its start already in the 16th century. It is quite common in Shakespeare: *the mariners ... who I have left asleep.*

Which was in the early 16th century still common with personal antecedents. The Prayer Book of Edward VI has *coumforte us, whiche bee grieued and weried.* In the next century it is already archaic as in the well-known *Our father which art in heaven.*

The compound relative *the which* was still common in EMnE but died out in the 18th century. Shakespeare has *Priams Troy, before the which is drawn the power of Greece.*

What as a relative with expressed antecedent is now substandard or dialectal (*I ain't none of them snobs what drink woine*).

At is a relative of Scandinavian extraction and has been known since ME. It is still used in Northern dialects: *to onything at's richt* 'to anything which is right'.

Ø-relatives

Ø as subject has survived colloquially in MnE after introductory 'there is, it is': The bosun's mate (to new crew). 'Now I'm goin' to read out some o' the things the board o' trade think you ought to know, an' if there's any of you don't understand English let 'im find out from the bloke next to 'im wot it's all about' (Punch). Other cases are dialectal or substandard: *A guy had an Airdale could herd sheep.*

As object the Ø-construction became increasingly common after the 16th century, though frowned upon by 18th-century purists. Dr Johnson called it 'a colloquial barbarism', but used it himself in his letters.

Interrogative pronouns in the OE period

The OE interrogative *hwā* has only masculine and neuter forms, and declines on the following model:

	masculine	*neuter*
N	hwā	hwæt
A	hwone	hwæt
G	hwæs	hwæs
D	hwǣm, hwām	hwǣm, hwām
I		hwȳ

MnE has the reflexes *who (whom, whose) – what,* besides the fossilized in-strumental *why.*

OE *whā* is used with personal reference: *Hwā mæg ēow nū trūwian?* 'who can now believe you?', *Hē ascode hwone hē sendan mihte* 'he asked who he could send' and *hwæt* primarily with non-personal reference: *Hwæt sægst þū, fuglere?* 'what doest thou say, fowler?'. *Hwæt* is treated as a noun and gov-erns a genitive as in *Hwæt gōdes?* 'what good things?'. *Hwæt* is used as a pre-dicative for *hwā: Nāt ic hwæt hē is* 'I do not know who he is'. In addition there existed two more interrogatives, namely *hwilc* 'which' and *hwæðer* 'whether', both following the strong adjective declension.

Hwilc (< earlier **hwi-līc* 'what kind') originally asked after the quality of a given object: *hē wiste hwæt and hwylc þis wīf wǣre* (AV has *who and what manner of woman*). It is commonly used to express selection from a definite number: *Hwilc ēower ne notaþ cræfte mīnum?* (: quis vestrum non utitur arte mea?). *Hwelcne cræft canst þū?* 'which trade do you know?'.

Hwæðer 'which of two' has preserved traces of the ancient dual: *Hwæðer þāra twēgra dyde þæs fæder willan?* 'whether of them twain did (his) father's will?'.

The ME period

Who showed only slightly modified inflexion in ME. As with the other pro-nouns, the old accusative *hwone* was dropped early in favour of the dative *hwǣm > hwām >* ME *whom.* The OE genitive *hwæs* became ME *whose.*

A few important ME developments should be noted. *Who* for object-case *whom* dates back to late ME: *thei wost ho I meant* 'they knew who I meant'. The predicative function of *who* as in MnE 'who are you?' was until about 1300 performed exclusively by *what: What art thou? – tell me thi name,* and throughout the rest of the ME period *what* continued to be used concur-rently with *who* in this function.

What, the old neuter form, became ME indeclinable *what.* It was in OE used exclusively as a noun (*hwæt þinga* 'what (of) things') but began to func-tion as an adjective (e.g. *what thinges*) in ME probably because of the disap-pearance of the genitive after governing *what.*

Which retained its strong adjectival forms (e.g. *hwilcne, hwilces, hwilcere*) only in early ME. It continued to be used in its original qualitative sense (= of what kind?): *Allas, man, whuch is þin heorte, herder þan eni ston?* and to express selection from a definite number: *I wille fayn, and I wiste wilk* 'I would gladly if I knew which', *which is the perfitest order?* 'which is the most perfect order?'

Whether with selective dual reference gradually began to be superseded by *which: Weþer is betere of þan twom?* 'which is the better of the two?'

The modern English period

Who had already in late ME approached the norm of present-day usage. *Who* displacing object-case *whom* began to be common in EMnE. Shakespeare has many examples: *Who hath he left behind him?* – some even after a preposition: *Yield thee, thief! To who? to thee?*

Today *whom* tends to be somewhat bookish and is obligatory only after a preposition.

What in EMnE could still be found predicatively with the value of *who: What is he that was not born of woman?* (Shakespeare) – but *who* is now the preferred alternative. *What* in this function died out after 1700.

Which has been the rule since ME with selective reference. *Which of you can rebuke me of synne?* (AV), *to live or die, which of the twain were better?* (Shakespeare). Colloquially, selective *which* now tends to be displaced by *who* or *what* (*What do you prefer, tea or coffee?*, *Who do you prefer, John or Peter?*) – except with partitive *of: Which of the two do you prefer?*

The original qualitative meaning of *which* (= what kind?) died out in ME and its place was taken by phrases like *what kind of, what manner (sort) of*, etc.

Whether died out in EMnE, and its function was taken over by *which*. AV has *Whether of them twaine did the will of his father?*

The personal pronouns in the OE period

The pronoun of the first person is inflected for three numbers:

	singular	dual	plural
N	ic	wit 'we two'	wē
A	mē	unc	ūs
G	min	uncer	ūre
D	mē	unc	ūs

The pronoun of the second person inflects for three numbers:

	singular	dual	plural
N	þū 'thou'	git 'you two'	gē 'ye'
A	þē	inc	ēow
G	þin	incer	ēower
D	þē	inc	ēow

The pronoun of the third person inflects for two numbers and three genders:

	masculine	feminine	neuter	plural (common gender)
N	hē	hēo	hit	hīe
A	hine	hīe	hit	hīe
G	his	hiere	his	hiera
D	him	hiere	him	him

It is worthy of note that only the pronoun of the third person has maintained accusative-dative contrast. In the two other pronouns they have coalesced early, polarizing the system into the subject – non-subject contrast we know today.

From the genitive forms were derived possessive pronouns, but in OE they could still, as in modern German, be used in a non-possessive sense as in *geþencst þū mīn?* 'gedenkst du meiner?', *hwilc hiera?* 'which of them?'.

Pronouns of address

The Anglo-Saxons consistently 'thoued' one another: *þū lēofa cyning* 'thou dear king', *þā cwæþ hē to þǣm bisceope, 'Ic þē hālsie ond bidde, þæt þū mē hit gesecge'* 'then he said to the bishop, 'I implore and beseech thee that thou sayest it to me'.

The so-called reverential plural, used with singular meaning in address to one person (cp. Danish *De*, German *Sie*, French *vous*, MnE *you*), is a ME departure.

Possessive and reflexive functions

From the genitive of the first and second-person pronouns were derived possessive adjectives declined on the model of the strong adjective: *ic healp mīnum fæder* 'I helped my father', *mid þīnre sweostor* 'with thy sister', *ealle mīne þing sint þīne* 'all my things are thine' (mark the plural concord also of the independent pronoun).

The genitive of the third-person pronoun is indeclinable when used as a possessive: *hēo hēalp hiere fæder* 'she helped her father', *on his hūse* 'in his house'.

OE possessed no reflexive pronoun proper, having lost its Germanic inheritance, the subject-referring **sik* (Danish *sig*, German *sich)* at some prehistoric stage[5]. Instead the personal pronoun has come to perform reflexive function: *hēo beseah hie to ānum his manna* 'she turned (herself) to one of his men', *se here gegaderode hine* 'the army gathered (itself)', *þæt folc gegaderode hit* 'the people gathered (itself)', etc.

The potential ambiguity caused by the loss of **sik*, however, is evident from cases like *hē acwealde hine* 'he killed him(self?)', *hēo hie ofslōg* 'she slew her(self?), etc. so to achieve greater clarity OE sometimes appended the adjective *self.* Orosius has *se cyning Hasterbald hine selfne acwealde, and his wīf mid hiere twǣm sunum hie selfe forbærnde* 'King Hasdrubal killed himself and his wife burned herself together with her two sons'.

A personal pronoun in the dative is common with intransitive verbs of motion or posture in a function which is usually classed as reflexive: *fār þē nū* 'fare thee now', *he him gewāt ūt of healle* 'he went (him) out of the hall', *sǣton him ætgædere* 'they sat (them) together'.

The ME period

The dual forms

Dual forms did not outlive early ME, and their function was taken over by the plural. The Ormulum (about 1200) has *unnc birrþ baþe þannkenn Crist* 'it befits us both to thank Christ'.

The pronoun of the first person

The subject form was usually *ik* in the North and *ich* in the Midlands and South. In accented position before a consonant, however, we get the weakened form *i/y* from about 1200 in the North and Midlands. This unaccented form gained currency, and gradually came to be used in all positions. Chaucer has *I*, but also uses *ich*.

It is from this unaccented variety that a new accented form [ī] is evolved – the ancestor of MnE *I* [ai].

The plural object form was OE *ūs*, so MnE *us* must derive from an earlier short unaccented variant.

The plural of majesty

This was unknown to OE. The Anglo-Saxon kings invariably used *I* about themselves, and a *we* always admitted of sociative interpretation, i.e. it might include others, for instance his councillors or entourage. A Latin plural of majesty was in OE always translated by the singular: *And ic bidde ēow ealle* (: *rogamus etiam vos*).

The plural of majesty seems to have originated in the Roman Dual Empire, where emperor and co-emperor used *we* (*nos*) about themselves, and were accordingly styled *you (vos)*. Later this courtly use of the plural fossilized into mere convention, and its sense was transferred to one ruler as a symbol of power and prestige. The next to adopt it was the Catholic church, through which it soon spread to most European countries. Pope Gregory writes to William the Conqueror *Rogamus etiam dilectionem vestram, ut ... defendatis* 'We also request your highness that you defend ... '(Note that also the king is addressed in the plural).

The first unambiguous instances of the plural of majesty (i.e. that it cannot be interpreted sociatively) emerged in the 13th century through French influence. One of the first examples is from the Proclamation of Henry III (1258) *in þe two and fowertigþe geare of ure cruninge (: de nostre regne)*.

The pronoun of the second person

This presents the following typical ME forms: the subject form of the singular is *þou/thou* and the object form is *þe/thee*. The plural has as subjet form *ȝe/ye* and as object form *ȝow/you*.[6]

Pronouns of address

Until about 1250 *thou* continued to be the only form of address to high as well as low, even in cases where translations from the French would seem to call for a plural: *þu havest woh (: vous avez tort)* 'thou art wrong', but already in the latter half of the century nearly all dialects seem to be familiar with the so-called reverential plural *ye* in address to one person: *Loverd, al Denemark I wile ȝou yeve* 'My Lord, I will give you all Denmark'.

This particular use of the plural for polite address, an offshoot from the plural of majesty, had through the intermediary of mediaeval Latin and the

Catholic church come to be known in most feudal states of western Europe long before it began to appear in England. Its late emergence in English seems to be due to the fact that the homogeneous and relatively classless Anglo-Saxon society provided no genial soil for the foreign importation. The Norman rulers employed the reverential plural in their native speech *(tu-vous)*, and with the fusion of the two races and the gradual ascendancy of English in the 13th century they began to carry their native mode of address over into their new language. A *thou-ye* distinction came to be the mark of refined and polite conversation. The Rule of St Brigit (about 1400) enjoins that *'none of you schall 'Thou' another in spekynge, but eche schal speke reuerently to other, the younger namely to the elder'*.

Already Chaucer is in keeping with the usage of the cultured circles of his day. *Thou* is used by superiors to inferiors (*And pardoner, I prey thee, drawe thee neer*), or with affective force as a mark of endearment (*And thow, Criseyde, o swete herte deere!*), familiarity (*And thow, my suster ... what thynkestow to do?*), or contempt (*Thou art a fool, thy wit is overcome!*). *Ye* is the norm in respectful address to superiors, as in *The hostiler answerde him anon, and seyde 'sire, your felawe is agon'*, or between equals as a gesture of courtesy: *'Sire', quod this squyer, 'whan it lyketh yow, it is al redy, though ye wol right now'*. In Chaucer persons styled *my lord, sir, lady, madame,* etc. almost consistently appear with *ye-* address.

The pronoun of the third person
This has undergone far-reaching morphological changes, notably in the feminine and plural forms. The OE paradigmatic dimensions (N A D) of the masculine and feminine singular (see p. 101) have now been reduced to a subject – non-subject contrast *(he-him, she-her)*, the old accusative having been superseded by dative forms already in early ME. The typical ME forms are:

	masculine	feminine	neuter	plural
subject	he	he, heo, sche[7]	hit, it	hi, he, they[9]
object	him	hir, her	him[8], it	hem, them

Reflexive functions
The simple personal pronoun used reflexively had already in OE begun to be reinforced by the adjective *self* (*mē selfne, him selfum, hīe selfe,* etc.). About 1200, however, the new possessive forms *miself, þiself* began to compete with the old object forms *meself, þeself.* These possessive forms are due to the weakening of *me, þe > mi, þi,* whereby they came to be easily associated with the possessive, and *self* came to be felt as a noun.

The plurals *usself(e)* and *youself(e)* began to generate corresponding possessive forms (*our-, your-*) somewhat later, about 1300.

Hitself and the original datives *herself, himself* were handed down directly from OE. *Themselfe* is also an old dative form (OE *hīe selfe – hem selfum*)

104

which is common from about 1300. The -s plurals, it should be noted, are not recorded till EMnE.

The personal pronoun continued to be used with reflexive force as in OE: *in no hole sall ye yow hide* 'in no hole shall ye hide (yourselves)', *holde hire still!* 'let her keep herself quiet!'

The reflexive 'dative' remained common particularly with verbs of motion: *Up him stod Peter and spec wid al his mighte, þau Pilatus him come wid ten hundred cnihtes* 'up stood Peter and spoke with all his might, though Pilate came with a thousand knights'.

Possessive functions

Rudimentary inflexion was preserved in the conservative South till about 1300 :*mines federes luue* 'my father's love', *on þinre side* 'on thy side'.

The dual died out in early ME. The Ormulum has *þeȝȝ shulenn lætenn hæþeliȝ off unnkerr swinnc* 'they should think scornfully of our toil'.

From early ME on the genitive of the personal pronoun was used only with possessive function. At the same time the possessive of the first and second persons began to drop the final -n before words with initial consonant, but the -n was retained before a vowel and *h: mi moder, þy name, min aunte,* but *þin appel, min honour.*

The possessive *its* is not attested till the 16th century, so *his* continued to perform the double function of a masculine and a neuter possessive throughout ME. Mandeville has: *the gode dyamand leseth his vertue* 'the good diamond loses its power'.

Independent possessives

The OE possessive, it will be remembered, had the same form whether it was used dependently as an adjective or independently. When, however, in ME differentiation according to the nature of the following sound set in, the possessive retained its final -n in independent position, probably because of the stronger emphasis it carried there: *Sir Edward, þine we are!* 'Sir E., we are thine!' A similar principle accounts for the retention of the -n in postposition: *Marie, moder mine* 'Mary, my mother'.

Independent possessives in -s

The pronouns *her, your, our, their* developed a kind of double possessive form in ME by adding -s. Barbour has: *dreidless it is ouris all* 'without doubt it is ours'. The process started in the North about 1300, but the new -s forms were not fully established in the conservative South till about 1600. Wiclyffe has *our stiriþ to iolité ...* and *here (=their) stiriþ to mornynge* 'ours induces mirth and theirs induces sorrow'.

The type 'a friend of mine'

This type began to appear about 1300 and was quite common in late ME. There is little consensus of opinion concerning the origin of this type, but it is very probably a native partitive construction, which was supported by the parallel French type 'un ami des siens'.

The so-called his-*genitive*

This was common in late ME and particularly in connection with personal names: *and sende Harold hys body to Harold hys moder* 'and sent H.'s body to H.'s mother'. This peculiar possessive type probably originated as a disconnected genitive suffix. For this view speaks the rarity of a *her*- variety, and the applicability of *his* also to feminine nouns and names.

The modern English period

The pronoun of the first person (ME *ich*) survived dialectally as *ich, uch* in the South till about 1800, and was until recently heard in parts of Somerset. It is also the form we find when Shakespeare imitates rustic speech as in *Chill (= Ich will) not let go, zur, withour vurther 'casion*[10].

The unaccented variety of the first-person pronoun is still heard in Northern dialects as [i].

The plural of majesty

This continues to be common in EMnE royal or proclamatory style: *What heir of York is there alive but we?* (Shakespeare). Queen Victoria is reported to have used it in her famous 'we are not amused'. More recent examples are more or less formulaic: *We Ernest Bevin – a member of His Britannic Majesty's Most Honourable Privy Council ... request and require ...* (British Passport).

The pronoun of the second person had in late ME the regular singular subject form *thou* and the object form *thee*. In the plural the subject form was *ye* and the object form *you*. In EMnE these two plural forms were still carefully distinguished by many writers, but because of the phonetic similarity of their unstressed forms, resulting in something like [jə], *ye* and *you* soon came to be confused, witness frequent examples like *I do beseech ye* (Shakespeare), *a southwest blow on ye and blister you all over* (id.). The AV of 1611, on the other hand, shows carefully distinguished *ye* for subject and *you* for object uses.

After a century or so of more or less indiscriminate use, however, *you* becomes the established form for both subject and object case, and *ye* disappears, but lingers on in liturgical use and in dialect, chiefly Northern. Tommy (to Jock on leave from France): 'What about the lingo? Suppose you want an egg over there, what do you say?' Jock: 'Ye juist say 'oof''. Tommy: 'But suppose you want two?' Jock: 'Ye juist say 'twa oofs', and the silly auld wife gies ye three, and ye juist gie her back one. Man, it's an awfu' easy language' (Punch). Note however its survival in a few phrases like [haudidu:], and in *lookee, thankee*, which are now archaic.[11]

Address

In ME refined speech, and as early as Chaucer, the use of *you* and *thou* had been fairly regulated, the former being the mark of respectful address whereas the latter was used to persons of inferior rank or to express familiarity.

In the 17th and 18th centuries *thou* was in a process of steady decline, and it is now confined to poetry and to liturgical language. It has however survived dialectally, particularly in the North. First: 'Wu't tak thy quoat off, then? Oi tell thee oi'm as good a mon as thee! Second: 'Thee a mon! Whoy thee be'st only walkin' about to save thy funeral expenses!' (Punch). The old singular pronoun *thou* is still in living use among the Quakers, who have stubbornly stuck to the pronoun 'used by God to Man, and Man to God' when it was being abandoned by others.[12]

The pronoun of the third person was by EMnE established in its present form with a few notable exceptions.

Hit was still usual as an accented form in EMnE. Queen Elizabeth uses both *hit* and *it* in her letters. Soon after 1600, however, the unaccented form became universal. The old dative form *him* was found sporadically in the standard language as late as the 17th century. For the neuter possessive form *his* see p. 105.

In the plural the Scandinavian-derived forms *they* and *their* were fully established by EMnE. The old native object form *hem* was displaced by Scandinavian *them* in the course of the 16th century, but has survived colloquially as unstressed *'em* (*take 'em, stop 'em,* etc.), often erroneously believed to be a clipped form of *them*.

Some other ME forms of the third-person pronoun have now only dialectal currency. The old *h-* form for *she* (see p. 104) lingers on in Lancashire as *hoo,* and the Yorkshire *shoo* could be a hybrid of the *she* and the *hoo* forms. The old masculine accusative *hine,* which was replaced in ME by the dative *him,* may still be heard dialectally as *en* or *un* in Southern dialects: *I 'vised 'un to gie up matrimony an' take to a trade* (Punch).

Reflexive functions
The old non-possessive forms *meself, theeself* die out in EMnE and have survived only dialectally.

The *-s* plurals, it should be noted, are late-comers, the forms *yourselves* and *ourselves* being only attested a couple of times in late ME.

The third-person plural *themselves* came into wider use in the 16th century, when the old *-s* less form could still be met with. Berners has *hwo bare themselfe so valyantly.*[13]

Oneself, used reflexively about the indefinite person, made its first appearance in the 16th century, but is not recorded in Shakespeare. The old use of the simple personal pronoun with reflexive meaning became increasingly rare after ME and is now dialectal. In Shakespeare we can still find *I'll withdraw me, we will rest us, stars may hide them,* etc. The usage is now only found in cases where the personal pronoun occurs after a stressed preposition with local sense: *I have no money about me, close the door behind you,* etc.

The old reflexive 'dative' is obsolescent in EMnE. Shakespeare has *run thee to the parlour, stay thee here, to sit him down.* Today it is non-existent except as a poeticism *(here my dear love sits him down).*

Possessives
In EMnE the *n*-less possessives seem to be the rule before consonants (*my dog, thy garden*), but before vowels and *h,* however, the old -*n* form may occur as late as the 18th century. Instances were particularly frequent with monosyllables like *eye, arm, ear, own.* Swift has *mine* before *eyes,* and Pope before *eyes* and *ears.* Soon, however, this purely phonetic distinction is abandoned, and *my* becomes the only possible form when used dependently as an adjective, while the old -*n* form becomes restricted to independent function *(the book is mine).*

Its, probably formed on the analogy of *his* or from *it* + the genitive -*s* of the nouns, is a product of the late 16th century. It is not found in Spenser, Bacon or the AV of 1611. In Shakespeare the old *his* preponderates: *How far that little candle throws his beams.* The AV has *But if the salt have lost his savour.* After about 1650, however, *its* (earliest form written *it's*) is the rule.

Her, the old native form for *their* (see p. 149,9), died out about 1500. Caxton has *her fader & moder cam & sawe how her doughter was biheded. Hisn, yourn, ourn, theirn,* formed on the analogy of *mine, thine,* are still dialectally widespread in the South and Midlands. Cp. the old rhyme *He that prigs what isn't hisn/ When he is caught must go to prison/ She that prigs what isn't hern/ At the treadmill takes a turn.*

The so-called his-genitive
This form was widely used in EMnE, because of the support derived from the phonetically similar -*s* genitive: *Ben Johnson His Volpone.* Addison has *Upon Pyrrhus his threatening to leave her.* In the 19th century the construction was obsolescent in non-dialectal use, cp. Dickens's famous *Bill Stumps His Mark* from the Pickwick Papers.

The indefinite article in the OE period
In most IE languages the indefinite article has developed out of the weakened numeral *one,* which early began to assume a secondary indefinite sense (= a certain). The process took place in the OE period, so it is often difficult without contextual aid to ascertain the degree of numeral force retained in *ān: hē wæs þǣr mid ānum brēðer wuniende* 'he was living there with a/one brother'. Numeral force is absent in *ān man hæfde twēgen suna (: homo quidam habuit duos filios),* but unlike present-day usage *ān* carries a strong notion of indefiniteness. In many cases where we today would use the indefinite article OE prefers Ø-form: *þæt mǣden hæfde unstille niht* 'the maid had an unquiet night', *hund is sāwullēas* 'a dog is soulless'.

Unlike MnE, the predicate noun generally takes Ø-article in OE: *þæt wæs gōd cyning* 'that was a good king', *hunta ic eom* 'I am a hunter'.

The ME period

Remnants of inflexion occur only in early ME (*in are tiden* 'upon a time', *in aness weress hewe* 'in a man's likeness'). As long as gender and case distinctions were preserved in early ME, numeral and article function could only be distinguished by contextual criteria as in OE. In the spoken language, however, article function was no doubt marked by a shortened vowel and absence of accent.

The 13th-century change of $\bar{a} > \bar{q}$ in all dialects south of the Humber (see p. 68), however, provides us with means of formal differentiation between the two functions. The indefinite article, because of its short unaccented vowel, came out of the change as *an,* and the numeral as *ōn.*

The loss of *-n* before consonants started about the 12th century in the North, and in the South the process was in the main completed by 1300. Before *h-,* however, instability has obtained till the present day.

In early ME the predicate noun was construed with Ø-article as in OE: *art þu angel?* 'art thou an angel?', but later in the period the article became more usual. In Chaucer it is the rule.

The modern English period

By EMnE *an/a* had become the regular forms before a vowel and a pronounced consonant respectively (*an apple, an hour, a dog, a horse*). However, forms like *an union, an European, an one* are frequent till the 19th century.

Before *h* in accented syllables *an* as well as *a* occurred in EMnE (*an home, an hundred, an hedge*). Today there is vacillation only if *h-* occurs in an unaccented syllable (*a/an hotel, an/a historical syntax, a/an Hungarian wine*).

For examples of metanalysis (*nickname, apron,* etc.), see p. 74.

The predicate noun in EMnE regularly took the indefinite article. Modern remnants of earlier Ø-constructions are examples like *he was more teacher than scholar, a spot into which he was not climber enough to venture,* etc. where the emphasis is laid upon the activity or quality inherent in the noun, which thus comes to approach the function of an adjective.

In cases where the predicate noun denotes unique position, Ø-article has been usual since late ME, e.g. *he was parson in Bishopthorpe.*

Numerals in the OE period

English, like most IE languages, counts in multiples of ten (the so-called decimal system), a practice originating in the use of the fingers as a handy unit.

The cardinals have the following typical forms: *ān, twēgen, þrȳ, fēower, fīf, syx, seofon, eahta, nigon, tȳn, endleofan, twelf, þrēotȳne, fēowertȳne ... twentig, ān and twentig ... þrītig* (30) *... hundseofontig* (70), *hundeahtatig* (80), *hundnigontig* (90), *hundtēontig (hundred)* (100), *hundendleofantig* (110), *hundtwelftig* (120) *... fīf hundred .. þūsend.*

Note that OE has the same order of units and decades as we find today in Danish and German (*fīf and twentig, seofon and þrītig,* etc.). The reversed order which we find in MnE is a product of late ME.

The first three cardinals are adjectives following declensions of their own. *Ān* has a special accusative *ǣnne* with umlaut. The masculine form of 'two' is *twēgen* (> MnE *twain*), and the feminine and neuter usually *twā.*

Numerals above three are sometimes treated as pronouns and govern a kind of partitive genitive of the item counted: *fīf scipa* 'five (of) ships', *xxx sciphlǣsta* 'thirty (of) shiploads', sometimes as adjectives, undeclined when used attributively: *fīf fiscas* 'five fishes', but declined when they occur alone: *būton fīfum* 'except five'.

The ordinals are *forma (fyrsta), ōðer, þridda, fēorða, fīfta, syxta, seofoða, eahtoða, nigoða, tēoða, endleofta, twelfta, þrēotēoða ... twentigoða,* and the rest of the decades in *-oða.*

The ordinals all follow the weak adjective declension except *ōðer,* which is always strong.

The Danish practice of stating numerals consisting of units and halves (1½ , 4½ 'halvanden, halvfemte') by combining half with the ordinal next above it reflects an ancient Germanic mode of reckoning, which is also represented in OE: *ōðer healf hund daga* '150 days' (cp. the same order in German *anderthalb*), *fīfte healf hund manna* '450 men'.

The ME period

On the formal dissociation of OE *ān* into numeral *one* and article *an*, see p. 109.

Survivals of inflexion are early ME: *be anun synfulle man* 'about one sinful man', *tweire kunne* 'of two kinds', but linger on in more or less fossilized form in Kentish as late as the 14th century.

Numerals, as we have seen, were in OE followed by a kind of partitive genitive of the item counted, but few traces of this original construction survived early ME. The Peterborough Chronicle has *And ðet lastede þa xix wintre wile Stephne was King* 'and it lasted 19 winters while Stephen was king'. Instead an *of*-phrase came to carry the partitive connotation: *syx of hethene kinges* 'six heathen kings'.

Vigesimal counting (i.e. counting in twenties) was introduced in early ME with the adoption of the Scandinavian loan *score*: *v scora scæp* 'five score of sheep'.

The OE sequence of units and decades was preserved throughout ME *(four and twenty, five and fifty).* The reversed order we know today began to appear in late ME, bur is not established till EMnE.

The modern English period

The old masculine form *twaine* has since ME been nothing but a poetic variant of *two*, sometimes preferred when the numeral follows the noun *(five loaves hath he and fishes twain).*

Vigesimal counting as in Shakespeare's *nine score and odd posts* is now confined to stereotyped rhetorical phrases like *fourscore and ten years ago.*

The ME practice of stating the units before the decades was still common in EMnE: *here is but two and fifty hairs on your chin* (Shakespeare). About 1700, however, the order was reversed, but the old system has persisted in many Southern dialects.

CHAPTER X

Verbs

The verb in the OE period

The Germanic simplifications discussed p. 21 are characteristic also of the OE verb. Only two inflectionally contrasted tenses (the present and the preterite) have been retained, besides two moods (the indicative and the subjunctive), one voice (the active), two numbers (the singular and the plural), and three persons.

Like her sister languages in the Germanic family, English was later to add new resources of tense, mood, and voice to this reduced system, chiefly by resorting to analytical structures.

Strong verbs

These can be grouped into six ablaut classes according to the variations in their root-vowel patterns, and are further characterized by having no dental element in the preterite and the past participle. The typical root-vowel patterns are the following:

Class I:

$\bar{\imath}$ (present) – $\bar{a}$ (preterite sing. 1st and 3rd persons) – *i* (preterite plur.) – *i* (past partc.) as in *grīpan* 'catch' – *grāp* – *gripon* – *gripen; rīdan* 'ride' – *rād* – *ridon* – *riden.* Similarly: *wrītan* 'write', *rīsan* 'rise', *scīnan* 'shine'. With Verner's Law (see p. 24): *līðan* 'travel' – *lāþ* – *lidon* – *liden.* With contraction (see p. 67) and Verner's Law: *þēon* (< * *þihan*) 'thrive' – *þāh* – *þigon* – *þigen.*

Class II:

$\bar{e}o$ – $\bar{e}a$ – *u* – *o* as in *bēodan* 'bid' – *bēad* – *budon* – *boden; scēotan* 'shoot' – *scēat* – *scuton* – *scoten.* Similarly: *flēotan* 'float', *flēon* 'flee', *gēotan* 'pour'. With Verner's Law (see p. 24): *cēosan* 'choose' – *cēas* – *curon* – *coren; frēosan* 'freeze' – *froren; sēoðan* 'seethe' – *soden.* With contraction (see p. 67) and Verner's Law: *tēon* 'draw' – *tēah* – *tugon* – *togen.*

Class III:

i (eo) – *a (ea)* – *u* – *u (o)* as in *findan* 'find' – *fand* – *fundon* – *funden; weorpan* 'throw, warp' – *wearp* – *wurpon* – *worpen.* Similarly: *climban* 'climb', *drincan* 'drink', *singan* 'sing', *feohtan* 'fight', *ceorfan* 'cut, carve'. With Verner's Law (see p. 24): *weorðan* – *wearþ* – *wurdon* – *worden.*

Class IV:

e – *æ* – $\bar{æ}$ – *o* as in *beran* 'bear' – *bær* – *bǣron* – *boren; teran* 'tear' – *tær* – *tǣron* – *toren.* Similarly: *cwelan* 'die', *stelan* 'steal', *helan* 'conceal'.

Irregular, but originally belonging to this class, are *niman* 'take' and *cuman* 'come' ($\bar{o}$ – $\bar{o}$ – *u*).

Class V:

e – æ – ǣ – e as in *metan* 'measure, mete (out)' – *mæt – mǣton – meten; drepan* 'kill' – *dræp – drǣpon – drepen*. Similarly: *sprecan* 'speak', *tredan* 'tread', *wrecan* 'fulfil, wreak (havoc)'. With Verner's Law (see p. 24): *cweðan* 'say' – *cwæþ – cwǣdon – cweden*. With contraction (see p. 67) and Verner's Law: *sēon* 'see' – *seah – sǣgon – segen; plēon* 'risk' – *plegen*.

Class VI:

a – ō – ō – a as in *faran* 'go, fare' – *fōr – fōron – faren; galan* 'crow' – *gōl – gōlon – galen*. Similarly: *wadan* 'go', *wascan* 'wash', *bacan* 'bake'. With contraction (see p. 67) and Verner's Law (see p. 24): *slēan* 'slay' (< * *slahan*) – *slōh – slōgon – slagen*.

Reduplicating verbs

These, in some grammars listed as ablaut class VII, are so called because they originally formed their preterites by reduplication of the initial consonant. They are remnants of a large IE group typified outside Germanic by forms like Latin *parco – peperci, curro – cucurri, tango – tetigi* and in Germanic by e.g. Gothic *haitan* 'call' – *haihait* 'called'. Only secondary vestiges of this peculiar type of verb have survived into OE, such as the contraction in the preterite resulting from the loss of the reduplicated syllable.

The two preterite vowels, either *ē* or *ēo,* are always identical, and the infinitive vowel corresponds to that of the past participle: *hātan* 'call' – *hēt – hēton – hāten; feallan* 'fall' – *fēol – fēollon – feallen*.

Similarly: *flōwan* 'flow' – *flēow; bēatan* 'beat' – *bēot; cnāwan* 'know' – *cnēow; lǣtan* 'let' – *lēt; blandan* 'blend' – *blēnd*.

This regularity is still retained in their MnE descendants: *blow-blew-blown; grow-grew-grown; fall-fell-fallen*.

Preterite-present verbs

So called because their present forms derive from a former strong preterite, and therefore there is no *-s* in the 3rd person present of their modern descendants. This original preterite had come to assume present meaning (cp. Lat. *novi* 'I know'), and to make up for the lack of a preterite, therefore, a new weak formation with dental suffix was introduced. The whole process can be illustrated by the verb *witan* 'know' which in the present singular is *wāt* (formally an old preterite), and the new preterite is *wiste*.

The preterite-presents constitute a small but extensively used group of verbs in English. Chief members are *witan* 'know', *sculan* 'be obliged to, owe' – *sceall – sceolde; cunnan* 'know, understand' – *can – cūðe; magan* 'be able' – *meahte; *mōtan* 'be allowed to, may' (the inf. has not been recorded) – *mōt – mōste, durran* 'dare' – *dear – dorste; āgan* 'have, possess' – *āh – āhte*[1]. Less important are *þurfan* 'need', *unnan* 'grant', *dugan* 'avail', *munan* 'remember'.

Anomalous verbs[2]

The verb *to be* in the Germanic languages is composed from different roots which are still obvious in MnE *be, am, is, are, was;* German *sein, bin, ist, war.*

The verb *to be* in OE composes its present indicative and subjunctive from two roots, one in **es/er* and one in **bheu* (cp. Lat. *sum* and *fui* respectively). The preterite has been supplied from a quite different verb, namely *wesan* of class V.

	present		*preterite*
		indicative	
1	eom 'I am'	bēo 'I am'	wæs 'I was'
2	eart	bist	wǣre
3	is	biþ	wæs
1-3	sind(on)	bēoþ	wǣron

		subjunctive	
1-3	sȳ	bēo	wǣre
1-3	sȳn	bēon	wǣren

Imperative sing. *wes/bēo*; imperative plur. *wesaþ/bēoþ*
Participles *wesende/bēonde; gebēon.*

The MnE plural *are* derives from an Anglian form *(e)arun*, which, heavily reinforced by its Scandinavian cognate *eru*, was to become generalized as recently as EMnE.

Other members of this group are *dōn* 'do, put, make', *gān* 'go', and *willan* 'wish'.

Weak verbs

As we have noted already p. 20, the weak verbs constitute a Germanic innovation, formed by means of a *-jan* suffix (hence the umlaut) from various other parts of speech, primarily nouns, adjectives, and preterites of strong verbs, a derivational mechanism which is still reflected in MnE *doom-deem, food-feed, sale-sell; full-fill, whole-heal; sit-set, drink-drench.*

The weak verbs fall into two major classes (I-II) and a less important class III.

Class I is characterized by umlauted root vowels throughout the paradigms, and has infinitives in *-an*, and preterites and past participles in *-(e)de*, *-(e)d*: *dēman* 'judge' (cp. *dōm*) – *dēmde* – *gedēmd; trymman* 'make strong' (cp. *trum*) *trymede* – *getrymed; fyllan* (cp. *ful*) – *fylde* – *gefyld.*

A significant number of weak verbs of class I are important in having no umlaut in the preterite and the past participle, because they lost the *-i-* at an early stage. Therefore only the present shows umlaut, e.g. *sēcan* < **sōkjan*, whereas the preterite *sōhte* presupposes **sōkda* and not the expected **sōki-da*, which would have given umlaut.

114

They include *þencan* 'think' – *þōhte* – *geþōht; þyncan* 'seem' – *þūhte* – *ge-þūht; sellan* 'give' – *sealde* – *geseald, tellan* 'count' – *tealde* – *geteald*.

It is important to emphasize that the vowel variation in the MnE descendants of this group *seek-sought, buy-bought, think-thought, tell-told*, etc. does not indicate strong verbs and has nothing to do with ablaut, but is, as we have just seen, due to lack of i-umlaut in two of the stems. The surest characteristic of a weak verb remains the dental preterite!

Class II is characterized by infinitive in *-ian*, no umlaut of the root vowel[3], preterite and participle in *-ode, -od: lufian* 'love' – *lufode* – *gelufod; folgian* 'follow' – *folgode* – *gefolgod; lōcian* 'look' – *lōcode* – *gelōcod; þancian* 'thank' – *þancode* – *geþancod*.

Class III comprises only four verbs, namely *habban* 'have', *hycgan* 'think', *libban* 'live', and *secgan* 'say'.

Indicative and subjunctive forms of the verb
The typical present and preterite forms of the OE weak verb were these. The weak class II differs only in having *-ode, -odest*, etc. in the preterite *(lufode* 'loved', *þancode* 'thanked')*.

		indicative	
		present	*preterite*
sing.	1	-e	-(e)de
	2	-(e)st	-(e)dest
	3	-(e)þ	-(e)de
plur.	1-3	-aþ	-(e)don

		subjunctive	
sing.	1-3	-e	-(e)de
plur.	1-3	-en	-(e)den

The strong verb differed from this paradigm on a few important points. In the 2nd and 3rd persons of the present indicative it had, if possible, umlaut, showing the endings to be earlier **-ist, *-iþ* (cp. German *fahre-fährst-fährt): ic cēose* 'I choose' – *þū cīest* 'thou choosest' – *hē cīesþ* 'he chooseth'; *ic fare* 'I fare' – *þū fœrest* 'thou farest', *hē fœreþ* 'he fareth', etc.

Further, the strong verb had no ending in the 1st and 3rd persons of the preterite indicative: *ic band* 'I bound' – *hē band* 'he bound', and the root vowel of the second person was formed from a different stem, namely that of the preterite plural: *þū bunde – wē bundon*. Similarly *ic grāp* 'I caught' – *þū gripe – hē grāp – wē gripon* (Class I). *Ic bēad* 'I bade' – *þū bude – hē bēad – wē budon* (Class II). The preterite subjunctive was formed from only one stem: sing. 1-3 *bunde;* plur. 1-3 *bunden*.

Uses of the subjunctive
The subjunctive forms have undergone drastic reduction since Common Germanic, there being in OE no contrasts left in person, only in tense and

number. The subjunctive is used extensively in OE and shows many parallels to modern German usage.

It is common in independent clauses expressing wish and command: *se ælmihtiga God ēow gescylde* 'Almighty God protect you', *geweorðe nu fæstnes tōmiddes þǣm wæterum* 'let there be land in the midst of the waters'.

In dependent clauses it is current in subject clauses, in object clauses (including indirect speech), in clauses of concession, condition, hypothetical comparison, finality: *gōd biþ men þæt hē sīe būtan wīfe* 'it is good for a man that he should be without a wife', *hīe sǣdon þæt min dohtor wǣre forþfaren* 'they said that my daughter was dead', *þeah hē hit self forswīge* 'although he himself is silent about it', *gif þu wille witan hwæt hē sīe* 'if thou wantst to know who he is', *swa hē slǣpende wǣre* 'as if he were asleep', *and gesette hīe on heofnan þæt hīe scīnen ofer eorðan* 'and placed them in the sky, in order that they might shine on the earth'.

The uses and non-uses of the subjunctive in OE, however, are often unpredictable. The indicative may occur in many of the above instances, particularly if the clauses contain some element of fact or certainty: *ic oncnāwe þæt þū eart wel gelǣred* 'I understand that thou art well educated', *gif þū Godes sunu eart* 'if thou art God's son'.

For periphrastic subjunctive equivalents, see p. 118.

Time and tense
As we have seen already p. 21, the existence of only two inflexional tenses, a present and a preterite, was one of the chief characteristics of a Germanic language.

In OE, therefore, the present must serve for all present and future time: *Lārēow, hwī gǣst þū āna?* 'master, why art thou walking alone?', *ic fare tō mīnum fæder* (: *ibo ad patrem*) 'I will go to my father'. Ælfric's Grammar recommends: *amabo = ic lufie tō dæg oþþe tō mergen*.

The preterite covers all past time. Perfect or pluperfect time relations may be implicit in the context or situation, or they may be brought out by some temporal adverb: *fæder, ic syngode* (: *pater, peccavi*), *hine hālig God ūs onsende* 'Almighty God has sent him to us', *hīe lange ǣr gierndon þæs cyninges dohtor* 'they had all long yearned for the King's daughter'.

In MnE the present, though with a limited choice of verbs and rarely without adverbial support, may still denote future time (*we leave at six, he does not return till next week*), but otherwise future, perfect and pluperfect time relations are now usually expressed by verbal periphrases.

The non-finite forms of the verb
The suffix of the OE present participle was *-(e)nde* (*sittende* 'sitting', *healdende* 'holding', *fremmende* 'performing', *lufiende* 'loving') as it still is in Danish and German. The past participle of the weak verbs ended in *-ed*, *-od* according to class (see p. 114), and that of the strong verbs in *-en*, which has in many cases survived to the present day (*taken, fallen, grown*, etc.).

116

The *ge-* prefix is a WGerm specialty and typical of the past participle (*ge-seten, gehealden, gefremed, gelufod*), but could also be prefixed to other forms, e.g. as a mark of aspect to mark non-durative action: *sēon* 'see', but *gesēon* 'catch sight of'. Cp. German *horchen* vs *gehorchen*.

The infinitive was originally a fully inflected neuter action noun, formed and used much in the same way as German *das Laufen, das Kommen, das Lachen*, etc. Traces of this former nominal status are preserved in OE in the so-called inflected infinitive after *to*: *to secganne* 'to say', *to witanne* 'to know', the *-e* indicating the dative case. Apollonius has *þa ēstas him beforan legde þe hē him tō bēodanne hæfde* 'put the provisions before him which he had to offer him'. Another nominal inheritance is its indifference to voice. The infinitive is always with active form even if the meaning is passive: *hē hēt hine behēafdian* 'he ordered him to (be) behead(ed)'.

The particle *to* is an old preposition meaning 'towards', and the infinitive it preceded thus denoted the goal towards which the activity of the main verb was directed (cp. Danish *at < ad*), so an OE sentence like *sēo fōr mid mē to onfōnne mīnum cynerīce* must originally have meant something like 'she went with me to(wards) the receiving of my kingdom'.

The use of *to*-less (uninflected) and *to* (inflected) infinitives in OE is in many respects parallel to our MnE norm. However, a few developments deserve mention. In the nominal functions a *to*-less infinitive is by no means unusual: *lufian his nīehstan...is crīstlic þing* 'to love one's neighbour is a Christian thing', *he ongan singan* 'he began to sing', *hē wilnaþ worldāre habban* 'he desires to have worldly fame'. It is common after verbs of motion where MnE requires a present participle: *hē cōm rīdan* 'he came riding'. The infinitive of a verb of motion is frequently left out after an auxiliary as in Danish and German; *hīe sceoldon tō Sandwic* 'they should (go) to Sandwich', *ic wille tō sǣ* 'I will (go) to the sea'.

Verbal periphrases

Elaborations upon the meagre two-tense framework of past and present inherited from ancestral Germanic began to appear already in OE. Perfect, pluperfect and future time relations could be alternatively expressed by verbal periphrases.

Perfect and pluperfect

A construction like **hē hæfþ/hæfde þone fisc gefangenne* may illustrate the first timid beginnings of what we now refer to as the periphrastic perfect and pluperfect. The verb *habban*, it will appear, has still retained its notional sense 'to possess', the participle *gefangen-ne* agrees in gender, number and case with the masculine object *fisc*. The construction translates literally 'he possesses (-ed) the fish as caught'. Soon, however, and probably already in late OE, the original construction tended to become obscured, the participle began to lose its grammatical concord and to become fused with the governing verb, which again assumed the function of an auxiliary: **he hæfþ/hæfde*

117

gefangen þone fisc. Next the construction began to connote not a state but the result of past action, but its original bearing upon the moment of speaking, however, has been carried down to MnE.

With some intransitive verbs, particularly of motion, the perfect and pluperfect are formed by means of the auxiliary *be* as in other Germanic languages: *þā hē þǣrtō gefaren wæs* 'when he had gone there'.

Shall and will

Futurity, besides being expressed by the simple present, could in OE also be rendered periphrastically by *sculan* and *willan*, both originally independent notional verbs. However, it is often difficult to ascertain the extent to which they have weakened into future-tense signs, for more often than not much remains of their inherent modal concepts of obligation and volition. Pure futurity is with least ambiguity attested in the first person: *wē sculon ende gebīdan* 'we shall await the end', *ic wille nū faran to þǣre stōwe* 'I will go to that place'.

Less linked up with modality is *weorðan*, which like its Danish and German counterparts *vorde* and *werden* was commonly used to express periphrastic future; *ēow weorðeþ forgifen hwæt gē sprecaþ* 'ye will be forgiven for what ye say'. Unlike German *werden*, which came to be the auxiliary par excellence for expressing futurity, English *weorðan* died out in the course of ME.

Periphrastic subjunctive equivalents

Modally marked action was in OE expressed by the inflexional subjunctive (see p. 116) or by periphrases containing some modal auxiliary, commonly *sculan, mōtan, willan* and *magan* – all originally full notional verbs: *hē wēnde þæt man hine sceolde ofslēan* 'he believed that the men would slay him' (...*hine ofslōge*, with the subjunctive, would also be possible). *Mīn dohtor gimþ þæt hēo mōte leornian æt þē þā gesǣlican lāre* 'my daughter yearns that she may learn from thee the blessed lore', *secge mē gewislicor þæt ic hit mæge understandan* 'tell me more plainly that I may understand it'. The periphrastic equivalents, which were undoubtedly felt as more emphatic carriers of modality than the crumbling subjunctive, came to attain an ever increasing currency throughout OE.

The periphrastic passive

Germanic, as we have seen (p. 21), early lost its inflexional passive, of which only fossilized *hātte* 'is/was called' remained in OE: *þā cwæþ hiera ān se hātte Ardalius* 'then said one of them who was called A. '. This early loss of a distinctive passive form, however, was remedied by periphrastic constructions containing *bēon/wesan* + the past participle: *Āsia is befangen mid Oceāno* 'Asia is surrounded by the ocean', *prēostas wǣron slegene* 'priests were slain'. Ælfric's Grammar has *amor = ic eom gelufod; osculator a te = ic eom fram þē cyssed* (note the marking of the agent by *fram*!).

Or it could be expressed by *weorðan: gif eaxle gelǣmed weorðeþ* 'if the shoulder becomes paralyzed', with much the same meaning as MnE 'gets paralyzed' (mutative passive).

The missing passive could also be expressed by the indefinite pronoun *man* + active verb: *gif man hine on fȳr dēþ* 'if it is set on fire'.

Be + the present participle

A periphrastic form made up of some connecting verb of the *be*-type + the present participle is indigenous to nearly all IE languages. In Germanic such periphrases are attested from the earliest beginnings of recorded speech. The construction exists in Gothic, in the Scandinavian languages, and is profuse in the WGerm branch. Only in English, however, was it to achieve importance.

The OE periphrases with *be* (*bēon/wesan*) + present participle usually denoted some kind of duration: *hē wæs feohtende in Āsia fīf wintra* 'he was fighting five winters in Asia = he spent five winters in Asia fighting', *þū eart rīxiende on heofonum* 'thou art (for ever) ruling in Heaven' – or it may have emphatic descriptive force, emanating from the adjectival heritage of the participle: *hīere onwald is nēa hrēosende* 'their power is nearly crumbling'.

Some authorities have tried to view the periphrasis as nothing but a calque on Latin constructions with *esse* + the present participle or on verbatim renderings of deponent verbs, etc. e.g. *erat docens* = *hē wæs lǣrende, locutus est* = *hē wæs sprecende, egressi eramus* = *wē wǣron ūt gangende*, etc. The scribes were often apt to translate such phrases word for word. It is true that the construction attains a particularly high frequency in translational works, but it is also found in poetry and texts where Latin influence can be excluded. Latin no doubt played a certain role in the proliferation of the periphrasis, but it is to all intents and purposes indigenous.

Why then did it have such a remarkable efflorescence in English, but remained marginal in the other Germanic languages? The support received from locutions of the type *hē cōm gangende* 'he came (was) walking' with weakened or quasi-auxiliary verb of motion + present participle, clause-equivalent constructions of the type *hē wæs in temple lǣrende* 'he was in the temple teaching', copula + predicative adjective constructions like *hit is scī-nende* 'it is shining' cannot have been decisive alone, for such constructions are shared by other Germanic languages as well.

More important for the growth of the construction in English is doubtless the gradual loss in OE and early ME of verbal prefixes (e.g. *ge-, for-, ymb-, æt-, tō-*, etc.) which have survived in the other Germanic languages and which were originally a common device for expressing intensity and non-durative (perfective) action in the verb.[4] Without any such prefix the verb was quite simply felt as durative. The loss of prefixes to mark the contrast durative – non-durative could then gradually be retrieved by the establishment from OE on of a new aspectual contrast: periphrastic form – simplex form. This also explains the rather unpredictable use of the periphrasis in

OE. As long as the prefixes (or some of them) were felt to be usable contrast makers, the choice between periphrastic form or simplex form was bound to be determined more by style than by necessity.

Another decisive factor for the spread of the *be + -ende* construction could have been the high incidence in OE of agent nouns in *-ende* to an extent unknown in other Germanic languages (*wealdend* 'ruler', *dēmend* 'judge', *wīgend* 'warrior', etc.). Bede has *þēos eorðe is berende missenlicra fugla* 'the earth is carrying (lit. 'is carrier of', note the genitive it governs!) various kinds of birds'. Similarly *hīe wǣron wealdende* 'they were ruling/they were rulers'.

Do + infinitive

Do was originally a full notional verb meaning 'place, put' (cp. German *etwas in den Kasten tun*, MnE *don, doff*): *hē dyde him on healse hring gyldenne* 'he put a gold ring round his neck'. Another notional sense was 'make, perform': *þū dydest eall gemǣre eorðan* 'thou hast made (created) all the boundaries of the earth'.

In all Germanic and many other IE languages, however, *do* may combine with the infinitive into a causative construction 'cause...to'. OE instances of this usage are few and supposed to be wholly or partially due to the Latin pattern *facere* + infinitive: *se gelōcaþ in eorðan and dēþ hīe cwacian* (= qui respicit in terram et facit eam tremere) '... and causes it to quake'.

The ME period

The drift from strong to weak form

OE possessed a total of about 300 strong verbs grouped into six ablaut classes and a seventh reduplicating class. In the transition period between OE and ME about one hundred of these strong verbs were lost, and in the course of ME and EMnE about 80 joined the weak conjugation. The drift towards weak form is primarily a tendency towards regularization caused by the analogy of the consistent weak majority pattern, and the absence of a written standard and the status of English as the speech of the uneducated masses made depletion of the strong category very swift. The verbs that acquire weak form in this period include *brew, glide, bake, creep, help, chew, read, knead, shear, shed, mete, ache, weep, laugh, step, carve, walk.*

The transition of course is gradual and many verbs appear for centuries with either form (*laughed/lough, wept/wope, ached/oke, helped/halp*, etc.).

Verbs that have moved the other way and developed strong forms through analogy are few. Most important are *wear* (on the analogy of *bear*, class IV), *stick* (on the analogy of *sting*, class III). Similarly *show* (OE *scēawian*), *sew* (OE *sēowian*), and *strew* (OE *strēowian*) have formed their strong past participles on the analogy of the *blow, grow* pattern. *Ring* (OE *hringan*) derives its strong form from the attraction of class III. All French verbs became weak except *strive* (OF *estriver*), where the attraction from class I was too strong. The analogy of this class also accounts for the strong forms of *thrive* (from Scandinavian) and *shrive* (from Latin).

Reduplicating verbs

Some have retained their characteristic regularity in ME such as *grow-grew-grown; know, fall,* etc., but a good many, including *walk, dread, sleep, weep, shed,* have joined the ranks of the weak conjugation.

The verb *haten* had by late ME fossilized into *hight* 'is/was called': *in a kynges tyme þat hyght Edward* 'at the time of a king who was called E.'

Preterite-present verbs

A few formal and semantic peculiarities of this category in ME deserve notice.

May (OE *magan – meahte*, ME *may – might/mought*). The commonest ME plural was *mowen* (OE *magon*), but later the form *may* was extended from the singular. The primitive sense 'be able to' recurred in ME; *a best...þat may se thurgh thik stane walles* 'a beast which is able to see through massive stone walls'. The modern senses of permission and contingency are in the main EMnE developments.

Must is the lineal descendant of the OE preterite *mōste*. In the 14th century it came to be used as a present: *Reymyld, quad Horn, ic moste wende* 'R., quoth H., I must go'. The original present, however, survives into EMnE: *do þi best, for y mot go* 'do thy best for I must go'. The semantic shift from permission (*he must not come in þe toun* 'he is not allowed to enter the town') to necessity and obligation (*Oon of vs moste bowen douteless* 'one of us must certainly yield') took place in ME and probably started in negative contexts (cp. MnE *may not/must not*).

Can (OE *cunnan – cūðe*, ME *can – couthe/coude*, the *-l* of MnE *could* being a 16th century innovation). *Can* retains its primitive sense 'know, understand' throughout ME: *I can no termes of astrologye* 'I know no astrological terms'.

Wit(en) (OE *witan – wāt – wiste*) is still current in ME; *þu wost wel* 'thou knowest well', *men wist neuer wher sche was bicome* 'they never knew what had become of her'.

Shall (OE *sculan – sceolde*) was in ME still used as a notional verb with the sense 'to owe': *the ferthyn þat y men shal* 'the farthing that I owe people'. The related sense of obligation is seen in: *we sculen alle deaþ þolien* 'we must all die'.

Owe (OE *āgan – āhte*) originally meant 'have, possess'. The semantic shift from 'possess' to 'be indebted' took place in early ME through uses like *hū mycel āht þū to geldanne hlāferde mīnum* (: ...*debes domino meo*), lit. 'how much hast thou to pay my lord'. With the related sense of obligation the old preterite (OE *āhte*) became current in ME as an auxiliary both with present and past meaning. Hence MnE *ought*.

The MnE regular weak forms *owe-owed-owed* were developed in ME, but the form *ought* both with its primitive sense 'possess' and its derived sense of obligation lingers on till about 1700.

Anomalous verbs
The forms of the verb *to be* call for a word of comment. In OE, it will be remembered, there were two plurals *bēoþ* and *sindon* (see p. 114), which in Anglian dialects were used concurrently with an alternative form *arun* (Lindisfarne Gospels have *gie aron leht middangeardes* 'Ye are the light of the world'). *Sindon*, however, was extinct by 1300, and its place was taken in the South and Midlands by the corresponding forms of *bēon*, which came to be the regular plural throughout ME: *þei ben ful harde* 'they are very hard'. In the North *are* held a strong position, and, supported by the Scandinavian cognate *eru*, expanded its territory southwards, but did not supersede the *be*-plural till EMnE.

The verb *will* (OE *willan*) retained its infinitive in ME: *to wylan to mak God felow of his violence* 'to desire to make God partner in his violence'. Current ME forms of the present were *wul* (through rounding) and *wol* (a back formation of the preterite *wolde*, and the ancestor of MnE *won't*): *and the smale wole wexen grete* 'and the small will grow big'.

The verb *to go* (OE *gān*) had the preterite *ēode* 'went' > ME *yode, yede*. The MnE preterite *went* is not in regular use till EMnE.

Indicative and subjunctive forms of the verb
The present indicative forms of the verb are important dialect criteria. The following are the typical ME forms:

	Midland	South	North
1	-e	-e	-e(s)
2	-est	-est	es
3	-eþ	-eþ	-es
plur. 1-3	-e(n)	-eþ	-es

The *-s* of the 3rd person singular is Northern and extends its territory southwards in the course of ME, supported by the analogy of *is-was*. By the 14th century it reached the London area, where Chaucer uses it a couple of times in rhyme-position.

In the plural, Southern *-eþ* continues OE *-aþ*, thus effacing the distinction between plural and third person singular. The Midlands introduce the plural *-en* (the ancestor of the MnE form after the loss of final *-n*), which probably derives from the plural of the preterite-present verbs or from the subjunctive. Chaucer has *-e* or *-en* as his rhyme prompts him.

The preterite of the strong verb in OE had vowels from two stems (*ic sang, þū sunge, hē sang, wē sungon*). Starting early in the North, however, these vowel distinctions began to be levelled in ME under that of the 1st and 3rd persons. This new kind of one-stem preterite is customarily referred to as a *northern preterite* and should be compared with the OE vowel patterns of their ablaut classes given in brackets. They include *sing* (class III), *begin* (III), *drink* (III), *ride* (I), *rise* (I), *smite* (I), *stride* (I), *write* (I), *see* (V), *give* (V).

Another type of preterite formation had its stem vowel extended from the past participle, the two thus becoming identical. Being a typically Western and South Western dialect feature, these kinds of formations are customarily referred to as *western preterites*. MnE examples are *bear* (IV), *bind* (III), *bite* (I), *break* (IV), *choose* (II), *cleave* (II), *fight* (III), *find* (III), *freeze* (II), *shoot* (II), *slide* (I), *speak* (V), *steal* (IV), *tear* (IV), *wear* (orig. weak), *win* (III), *wind* (III).

The levelling of course took place over a long period of time, and many verbs preserved their original stem vowels till well on into EMnE. Preterites like *bare* 'bore', *spake* 'spoke', *brake* 'broke', *fond* 'found' were still widely current in late ME.

The *-est* of the 2nd person (*foundest, borest*) was extended from the weak preterites and the present in the 14th century (see paradigm p. 115).

The subjunctive

The subjunctive present in OE had the endings *-e* (sing.) and *-en* (plur.), which were preserved in all dialects of ME, but in the Midlands *-en* had come to coincide with the present indicative plural (see p. 122). In the South where the prevailing plural was *-eþ*, the subjunctive remained distinctive until about 1400 when *-eþ* began to be ousted by the Midland *-en* type. In the North the subjunctive remained distinctive throughout ME.

Uses of the subjunctive

Though encroached upon by the indicative and by periphrastic equivalents (see p. 126), the ME subjunctive was still fairly commonly used, above all in independent clauses expressing wish and command: *God gife uss mahht* 'God give us power', *ylkon take hede to thys thyng* 'let everyone pay attention to this'.

Examples of the subjunctive in dependent clauses (subject and object clauses, clauses of concession, condition, hypothetical comparison, finality): *For betere is þat heo wepen here* 'for it is better that they should weep here', *he askede wat lond it were* 'he asked what country it was', *and alle thoughe he were a payneme, natheless he served wel God* 'and although he was a heathen, he served God well', *yf the fruyt of a tree be badde, the tree is badde* 'if the fruit of a tree is bad, the tree is bad', *starinde als he ware wod* 'staring as if he were mad', *sikerliche þe feond fliþ, leste he beo forschaldet* 'surely the devil flees, in order not to be scalded'.

Time and tense

In ME the establishment of a periphrastic future gradually effected a decline in the use of the futuric present inherited from Germanic. It did continue to exist, but futurity was more often than not brought out by some ad-

123

verbial time-indicator: *Bot ar ye in this towne to-day?* 'will you be in town to-day?', *he gothe forward as uppon Tewesday* 'he will leave on Tuesday'. As in OE, the simple present continued to cover action going on at the moment of speaking, where MnE would require an expanded tense: *Wat dest þou þere nou?* 'what art thou doing there now?'

The MnE rigid distinction between preterite and perfect was not yet established in ME: *þe fayrist þat I seigh þis seuen yere* 'the fairest that I have seen during the last seven years', *for y cam to departe a man ayens hys fadir* 'for I have come to separate a man from his father', and inversely: *Hanybale that Romayns hath vanquysshed tymes three* 'H. who conquered the Romans three times', *aventures that whylom han befalle* 'adventures that took place in old days'.

Non-finite forms of the verb

The present participle in ME is a handy clue to dialect. In the South and the South West it ended regularly in *-inde* (*cuminde, stondinde*). The Midlands favoured *-ende*, and the North *-ande* (supported by the analogy of Scandinavian *-andi*). About 1200 the modern suffix *-ing* began to appear in the Southern dialects. The new suffix originates from OE *-ing/-ung*, used to derive action nouns chiefly from verbs (*bletsing* 'blessing', *leornung* 'learning').

In early ME the unaccented *-ng* of the verbal noun, the *-nd* of the present participle and also the *-nn-* of the inflected infinitive (see p. 117) were often confused phonetically, witness common hybrid forms like *to cominde, to comende, to cominge*. Rhymes like *higinde – kinge, forsakyng – takyne* and spellings like *þousen, þousyng, þousend* 'thousand' tell a similar tale. This confusion of form and subsequently also of syntactical function is probably what caused the *-ing* suffix to become extended to all present participles after 1400 and the old noun in *-ing* to begin to acquire verbal force. That the new form in *-ing* is thus probably due to its coalescence with the *-ind* participle is further supported by the fact that the whole process started in the South, where the suffix *-ind* was the prevailing variant.

In the North, it should be noted, the endings of the present participle and the *-ing* noun have been kept apart in dialect till the present day.

The past participle lost its *ge-* prefix early in the North, probably under the influence of Scandinavian where it was unknown. In the other dialects it was gradually reduced to *y-, i-* (*icume* 'come', *ytake* 'taken'). The strong participle retained its final *-n* in the North, but lost it early in the South and Midlands. Thus *comen, taken* represent the prevailing Northern type, and *ycume, ytake* the corresponding Southern and Midland varieties.

The infinitive dropped its final *-n* early in the North, but it was preserved in the South till late ME. In many 14th-century poets the choice of suffix is determined by metre: *wel koude he synge and pleyen on a rote* 'Well could he sing and play on a harp'. Remnants of the inflected infinitive after *to* lingered on till the 14th century. Chaucer has a few examples in rhyme position: *... colour fresh and grene... which joye was to sene* 'colour fresh and green... which it was a joy to see' (cp. OE *tō sēonne*).

The particle 'to'. The gradual reduction of the former preposition to an empty infinitive sign in early ME is evident from several new developments, e.g. the use of prepositions like *for, from, with* etc. before the infinitive (*it be-gynneth ... for to swete* 'it begins to sweat', *wiþþ to letenn swingenn himm* 'by having him flogged'),[5] the rise in late ME of the so-called split infinitive (*synful men for to þus lede in paradise* 'to thus lead sinful men into paradise'), the expansion of *to*-infinitives at the expense of the simple type.

As far as the distribution of *to* and *to*-less infinitives is concerned, the norm of today is reached in late ME. In subject function the *to*-infinitive had become practically universal by early ME. In object function some vacillation still obtained with a great number of verbs, such as *gin* 'begin', *help, let, think, do, begin: gretter wexen hit began* 'it began to grow bigger'.

The passive infinitive. In origin a noun, the infinitive was originally indifferent to voice (see p. 117), and in early ME the active infinitive continued to be used also with passive content: *þe king heet halgien þe stude* 'the king ordered the place to be consecrated', *God is swuþe to luvien* 'God is to be loved dearly'. However, in late ME the *be*-type prevails.

The noun in -ing and the gerund. In OE the form in *-ing/-ung* was treated exclusively as a noun, inflexionally as well as syntactically. In early ME it still kept nicely within the syntactical boundaries of a noun, but from about 1300 it began to operate also as a verb, taking a direct object (i.e. non-genitival and non-prepositional) and adverbial modifiers. There is little consensus as to how these gerundial features have been acquired, but they are very probably due to a confusion of syntactical properties as a result of the phonetic coalescence of the suffixes of the present participle, the infinitive and the noun in *-ing* (see also p. 124). French influence through translations of forms in *-ant*, common to both the gerondif and the present participle, may also have been a contributory factor.

Examples with direct object are increasingly common in ME: *in bryngynge hire servyse* 'in offering their service', *fro kepynge Goddis hestis* 'from obeying God's commands', but the original genitival, later also *of*-object type recurs throughout the period: *ac þar is Cristes heriinge* 'but there is the praising of Christ', *in releuynge of þe pore commouns* 'in relieving the poor lay people'.

The form in *-ing* is by heritage indifferent to voice: *he was bounden by prisonyng in Rome* 'he was prevented by being imprisoned in Rome'. The verbal feature of a distinctive passive form is not in evidence till the 15th century. Tense distinctions are even younger and belong to the EMnE period (see p. 133).

Verbal periphrases

Perfect and pluperfect
The development of a full-fledged periphrastic perfect and pluperfect took place in the early ME period. The loss of semantic content in the verb *have*, the abandonment of inflexion in the participle and a change of word order

all point to an intimate fusion of the two into the modern compound tense. The OE type *hē hæfþ þone fisc gefangenne* becomes ME *he hath fangen þe fisch*, connoting now the result of past action.

The typically Germanic feature of using the auxiliary *be* particularly with intransitive verbs of motion is continued in early ME: *he wass risenn upp off dæde* 'he had risen from the dead', *Jhesu wes to helle y-gan* 'Jesus had gone to Hell'. The tendency to employ *have* with such verbs started about 1300 (*If þu haddest þider igon* 'if thou hadst gone there') and has been carried further in English (and Swedish) than in other Germanic languages. One of the chief reasons may be the increasing use of *be* in English as an auxiliary of the passive and also the coalescence in sound of the unaccented forms of *has* and *is* in some ME dialects.

The compound tenses of *be* have been formed with *have* since early ME: *longe habbe ich child ibon* 'long have I been a child'.

Shall and *will* were in OE heavily linked up with modality, so instances where they were used as pure future signs were few. In ME, however, *shall* became the auxiliary most commonly used in forming the periphrastic future of all persons, whereas *will* still seemed reluctant to disconnect itself from its inherent volitional connotations: *þeȝȝ shulenn lætenn hæþeliȝ off unnker swinnc* 'they will think scornfully of the labour we have both had', *Noe go cloute thi shone, the better will they last* 'Noah, go and cobble thy shoes, and they will last the longer'.

Worthen (German *werden*, Danish *vorde*) often denoted futurity as in OE: *what þou be, þou worst yfet* 'whoever thou art, thou wilt be fed'. For other functions of *worthen*, see p. 127.

Be going to in ME denoted motion. A sentence like *I am going to visit my father* meant 'I am on my way to visit my father'. It was only in late ME that the construction was used to express immediate futurity: *thys onhappy sowle...was goyng to be broughte into helle* 'this miserable soul was going to be taken to hell'.

Periphrastic subjunctive equivalents

The subjunctive began to lose ground in ME, its functions being taken over by the indicative, by object + infinitive constructions (*he commanded that he go* > *he commanded him to go*), or by periphrases with a modal auxiliary. The auxiliaries most commonly used were *shall* and *may*, capable of forming periphrastic equivalents of nearly all functions of the subjunctive: *and alle hoped it myghte be so* 'and all hoped that it might be so', *þanne het he him þet he his ssolde yeve to þe poure* 'then he ordered him to give his (money) to the poor'.

The auxiliary of the hortatory subjunctive was from the 13th century *let*: *Nou late us sitte and drynke* 'Now let's sit and drink'.

The periphrastic passive

The form *hight* 'is/was called', the last trace of the ancient inflected passive, survives into ME: *in a kynges tyme þat hyght Edward* 'in the days of a king who was called Edward'.

The most commonly used auxiliary of the passive is *be, worthen* being increasingly marginal after early ME. Chaucer does not use it at all.

The past participle in the passive construction, in OE treated as a normal predicative adjective, ceased to observe concord in early ME; the old construction is seen in *fewe beoþ icorene* 'few are chosen'[6].

Worthen (OE *weorðan*, German *werden*) as an auxiliary of the passive was in the course of ME slowly replaced by *be*, and the language lost the convenient means of distinguishing between statal/descriptive (*be*) and the actional/mutative aspect (*worthen*) which German still has: *the shop was closed* (: *war geschlossen*), but *I don't know when it was closed* (: *geschlossen wurde*, ME *worth yclosed*). The loss of *worthen* to express the idea of 'becoming', however, was made up for through the rise in late ME of equivalents like *become, fall, grow, turn, wax* and in EMnE of *get*.

The ousting of *worthen* from important functions as an auxiliary of the future by *shall* and *will* and of the passive by *be* has never yet been satisfactorily explained and remains one of the major puzzles of English historical syntax.

Be + present participle. Throughout early ME this construction continues to be functionally remote from our present-day norm. It is still comparatively rare in early ME but becomes increasingly common and is found in all dialects in late ME. Its use in ME is still unpredictable, but it seems to occur primarily with descriptive and durative force. In many writers its use or non-use is determined by considerations of metre and rhyme.

In late ME, however, the *be* + present participle construction came to coincide formally with the OE type 'he wæs on huntinge', which in ME eventually dropped the preposition via the reduced stage 'he was a-hunting'. The merging of these two constructions no doubt played an important part in determining the notion underlying the modern expanded tense.

French influence through the identical type 'il était parlant' may also have played an important part, and is doubtless one factor behind the growing popularity of the expanded form down through ME.

Because of its adjectival origin the present participle is inherently indifferent to voice, so *be* + *-ing* was commonly used with a passive sense: *þere are dedis doand neu* 'there are deeds being done now'. The modern type 'the book is being printed', with passive form, is a 19th-century departure (see p. 135). In OE and throughout most of the ME period the expanded form seems to have been confined to the present and the past tense. Additional tenses are later. Late ME was to see the development also of a perfect, a pluperfect and a future, but none of these can be said to be really current till about 1700.

For the type 'be going to', see p. 126.

Do + infinitive. The independent notional senses outlined under OE were in the main preserved in ME.

As a causative auxiliary *do* was slenderly evidenced in OE and probably due to Latin influence, but it becomes increasingly common in ME, no doubt supported by a parallel French construction with *faire* + infinitive: *King Aþelwald me dide swere, þat...* 'King A. made me swear that...', *þatt dide menn to trowenn* 'that caused people to believe', *þe king did writte a pair o letteris* 'the king had a couple of letters written'.

It is particularly the last type (with the subject of the infinitive unexpressed) which in the opinion of some authorities is the ancestor of the modern *do*-periphrasis. They explain it as the ultimate result of a gradually weakening causative *do*. In a sentence like 'the king did build a castle' the causative aspect is unambiguous, but in a type like 'the king did write a letter' it is not immediately obvious whether the king performs the act himself or has it done by someone else (: 'wrote a letter himself?' ... or 'caused a letter to be written?'). Either interpretation is possible[7]. It is this ambiguous type which is supposed to have paved the way for the later purely periphrastic type 'the king did read a book', which began to spread late in the 13th century.

The origin and regulation of the *do*-periphrasis is one of the most intriguing and debated problems of English historical syntax. The 'weakened causative' theory is only one of several theories, but probably the one upheld by most authorities today.

The ME examples of purely periphrastic *do* occur chiefly in positive declarative statements and mostly in poetry where an empty *do* proves a convenient device which gives the option of two different rhymes e.g. *wrote/did write, saw/did see*, or which might fill the metre better: *Noach did þam alle out driue / Beist and fuxul, man and wiue* 'N. drove them all out, beast and fowl, man and woman'.

Its use in prose and in negative and interrogative sentences, it should be noted, is in the main a post-15th century development.

The Modern English period

The drift from strong to weak form
This continues in EMnE though now only at reduced speed, owing largely to the stabilizing influence of education and printing. Verbs that can still be found with strong preterites in EMnE include *help (holp), climb (clomb), burst (brast), wade (wode), gnaw (gnew), abide (abode), crow (crew), dread (drad), wash (wesh), delve (dolve), cleave (clove/clave), creep (crope), sow (sew), yield (yold), laugh (low), slide (slode), bite (bote), rake (roke), dive (dove), melt (molt), swell (swoll), lade (lode), shave (shove), weigh (wogh)*. Many of these older strong forms are still dialectal.

Other verbs such as *blow, grow, shine, swing, shrink* were common in EMnE as weak verbs, but their strong forms have prevailed, and the former weak alternative is now dialectal or non-standard.

On the whole the drift from strong to weak form has gone much further in the dialects where forms like *drinked, speaked, weared, seed, stealed, gived (gied)* can still be heard.

Reduplicating verbs

Many verbs originally belonging to this old category have assumed weak forms. We have already mentioned *sow, crow, dread,* and might add *blend, claw, flow, glow, leap, row, wield, swoop, wax, walk.*

Hight 'is called' was already archaic by EMnE. Shakespeare has *that grislye beast which lion hight by name.*

Of *hold* (OE *healdan*) the strong participle has survived in *beholden,* now slightly archaic.

Mod. Eng. *hang-hung-hung,* and the weak forms in *-ed* (with the sense 'execute') are from two verbs. The former is from the OE reduplicating verb *hōn* and the latter from the OE weak verb *hangian,* which in ME became *hangen.* In ME *hōn* became *hongen* through analogy, and in EMnE the two presents became identical with both strong and weak forms remaining.

Preterite-present verbs

The preterite-present verbs have by and large attained their Mod. Eng. forms and functions by EMnE. However, a few deviations should be noted.

May retained its variant preterite *mought* throughout EMnE. The old notion of ability died out in the 17th century. Drayton has *Thy mighty strokes who may withstand?*

Must has been used as a present since ME. The old present *mote* was in EMnE already poetic. Spenser has *Now mote ye understand that ...* Byron is deliberately archaic in *Nor mote my shell awake the weary Nine* (Childe Harold). *Must* denoting inference as in *he must be sixty now* has been on record since the 16th century.

Can retained its primitive sense 'know, understand' till about 1700. Ben Jonson has *she could the Bible in the holy tongue.* For ME *cuthe* > Mod. Eng. *could,* see p. 121. For the form *uncouth,* see p. 77.

Wit died out in EMnE. Shakespeare has *Now please you wit, the Epitaph is for Marina writ.* It has survived in the archaic phrase *to wit* 'namely', until recently current in legal parlance.

Shall has preserved its primitive sense of obligation in the Biblical *Thou shalt not steal,* but in Mod. Eng. chiefly in preterite uses like *you should go to church more often.*

In the present it now functions mainly as an auxiliary of the future, see p. 133.

Anomalous verbs

Be competed with Scandinavian-supported *are* in EMnE as the regular form of the plural. *Be*-plurals are still common in Shakespeare: *Where is thy Husband now? Where be thy Brothers?* Shortly after 1600, however, *are* was victorious, but *be* is still common in the dialects, where it is sometimes even carried through the whole of the present paradigm. Oldest inhabitant (to district visitor): I be ninety-four, an' 'aven't got an enemy in the world. D.V.: That's a beautiful thought. O.I.: Yes, miss. Thank God, they be all of 'em dead long ago (Punch).

The preterite of the 2nd person singular indicative was *were* until EMnE, when the forms *wast* (under the influence of the Bible) and *wert* (on the analogy of *art*) began to appear. Particularly the form *wert* has been an extremely common poeticism right down to the present century.

For the form *you was,* see p. 149, note 11.

The history of the non-standard negative contraction *ain't* is difficult to account for, because functionally it expresses not only *am, is, are* + *not*, but also *have, has* + *not*.

The spelling *an't* began to appear in the 17th century and the variant *ain't* about a century later. The diphthong in *ain't* presupposes ME *ā*, which could be derived both from ME *am not* and from *are not* (after the loss of preconsonantal *r* (see p 80)). The link with *have* could be established through its pronunciation in accented position (cp. *behave*) and the later dropping of *h* in non-standard speech (see p. 79).

Will. For distinction the variant form *wol* (see p. 122) was frequently used in EMnE in negative statements where it often appeared with loss of *l* as *wonnot*. Scott has *To leave the place while the lad is in jeopardy, that I wonot.* For *will* as an auxiliary of the future, see p. 133.

Indicative and subjunctive forms of the verb

The present indicative and subjunctive forms of the verb in EMnE were the following:

	Indicative	Subjunctive	
1	(-e)	(-e)	
2	-(e)st	(-e)	
3	(-e)s, -(e)th	(-e)	plural 1-2-3 (-e)

The Midland *-en* plural was obsolescent at the beginning of EMnE, giving way to a zero-form. Ben Jonson says in his grammar that the *-en* plural was used 'till about the reign of Henry VIII', but 'hath now grown quite out of use'. The Southern *-th* plural survived into the 16th century. Shakespeare has a couple of examples of both, no doubt to achieve an archaic effect: *All perishen of man, of pelf* (Pericles), *Looke how thy woundes doth bleede* (Troilus).

The typically Northern *-s* of both the plural and the singular paradigms was occasionally recorded in EMnE. Peele has *That all his barons trembles at my threats,* and it has maintained itself to the present day in non-standard speech. Police Constable: 'Your 'usband won't be 'ome tonight, missus. We've just run 'im in'. Lidy (sic!): 'Well, you knows your own business best. I've just run 'im aht' (Punch). – Sailor: 'It's a remarkable thing, sir, but when I woggles me leg like this I gets a 'orrible pain in it'. Irritable ship's doctor: 'Then why the Hell do you woggle it?' (Punch). Some authorities, however, hold that this *-s* should be regarded as an extension from the third person singular rather than as a Northernism.

The -s of the third person singular on the other hand is undisputedly Northern in origin. It is slow to penetrate into the London area, and throughout the greater part of the 16th century -th forms still predominate. It is not until the 17th century that -s finally prevails and -th forms seem to be confined to more elevated style. The Bible of 1611 has thus -th throughout. Shakespeare has both varieties: *Cæsar doth bear me hard, but he loves Brutus.* Particularly the short forms *hath* and *doth,* it should be noted, seem very tenacious of life and persist in that form right down till about 1800. It is believed by some authorities that the penetration of the -s form into London speech and the later standard should be explained not as due to Northern dialectal influence but as an independent development, as a colloquialism formed on the analogy of *is/was.*

The -st of the second person became obsolescent in the 17th century along with the pronoun *thou,* but has survived as a poeticism and in liturgical and dialectal speech till the present day.

The indicative preterite in EMnE had no ending except for the 2nd person singular having occasionally *-(e)st (beganst, camst),* which, however, began to die out in the 17th century along with *thou.* For the preterite forms *wast, wert,* see p. 130.

Uses of the subjunctive
Though increasingly encroached upon by the simple indicative and by modal periphrases, the subjunctive was still holding some ground in EMnE, where it may occur in all the functions it had in the previous periods of the language. But the use or non-use of the subjunctive was increasingly becoming a matter of style.

In independent clauses the subjunctive is now alive only in more or less petrified phrases expressing wish or exhortation: *Heaven forbid!, God save the Queen, suffice it to say,* etc.

In dependent clauses only the subjunctive form *were* is idiomatic in Mod. Eng. It is found in object clauses of concession, condition and comparison introduced by *(even) if, (even) though, as if, as though: I wish it were over; even if it were true; if I were you; he reeled as if he were drunk,* etc.

Remarkable is the American use of the subjunctive, which particularly in dependent clauses has many features in common with EMnE usage (*I suggest that he leave tomorrow and the children be looked after by their aunt; it was my idea that she sit next to her father,* etc.).

Time and tense
The futuric present had already in ME begun to require the accompaniment of some adverbial indication of time. From EMnE it underwent further restrictions to its use, being current now only with verbs connoting coming and leaving, or when the reference is to something prearranged (*the train leaves at six; he comes back tomorrow; we dine with the Smiths tonight,* etc.).

The modern clear-cut distinction between the perfect and the preterite –

observed to an extent unknown in other Germanic languages – was not yet firmly established in EMnE. Shakespeare has *You spoke not with her since?* or *I saw not better sport these seven year's day.* And inversely: *When you saw his chariot appear, have you not made an universal shout?*

Before the regulation of the use of the expanded form in the 17th century the simple present could still be found with that function: Polonius to Hamlet, 'What do you read, my Lord?'. The AV has *Thy mother and thy brethren stand without.*

The non-finite forms of the verb

The present participle. The old *-nd* ending of the present participle has until recently remained distinct from the *-ing* of the noun in the Northern dialects (cp. *a singan' burd* but *the singing o' the burds*).

The past participle. The old *i/y* prefix (OE *ge-*) was archaic already in EMnE. Spenser has numerous examples: *so forth the noble ladie was ybrought.* Byron has *Spring yclad in grassy dye* as a conscious archaism in 'Childe Harold'. Dialectally the old *ge-* prefix has survived today as *a-* [ə] mainly in the South West (*afound, adone, an' we have all a-left the spot, To tëake a-scatter'd, each his lot* (Dorset)).

The *-n* ending of the strong participle has been lost after a stem in two consonants or a nasal (*bound, fought, held, stung, come, spun, won,* etc.). When *-n* is retained in these forms it is often a Northern dialect feature. Scott has *the field must be foughten in our presence.*

Note, however, adjectival forms like *bounden (duty), shaven (cheek), sunken (eyes), molten (lead),* etc.

The infinitive by late ME had come to be identical with the verbal stem. The old form in *-en,* however, was sometimes used by 16th-century poets as an archaism. Shakespeare has *For though he strive to killen bad* (spoken by Gower in 'Pericles').

During the ME period the simple *to*-less infinitive had seen its range of application constantly narrowed down, and by 1500 it had come to be used, as today, only after auxiliaries and in some nexus constructions *(I saw him come, I made him laugh,* etc.).

The infinitive, it will be remembered, is an old action noun, which down through its history has acquired an ever increasing number of verbal features (tense distinctions (OE), passive form (ME), expanded form (17th century)). Modern reflexes of its nominal past are primarily its power to function as subject, object and predicative complement, and its indifference to voice in some more or less fixed phrases (*the house is to let, what is there to pay?,* etc.).

The so-called split infinitive, rare in ME, remained sporadic throughout EMnE. It is not recorded in Shakespeare, and was until the 20th century frowned upon by prescriptive grammarians.

The noun in -ing and the gerund. The *-ing* noun had begun to develop gerundial force in ME, i.e. it had acquired the additional features of a verb. The norm of present-day usage was achieved in EMnE.

132

A direct object is now the rule unless the *-ing* form is preceded by the definite article (*don't be afraid of asking questions* but *co-operation is based upon the asking of questions*). But EMnE was still inconsistent with regard to the form of the object. Bacon has *and set their hearts ... upon erecting of an order, sometimes upon the advancing of a person*). Hazlitt has *the balancing the artificial tree.*

The *-ing* form originally had its subject in the genitive (*I insist on his/the soldier's obeying orders*), and from ME on it could also be in the form of an *of*-phrase. A common-case subject (or in the case of pronouns an object-case one) has been sporadically recorded since late ME, but gains increasing currency down through EMnE (*I have nothing against him/the man trying to do it*). The proliferation of this type of subject is no doubt due to the incapacity of many words, or word groups, to appear in the genitive (*both, the old, the French, the master of the house,* etc.).

Until ME the *-ing* form had largely remained true to its nominal heritage in being indifferent to distinctions of time. In EMnE, however, it began to set up the verbal feature of a compound perfect tense. Spenser has *After having whispered a space.* In the 18th century it added also a compound perfect passive (*after having been*) to its verbal properties.

The inherent nominal indifference to voice was still a prominent feature in EMnE: *How 'scaped I killing* (Shakespeare), *Jove keep thy chain from pawning* (Ben Jonson), but passive form is an increasingly frequent alternative after 1600.

Verbal periphrases

Perfect and pluperfect
The tendency to use *have* with transitives and intransitives alike has been increasingly perceptible since ME. EMnE still retained ME practice with many intransitives of motion. Shakespeare has *Brutus and Cassius are rid like madmen through the gates of Rome.* The Prayer Book of Edward VI has *And when he was come nere to Hierusalem.*

The verbs *become* and *grow* were almost invariably construed with *be* down to about 1800: *it was become a matter of indifference* (Jane Austen); *their parties are grown tedious and dull* (Jane Austen).

Modern idiom has retained *be* only when the desire is to express a state or resulting condition, and the participle approaches the function of an adjective (cp. *he is/has gone; we are/have started; they are/have disappeared,* etc.).

Shall and *will. Shall* was in EMnE still the prevailing auxiliary for all persons of the future: *She gives it out that you shall marry her* (Shakespeare), *He that questioneth much shall learne much* (Bacon). In Shakespeare and in the AV of 1611 *shall* is the normal auxiliary of the future, instances with *will* being more often than not volition-coloured. In some writers, however, there is considerable vacillation, and in the 17th century *will* finally seems to be gaining momentum.

Our present-day distribution of *shall* and *will* is a product of the 17th century. The first to lay down its rules was John Wallis in his 'Grammatica Linguae Anglicanae' (1653), and they were since elaborated upon by prescriptive grammarians like Bishop Lowth (1762) and William Ward (1765).

Our present *shall/will* distribution, in other words, is the triumph of prescriptive grammar, of the prevailing rationalist tendencies to reduce usage to codified rule.

In the dialects, including American idiom, the development has taken its natural course, and *will* seems to have come to be used indiscriminately for all persons.[8]

Worth (OE *weorðan*) as an auxiliary passed out of use in late ME. The only non-dialectal trace of it in Mod. Eng. is the archaic imprecatory phrase *woe worth*: *woe worth me, when Agatha sets eyes on it* (Conan Doyle).

Be going to, it will be remembered, had come to denote futurity in late ME, but in EMnE it is still comparatively rare with that function. In Milton, Bunyan, Pope, and (with one exception) in Shakespeare the construction still denotes actual motion: *I am going to visit the prisoners, fare you well* (Shakespeare). By the 18th century, however, it seems to be used according to the norm of today. Richardson has *Judge, dearest Madam, by what I am going to confess.*

Periphrastic subjunctive equivalents

Mod. Eng. differs from late ME and EMnE usage only with regard to the extent of their application. Modal periphrases are now the usual construction, the subjunctive having survived only in more or less fossilized phrases.

The periphrastic passive

Hight 'is/was called' was already a conscious archaism in Spenser and Shakespeare. It turned up as an archaism also in the Romanticists: *Childe Harold was he hight* (Byron), and was until recently used in Northern dialect.

The passive type 'I was offered a job' is essentially an EMnE development. The prevailing OE and ME type was 'me was offered a job' (cp. Chaucer *me was tolde certayn ...*). The subject-case construction, however, has been explained as due to the analogy of types like 'the man was offered a job', where *man*, originally a dative, had come to be looked upon as the subject because of its pre-verbal position.

Be + the present participle. Expanded forms were on the whole more sparingly used in ME and EMnE than now, and until recently that feature was still reflected by the dialects (*it rains now, the sun shines again,* etc.).

The difference between EMnE and today's usage is tellingly brought out by a collation of the two Bible versions of 1611 and 1961:

Now while Peter doubted in himself what this vision he had seen should mean, behold, the men which were sent from Cornelius had made inquiry for Simon's house, and stood before the gate and asked whether Simon, which was surnamed Peter, were lodged there. While Peter thought on the vision, the Spirit said unto him, 'Behold, three men seek thee'.

While Peter was still puzzling over the meaning of this vision he had seen, the messengers of Cornelius had been asking the way to Simon's house, and now arrived at the entrance. They called out and asked if Simon Peter was lodging there. But Peter was thinking over the vision when the Spirit said to him, 'Some men are here looking for you'.

The early 18th century, however, was to see the emergence of the PE functions of the expanded form. The present connotation of limited duration is no doubt due in part to its late ME coalescence in form with the *be + on + -ing*[9] *> be + a + -ing > be + -ing* type *(he was on hunting > he was a-hunting > he was hunting)*.

Because of the adjectival heritage of the participle the expanded form is slow to develop tenses. The perfect, pluperfect and future are of limited occurrence throughout early Modern English. An expanded perfect infinitive *(to have been reading)* is first attested in the 17th century.

The first examples of the PE passive type *the book is being printed* began to appear sporadically around 1800. Until that time a sentence like *the lion is hunting* could have a passive as well as an active content. The context was decisive. Typical early Modern English types are: *while the operation was performing* (Swift), *while supper was preparing* (Addison), *while his leg was cutting off* (Boswell).

The old construction, however, is still alive in more or less set phrases like: *dinner is cooking; tea is brewing; the book is printing; the film is still showing; the house is building,* etc.

The type *is being* + adjective *(you are being naughty)* is even younger, and not frequent till about 1900.

Do + infinitive. The old causative construction died out in the course of early Modern English, its function being taken over by more pregnant causatives like *cause* and *make*. Spenser uses causative *do* only archaically: *sometimes to do him laugh, she would assay to laugh.* Later examples are of a more or less formulaic nature: *to do somebody to wit* ('know, understand').

The late ME period had seen periphrastic *do* firmly established in affirmative declarative sentences, particularly in poetry where it remained common till about 1700; in prose it is obsolescent already after 1600: *else the new wine doth burst the bottles* (The Bible). In PE the usage is now archaic or poetic.

In negative and interrogative sentences the *do*-periphrasis has been attested since late ME, but is not current till early Modern English. Shakespeare has *do* in about half of the cases where it would now be obligatory: *if I mistake not, thou art Harry Monmouth; Now sir, what make you here?*

Negative interrogative sentences have required the periphrasis since the 16th century. In Shakespeare it is already common: *Do we not likewise see our learning there?*

The restriction of *do* in the course of early Modern English to negative and interrogative sentences seems to be bound up primarily with word-order factors. Already in the 15th century inversion was becoming increasingly rare with verbs other than auxiliaries, and the *do*-periphrasis came to be a convenient means of allowing the word-order to remain normal *(come you now? do you come now?)*.

In the case of negative statements a word of comment is necessary. *Ne*, it will be remembered, had disappeared in the course of the 15th century, and *not*, originally only a strengthener of the negation, had come to occupy a position after the main verb *(I ne seie noht > I say not)*. The *do*-periphrasis *(I do not say)* was here felt to offer the advantage of placing the negation more emphatically between auxiliary and main verb.

Emphatic do has been recorded since late ME. Caxton has: *that his antecessours of old had and yet dyde here them.* But the usage is by no means common till early Modern English.

Notes

Notes to chapter I

1. All IE languages are inflective, grammatical functions like case, number, person, tense, mood, etc. being expressed through variation in the form of a word or word-stem.
2. A traditional classification divides the IE languages into an eastern satem and a western centum group named after the Old Persian and Latin words for 'hundred'. In the satem group Proto-IE *k* developed into *s*, whereas in the centum group it was retained, but shifted in Germanic to *h* (see p. 23). The borderline between the centum and satem split is roughly one running from Sweden to Greece.
3. Gipsy (sometimes called Romany) descends from the dialects of north-western India. In Europe the Gipsies were mistakenly believed to have come from Egypt. Hence the name.
4. It is important to note that the Celtic-speaking pocket in French Brittany is in no way to be connected with the ancient Gauls, but are descendants of the British Celts who were driven out by the invading Angles and Saxons in the 5th century (see p. 27).
5. But one glance at hundreds of basic-vocabulary items like e.g. English *night*, German *nacht*, Danish *nat*, Irish *nochd*, Lithuanian *naktis*, Russian *noche*, Latin *noctis* (gen.), Sanskrit *nakta-*, etc. is enough to convince anyone that these languages must be descended from one common ancestor at some time in the pre-historic past.
6. Change in the verbal form to indicate whether the activity of its semantic content is viewed with regard to beginning, iteration, perfectivity, imperfectivity, etc.
7. We should be wary of arguments like the absence of words for monkey, tiger, camel, olive, etc. from the common vocabulary. It does not necessarily indicate that the Indo-Europeans must have dispersed from regions where such phenomena were unknown. We should not conclude ex silentio.
8. The beech does not grow east of a line running roughly from Poland to the Crimea, and the honey-bee is not indigenous to those parts of Asia which could be a likely IE homeland.
9. Here again we should be sceptical. The homeland of the Indo-Europeans does not necessarily coincide with the present location of one of their most archaic languages. We could then with equal justification place it in India (Sanskrit) or claim that the Germanic tribes all came from Iceland.

Notes to chapter II

1. Traces of Spain's Germanic past are few and, not surprisingly, represented chiefly by place-names, e.g. *Andalucia, Andalies, Puerto del Alano, Suegos, Puerto de Sueve, Gotones, la Goda, Godos, Catalonia (< * Goth-alan-ia),* etc., reflecting important tribal names (Vandals, Alans, Swabians). Names of Germanic chieftains linger on in such hybrid formations as *Villabertran, Casadoufe (< Andulf), Castro Adalsindo (< Adalsind).* The Visigoths had abandoned their Germanic tongue by the 7th century, but a few words like *estaca* 'stake' and *brotar* 'bud' have survived in the Iberian languages to the present day.

2. Vestiges (about 60 words) of what was probably the Ostrogothic language survived in isolated pockets in the Crimea till the 16th century when they were accidentally recorded.

3. The negligible heritage of Celtic words in English (see p. 39) prompted earlier historians to assume a swift extermination of the Celts by the invading Anglo-Saxons. This view is no longer tenable. The increased number of Celtic river and place-names as one moves westward suggests that the expansion of Anglo-Saxon settlement must have proceeded gradually and taken well over 300 years, which must have left time for some co-existence and bilingualism.

4. e.g. *Kerbu* (Danish *Kærby*), *Carqueby* (: *Kirkeby*), *Houlbec, Carbec, Esquilbec, Appetot* (: *Æbeltoft*). The vast majority of them contain Viking personal names, *Grimouville* (: *Grim*), *Auberville* (: *Asbjørn*), *Touteinville* (: *Thorstein*) and have had the second component gallicized.

5. Only a handful of personal names have survived to the present day. Still current are names like *Oleg* (ON *Helgi*), *Rurik, Igor* (ON *Yngvarr*), *Olga* (ON *Helga*), which last, curiously enough, has always been looked upon as a typically Russian name. Many more Scandinavian personal names are found imbedded in place-names. There are about 150 Scandinavian place-names, most massively in the north and along the Volga. Most of them are slavicized, ending typically in *-ovo* or *-ino: Zizlovo* (ON *Gisli*), *Koloberovo* (ON *Kolbjörn*), *Turikovo* (ON *þjodrekr*), *Monino* (ON *Manni*), *Rognedino* (ON *Ragnheiðr*), etc. Scandinavian names like *Björn, Einarr, Hakon, Ivarr, Sigvaldr, Steingrimr, Sveinn, þorleifr,* etc. are also quite common components in Russian place-names.

   Further examples of Scandinavian place-names include *Varegovo Boloto* 'the Varangian moor' (Varangian being the Russian name for Viking), *Svinord* 'swine fiord', *Kolbagi* 'club bearer' (cp. Danish *kølle*), etc. A secondary loan is the word *rus*, which appears in the name *Rusland* (Russia). It was probably introduced via Finnish where it meant 'Swedes' (cp. *Ruotsi*). In mediaeval sources the word was often used to denote the Scandinavian tribes in Northern Russia, but later came to be extended to the whole nation.

6. A change of consonants about 600 A.D. that set apart Old High German from the other West Germanic dialects. The unvoiced stops became

OHG fricatives or affricates, e.g. *p* > *pf* (cp. *pound-Pfund,* but medially and finally > *f* (cp. *sleep-schlafen, ship-Schiff); t* > *z* (cp. *tongue-Zunge)* but medially and finally > *ss* (cp. *eat-essen, foot-Fuss*); *k* medially and finally > *ch* (cp. *make-machen, book-Buch*), etc.

7. Traditionally the dental is explained as the last trace of an independent word, namely the preterite of a verb related to *do (I loved < * I love + did).* Such tense formation through agglutination is well known in other languages (cp. French *je chanter-ai* 'I will sing' < Latin *cantare + habeo*). However, the theory has met with grave objections, and some linguists prefer to trace the dental back to the *-t-* of the perfect participle, where it was present already in IE (cp. Latin *amatus*).

   It is important to note that it is alone the presence or absence of a dental preterite suffix which is decisive for whether or not a verb should be classed as weak or strong. Verbs like *buy-bought, bring-brought, sell-sold, tell-told,* etc. are weak and the vowel variation is not ablaut, but can be otherwise explained.

8. Ablaut (or gradation), i.e. qualitative or quantitative variation of the radical vowel, is thus not a specifically Germanic feature, but can be observed in other IE languages (e.g. Latin *ago-egi-actum*). Germanic is the only language group, however, which has exploited this inheritance systematically as a tense marker in the so-called strong verbs (see p. 112).

9. In the Scandinavian languages additionally by means of what used to be reflexive constructions, the suffix *-s* being the last trace of the pronoun *sig* (Dan. *elskes, findes* 'is loved', 'is found').

10. In Latin, it should be noted, IE aspirated *bh* becomes *f.* Hence correspondences like *frater – brother, ferre – to bear.*

11. Similarly IE *dh* becomes *f* in Latin, witness correspondences like *foris – door, facere – to do.*

12. The principle involved, as we shall see below (p. 78), has been operative much later in English in what is sometimes referred to as Jespersen's Law (cp. pairs like *ex'hibit* /ig'zibit/, but *exhi'bition* /eksi'biʃn/.

13. It will be pointless to use examples from other Germanic languages, because developments there are as often as not blurred by later soundchanges.

Notes to chapter III

1. Unlike the other invaders, the Jutes left no modern place-names pinpointing their settlement area. An 11th-century chronicler, however, informs us that the New Forest (Hampshire) in his day went by the name *Ytene* (: belonging to the Jutes).

2. Tribal names are embedded in place-names like *Swaffham* 'homestead of the Swabians', *Friston* (: Frisians), *Saxham* (: Saxons), *Exton* (: East Saxons), *Englebourne* 'brook of the Angles'.

   Dorset and *Somerset* are also earlier tribal names, containing the OE element *-sæte* 'dwellers' (cp. German *Elsass*).

3. The West Germanic pantheon is also represented in the days of the week: *Tuesday, Wednesday,* OE *þunresdæg* (later to be superseded by Scandinavian *Thursday* (see p. 43)), *Friday,* all originally modelled on the Roman deities Mars, Mercury, Jove, Venus (: *dies Veneris*) and reflected by the corresponding French names for the days of the week.

4. Not all the place-names, however, point unilaterally to Danish settlement. Many, particularly in the north-west, are distinctively Norwegian in character, containing such elements as *-sett* (ON *-setr* 'pasture') as in *Appersett, Wintersett,* -*brick* (ON *brekka* 'slope') as in *Larbrick, Scarisbrick,* -*gill* (ON *gil* 'ravine') as in *Howgill, Scargill,* – *fell (ON fjall* 'mountain') as in *Harter Fell, Hest Fell.* These names reflect settlement activity by Norwegian Vikings who had set out from Ireland. That some of them had already adopted Celtic names can be seen in the first element of many of the place-names in the area, e.g. *Melmerby (: Maelmuire), Duggleby (: Dubhghall).* Further, according to Celtic practice the order of the elements is often reversed as in *Aspatria* 'ash Patrick', *Brigsteer* 'bridge Styr' (: Styr's bridge).

5. Particularly the Germanic initial accent causing slurred final syllables and the incompatibility of the grammatical systems with the accelerating loss of grammatical concord in English must have been detrimental to Anglo-Norman.

   Chaucer's prioress in the Canterbury Tales gives us a vivid picture of the linguistic situation in 14th-century England. She spoke, as he says, 'French ful fayr and fetyslie' (: neatly), but it was the Stratford variety, 'for French of Parys was to hir unknowe'.

6. Even after English had been restored as the language of the Law Courts, the curious mixture of English and French known as *Law-French* persisted for centuries and was finally abolished by act of Parliament in 1731.

7. The rise of one particular dialect to being the received standard of the educated will inevitably cause the other dialects, in ME a symbiosis of equally important, prestige-neutral dialects, to be slowly pushed into a marginal position with the lowered status of provincial or substandard varieties of what now comes to be felt as the 'national' tongue. In the London area, however, uneducated speakers continued their native speech habits, which in the course of the 16th century developed into the regional dialect now commonly referred to as *Cockney.*

8. Many of the colonies both in America and elsewhere owe their foundation to private initiative. Many were shelters for religious minorities, e.g. Maryland for the Catholics, Pennsylvania for the Quakers, and the New England States (Massachusetts, Connecticut, Rhode Island, and New Hampshire) for the Puritans.

9. American English, to take an example, is in many respects highly reminiscent of earlier stages of British English. The American preservation of /r/ finally and before a consonant and its pronunciation of *a* as /æ/ in

words like *bath, cast, demand,* and of /ɔ/ as /a:/ in words like *frog, dog* were typical of 17th and 18th-century British English and still retained there dialectally.

Australian English has strong roots in 19th-century Cockney and preserves many features from that dialect.

Notes to chapter IV

1. The Celtic stem *-rīg,* which we see in OE *-rīce* 'power' (and still retained in PE *(bishop)ric* and in proper names like *Frederic*) is much older and reflects the contact between the Celts and the Germani on the Continent (cp. German *reich,* Danish *rig*). A word of similar provenance is OE *ambeht* 'servant' (cp. Danish *embede,* German *Amt*).

2. Native resources were also exploited to meet the demands of the new faith. New meanings came to be assigned to what used to be pagan concepts. *Easter* originally denoted a pagan Germanic cult celebrating *Eostre,* the goddess of the dawn, at vernal equinox. Similarly *Hell,* originally that which 'hides or covers up', is transferred to a Christian sense. With heathen background are also *bless* (OE *blētsian* orig. 'to sprinkle with blood'), OE *hūsel,* 'housel, Eucharist', orig. a heathen sacrifice, and OE *wēofod* 'altar' (< *wīgbēod* 'idol table').

3. Still surviving in Scandinavian as *knar* 'type of racing yacht' and *skægde* 'small sailing boat'.

4. From ON *vapnatak,* a territorial division still used in many parts of the old Danelaw, e.g. in Lincolnshire and Yorkshire.

5. From ON *þriðjungr* 'the third part of something'. Hence the division of Yorkshire into North, East and West Riding.

6. Surviving today as *(black)mail,* lit. 'the black agreement' by way of Northern dialects.

7. OE had *niman* (cp. German *nehmen*), which survived till about 1600 with the meaning of 'steal'. The past participle *numen* is found in *numb* (with cold).

8. OE had *weorpan* (cp. German *werfen*), surviving as *warp.*

9. OE had *steorfan* (cp. German *sterben*) and *sweltan,* surviving today with marginal senses as *starve* and *swelter.* PE *dead* and *death,* however, are native.

10. OE had *ceorfan* (PE *carve*) or *snīðan.*

11. Numerous Scandinavian words are still alive in the modern dialects of what was once Danelaw territory. They include words like *addle* 'earn', *lathe* 'barn', *flit* 'move', *lait* 'seek', *kist* 'chest', *sark* 'shirt', *loup* 'jump', *lake* 'play', *lea* 'scythe', *ket* 'rubbish, carrion', *stee* 'ladder', *neave* 'fist', *lop* 'flea', *haver* 'oats', *ing* 'meadow', *carr* 'swampy ground', etc. As recently as last century such dialectal survivals could be counted by the thousand, but they are now slowly dying out with the dialects that house them. Words like *oast* 'cheese', *seng* 'bed', *gool* 'yellow', *grice* 'pig' are long gone.

To these should be added the many Scandinavian words that we only know from ME sources, such as *blout* 'soft' (cp Dan. *blødt*), *dreng* 'warrior' (cp. Dan. *dreng* 'boy'), *ande* 'breath' (cp Dan. *ånde*), *derf* 'bold' (cp. Dan. *djærv*), *rowst* 'voice' (cp. Dan *røst*), *twinne* 'two' (cp. Dan. *tvende*), *sperren* 'to close' (cp. Dan. *spærre*).

12. The word in its alcoholic use seems to go back to the visit of James VI to Denmark in 1589 to collect his bride Anne, the elder sister of Christian IV. The word was long confined to Scottish idiom where it is recorded from 1600.

13. Surviving in PE as an appellative noun in *by-law* 'town law'.

14. Place-names are often tricky, and this and the following example should warn against rash interpretations before a 'pedigree' of all ascertainable earlier forms has been established. The pedigree *Oxton* – *Uxtoun* (1654) – *Ugistoun* (1464) – *Ulkistoun* (1273) – *Ulkilstoun* (c. 1220) – *Ullfkelistoun* (1206) shows that the present form has nothing to do with 'ox', but contains the Scandinavian personal name *Ulfketill*. In *Oakesthorpe* the same name was confounded with 'oak' by mediaeval people trying to read some sense into a name they no longer understood.

15. Sometimes the Scandinavian population in certain areas were numerous enough to permanently 'scandinavianize' original English place-names, witness pairs like *Keswick* (Cumberland) vs. *Chiswick* (Essex), *Carlton* (Yorkshire) vs. *Charlton* (Somerset), *Skelton* (Yorkshire) vs. *Shelton* (Bedfordshire), *Skipton* (Yorkshire) vs. *Shipton* (Dorset), *Stainley* (Yorkshire) vs. *Stanley* (Gloucestershire), *Oustwick* (Yorkshire) vs. *Eastwick* (Sussex).

16. Some names like *Acon* (ON *Hakonn*), *Canut* (ON *Knutr*), *Turstin* (ON *þorsteinn*) show unmistakable signs of having suffered in the pens of Norman scribes.

17. The fact that many sources seem to contain about 50% Scandinavian names should not be taken to indicate that half the population in certain areas were Viking descendants. There is ample evidence that Scandinavian names became popular among the Anglo-Saxons.

18. Numerous 12th-century entries in Danelaw documents like *Roberto filius Grimkelli, Willelmus filius Asgar, Huche* (: Hugh) *filius Fin,* etc. vividly illustrate the process.

19. Family names like *Thackeray, Gaitskell, Ormerod, Asquith, Copeland* are types derived from original Scandinavian place-names.

Survivals through Scottish include *Mac Manus* (ON *Magnus*), *Mac Queen* (ON *Sveinn*), *Mac Cloud,* anglicized from *Mac Leod* (ON *ljotr* 'ugly'), *Kerr* (ON *kjarr*), *Gunn* (ON *Gunni*).

20. The French form with long vowel has survived in English as *sire* used in addressing the sovereign.

21. Walter Scott points out this distinction in a conversation between two Saxon serfs Gurth and Wamba in 'Ivanhoe'. The observation is correct but probably antedated. According to OED there are no examples of these correspondences before after 1290.

22. Note the use of this word in imprecations like *deuced(ly), what the deuce,* etc. probably going back to *deuce* being an unlucky throw (cp. German *was der Daus!,* Danish *(sinka)dus*).

23. Participation or non-participation in English sound changes can be used as a rough indication of the period of borrowing. Words like *crinoline, facade* and *soup* must have been adopted after the Great Vowel Shift (see p. 74).

   For consonantal criteria in words like *jabot, rouge, chef, mirage,* etc. see p. 50.

   The position of the stress may also afford some clues, early loans having had time to adopt English stress habits, cp. ¦*college* vs. co¦*llage,* ¦*vestige* vs. pre¦*stige,* ¦*valour* vs. ve¦*lour.*

24. Pronounced as in French. Note *corpse* 'dead body', originally the same word, but of earlier introduction with its *p* written and pronounced through the influence of Renaissance Latinists (cp. Lat. *corpus*).

25. It should be borne in mind that these names are not of Romance but of Continental Germanic (i.e. Frankish) origin, cp. *William* (OHG *Willahelm*), *Robert* (OHG *Hrodebert*), *Alice* (OHG *Adalheidis*).

26. A few Anglo-Saxon names like *Edmund, Edward, Alfred, Edgar, Hilda, Mildred* survive the Middle Ages probably because they had been borne by kings or canonized saints, but they owe their existence today largely to later reinforcement through the Gothic Revival or through Romanticism. Some came to enjoy brief popularity through revival by authors like Tennyson and Scott *(Cedric, Wilfred, Ethelbert, Aylmer (Elmer), Edwin)*.

27. From the Spanish place-name Jerez (de la Frontera) near Cadiz. The form *sherry* was evolved because the early spelling *Xeres* or *Sherris* was mistaken for a plural.

28. From Low German *būr.* The much later *Boer* is of Dutch origin.

29. Dutch *taptoe* – originally a signal urging inn-keepers to close taps and send carousing soldiers back to their quarters (cp. Dan. *tappenstreg,* Germ. *Zapfenstreich*).

30. The Italian contribution to the mercantile and financial vocabularies of the other Germanic languages is much more spectacular (cp. Dan. *konto, ditto, brutto, netto, kasse, risiko, fallit, giro, porto,* etc). Already in the Middle Ages the word *Lombard* was in many European languages synonymous with bank(er), cf. also Lombard Street in London which is the seat of many banks, Lombardsbrücke in Hamburg, Rue des Lombards in Paris, etc.

31. The word has been explained as deriving from Hindi *panch* 'five', which came to denote a drink consisting of five ingredients.

32. From Chinese *jin* 'man' + *shen* 'image' from the shape of the root.

33. The word must be of very early introduction in the Germanic languages (OE *seolc,* ON *silki*).

34. From Arabic *hashishi* 'drinkers of hashish', which was first used about a sect of religious fanatics in 13th-century Palestine, who stabbed Crusaders.

35. From Persian *shah* 'king', cp. also Persian *shah mat* 'the king is dead'.

143

Notes to chapter V

1. Hence maybe the etymological relationship between *book* and *beech*. Similarly the verb *to write* originally meant 'carve' or 'engrave'.
2. So called because the first six letters were fuÞark, just as the Greek system is known as alpha-bet and ours as the A-B-C.
3. So called because this important type of calligraphy was the outcome of a decree by Charlemagne in 789 to revise all church books.
4. A few native words like *vat, vane, vixen*, it should be observed, were introduced from dialects where *f-* was voiced initially (see p. 72).
5. In late ME ʒ was gradually disused but continued to be written in Scotland, but early compositors having no ʒ in their fonts often substituted a *z* for it, hence personal names like *Menzies, Clunzie, Dalziel, Kenzie*. The historical pronunciation with [j], however, can still be heard.
6. Final *-e* had come to be associated with length because of the analogy with the numerous dissyllabic words where the stem vowel had been lengthened in syllables opened by the *-e* (OE *wicu* > ME *wēke*, OE *nama* > ME *nāme*, etc). See further p. 71.
7. In the North *i* was frequently used after a vowel to indicate length: *maid* 'made', *noin* 'noon'. Hence Scots dialectal spellings like *buik* 'book', *muir* 'moor', *guid* 'good'. PE *raid*, historically the same word as *road* (OE *rād*, see p. 68) is an instance of Scots spelling in the modern standard.
8. Which, as its name eloquently points out, was originally written *uu*.
9. The capital *I* in the pronoun of the first person sing. is a result of late ME scribes, after the French fashion, often using a lengthened *i* when it was alone or final. This *j* was later raised above the line and came to resemble an *I* by which it was represented by the early printers.
10. The fact that clerks were on piece rates (paid by the inch) could also be an incentive to add superfluous letters.
11. A few words like *done, some, come, gone* were shortened after the fixation of spelling. Hence the short vowel + *-e*.
12. The old form is reflected by the verb *saunter* < OF *s'aventurer* 'take one's chance'. *Advance* and *advantage* should perhaps appear in the next paragraph, for they contain French *avant* which has been wrongly associated with Lat. *ad-*.
13. *Catherine* is now pronounced with [θ], but *Kate, Kit* reflect the historical sound. Cp. also *Arthur* (but *Art*), *Elizabeth* (but *Betty, Bettina, Babette*).
14. One of the important rules attributed to Mulcaster is the use of silent *-e* as a length marker and the useful principle that individual words should always be spelt the same way.

Notes to chapter VI

1. Unless otherwise stated, the features discussed are those of classical WSax, the only dialect of which we have reliable and continuous information.

2. The fronting of Germ *$\bar{a}$ > OE $\bar{æ}$ took place when the Anglo-Saxons were still on the Continent, so the word must be a very early loan (cp. later Latin loans like *castel* 'village', *sanct* 'saint').

3. It is important to note that when followed by the back vowels *a, o* and *u* in the next syllable, *æ* was retracted to *a* (e.g. *dæg-dagas* 'days', *fæt-fatu* 'vats').

4. Breaking takes place in the Continental period and can consequently have affected only very early Latin borrowings like *cealc* 'chalk', *sealm* 'psalm'. But *alter* 'altar', *carte* 'document' must be later.

5. WSax has *healdan, eall, tealde,* which would have given something like **heald, *eald, *teald* today. One of the many instances of dialectal influence in the modern standard. Cp. also regionally distributed place-names like the *Weald* (Kent), the *Wolds* (Yorkshire), *Easingwold* 'the forest of Esa's people' (Yorks.) – containing what corresponds to German *Wald*.

6. MnE reflexes of such umlauted *-iðu* formations from adjectives are *strong-strength, long-length, foul-filth, whole* (OE *hāl*)-*health*.

7. But they are affected in different periods. In English it probably started to operate in the 6th century. Some Lat. loans were caught by i-umlaut and must consequently have been adopted by that time, e.g. *mynet* 'coin' < earlier **munit,* Lat. *moneta,* but *calic* 'chalice' and *magister* 'teacher' must be after the operation of i-umlaut.

8. On the formation of weak verbs by *-jan* suffix, see, p. 20.

9. If we compare these developments with their modern reflexes, it appears that many such lengthenings must have been lost again in ME. They were, however, generally maintained before *ld* and, in the case of *i* and *u*, also before *nd*: ME *wīld*, 'wild', *ōld* 'old', *gōld* 'gold', *fēld* 'field', *būnden* 'bound', *wīnden* 'to wind'.

10. MnE *sheaves* thus represents OE *sceafas.* Similarly OE *līf* gives MnE *life,* but *alive* represents an OE dative *on līfe,* and the verb *live* OE *lifian.*

11. Cp. MnE *oath* (OE *āÞ*), but *oaths* (OE *āðas*). Similarly *path* (OE *pæÞ*) but *paths* (OE *paðas*), *cloth – clothe* (OE *clāÞ – clāðian*).

    Warning! The symbols *ð* and *Þ* occur in OE texts more or less interchangeably and not consistently as we use them here. Forms like *wearð, ðōht, paÞas* are equally possible.

12. Palatalization (see p. 67) precedes i-umlaut, so if the front vowel represents an original i-umlauted back vowel, there is no palatalization of [k]: *cyning* 'king' < earlier **kuning.* Often the MnE reflexes may serve as a guide: *kiss* (OE *cyssan*), *keen* (OE *cēne*), *keep* (OE *cēpan*). For the ME *k*-spelling, see p. 57.

13. Of the *h* + consonant combinations only *hw* survived into MnE, but although it came to be spelt *wh* in ME on the analogy of the frequent use of *h* in that position as a mere diacritic (cp. *sh, th, ch*), it represented a genuine aspirated sound, which can still be heard in Northern dialects.

14. But cp. *brimstone* and place-names like *Brent Pelham, Brant Broughton* where it means 'burnt'.

15. The *h – g* interchange is due to Verner's Law, as will remembered (see p. 24).

16. The term ME, unless otherwise stated, will in the following be used about the East Midland dialect. The symbols are those traditionally used in historical phonology, $\bar{e}$, $\bar{o}$ denoting open and $\bar{e}$, $\bar{o}$ closed sounds; *ü* and *ö* are pronounced with the values we know from German. The diacritical marks, it should be noted, are added here to show the value of the vowels and were not used in ME script.

17. According to whether OE $\bar{æ}$ derived straight from WGerm *$\bar{a}$ through isolative changes as in *slǣpan* (see p. 64) or from i-umlauted WGerm $\bar{a}$ as in *hǣlan* (see p. 65). These two are sometimes distinguished as $\bar{æ}^1$ and $\bar{æ}^2$.

18. In Northern dialects, however, $\bar{o}$ became *ü* (usually written *ui* as in *guid* 'good', *buik* 'book'), which has been retained down to the present day in Scots dialects.

19. The *e + r > ar* change was originally much more extensive, witness dialectal forms like *desarve, sartin, sarvint* (: servant) and the colloquial form *Varsity* for 'university'.

20. Similarly MnE *gold* cannot be explained from ME *gōld*, which would have given something like **goold* in MnE, and which was indeed the received pronunciation till the 18th century (cp. the personal name *Goold*). But MnE *gold* presupposes a short vowel, which may have developed on the analogy of inflected adj. forms like *goldene, goldne*.

21. Southern voicing has never been fully explained. It was probably a characteristic already of spoken WSax, but concealed from our view by the written standard. Dutch may have exerted some contribution (cp. words like *vader* 'father', *zoon* 'son', etc.).

22. Quite a few place-names of the type *Clanville, Longville, Turville*, etc. in the South and West today had OE *feld* 'open land', ME *-veld* as the last element, and it was probably the *f > v* voicing in these dialects that contributed to this element being later confused with French *-ville*.

23. MnE *reeve* shows the normal development. Inversely MnE *five* cannot be explained from OE *fīf*, but presupposes some inflected form with the fricative in position for voicing. Similarly *alive* (OE dat. *on līfe*).

24. In the North, however, the *hw-* sequence retained its strong aspiration and was written *qu-* (*quhel* 'wheel', *quhat* 'what'). Many Scots dialects of the present day distinguish *Wales-whales, witch-which*, etc.

25. As when Florio, lexicographer and reader in Italian to the Queen, stated (1611) that the vowel of *bone, stone, God* should be pronounced like the open *o* of Italian *rosa, torre*.

26. Such 'private' spellings (or what we today would call misspellings) are valuable in that they do not conform to professional scribal convention, but are more spontaneously 'phonetic'. When the Paston Letters in the late 15th century begin to spell *shype* for 'sheep' or Queen Elizabeth *swit* for 'sweet', *nide* for 'need', it suggests that the shift from ME $\bar{e}$ to $\bar{i}$ is in operation.

27. Note the reflexes of the late ME practice of marking long vowels either by doubling or by final -*e*.

28. There are, however, indications that the change may have been somewhat earlier in some dialects, witness common 16th-century 'private' spellings like *Samerset, camyth* 'comes', *saden* 'sudden'.

29. Dryden rhymes *flood-mood-good,* suggesting an alternative short variant of *mood.* It could, however, be an eye-rhyme.

30. MnE *one* is difficult to explain. The normal development would have given us *[oun] as we still see it in *alone, only.* Shakespeare still pronounced $\bar{\varrho}n$, rhyming *stone* with *thirty-one,* Cowley *grown-one,* Dryden *one-thrown.* The development $\bar{\varrho}n > w \wedge n$ is best explained as due to the influence of dialectal overrounding which also gave forms like *wuts* for 'oats' (now dialectal), or *wuther* for 'other'. The stages are then presumed to have been something like $\bar{\varrho}n > w\bar{\varrho}n > w\bar{\varrho}n > w\bar{u}n > wun$, and may have penetrated into the early standard from low-class dialect. A grammar from about 1700 outright condemns the pronunciation 'wun' as vulgar. The spelling *wone,* however, is already found in the letters of Henry VIII and Queen Elizabeth. MnE *none, nothing* (ME *nōn*) may have been influenced by the vowel in *one.* *Broad* (ME *brōd*) is another case of dialectal (South Western) interference in the modern standard. *Groat* was similarly pronounced till about 1800.

31. Forms like *boil* 'carbuncle' (ME *bīle*), *groin* (ME *grīne*) are survivals in MnE of forms that testify to the *oi*-spelling having been readily associated with the sound [ai] in EMnE.

32. In many dialects e.g. in Cockney, *h* has ceased to be pronounced at all ('*orse, 'ouse, 'enry*). Conversely it was in Cockney and other dialects until recently habitual to place an unetymological *h* in front of words beginning with a vowel not only as hypercorrection, but also as a mark of emphasis (*haccident, my hown, hextra power,* etc.): 'Arry: 'Ever lose any money backin' 'orses, coachie?' Driver: 'Not 'alf! Lost twenty quid once – backed a pair o' 'orses and a homnibus into a window in Regent Street!' (Punch). In Northeastern regional dialect and by Irish and Scottish speakers, however, *h* is usually retained.

Notes to chapter VII

1. The feminine genitives are *s*-less as in German. There are few PE survivals of this pattern, e.g. *Lady Day, Lady Chapel* ('our Lady's Chapel').

2. The genitive plural, it should be noted, was not differentiated graphically from the rest of the plural paradigm in ME, the apostrophe being an early Modern English introduction (see p. 86).

3. Cp. *ich sage es (zu) dir; he gave it (to) me.* Latin: *Romam ire/ ad Romam ire* 'go to Rome'.

4. Plural -*en* was sometimes even grafted on to French nouns (*chainen, unclen, chaumbren* 'chambers') – but more usually they took -*s* as in French (*floures, servaunts*).

5. The adverbial genitive -s has been an extremely prolific formative element particularly in the dialects to which belong expressions like *togethers, nowheres, somehows, anyways, alives*. In some cases a -t has been added: *acrost, onst* (= *once*). The PE standard has: *against, amongst, amidst.*

6. Their original Germanic gender, it should be remarked, was the reverse of their Latin (cf. German *der Mond, die Sonne*).

Notes to chapter VIII

1. The strong adjective, it will be observed, has retained the distinctive instrumental case which in the nouns had come to be expressed functionally by the dative (see p. 82).

2. The strong form is usual, but weak *gōdena* is also found in this case.

3. The -e had probably ceased to be pronounced by Chaucer's day. He uses it in his works as the metre prompts him.

4. The last component is an old Germanic noun meaning 'creature, thing' (cp. German *(Böse)wicht*, Danish *vætte*).

5. And even more so when it was revived by the Romantic poets in the 18th century: *A Youth, who ne in virtue's ways did take delight* (Byron).

Notes to chapter IX

1. *Yon, yonder* go back to OE *geon* (cp. German *jener*) and the genitive-dative feminine form *geonre* respectively. They are still common in Shakespeare, but now typical of Northern or Scottish dialect (*by yon bonnie banks, on yonder hill*, etc.).

   Slike (< ON *slikr*, cp. Danish *slig*) is common in ME Northern dialect but died out about 1500. Chaucer uses it in his 'Reeve's Tale': *Hwa herkned euere slyk a ferly thyng?* 'who ever heard such a strange thing?'.

2. Ø-relatives are extremely rare in OE and are essentially a ME development, see p. 98.

3. *That*, unlike *which* and *who*, invariably thrusts a governing preposition to the end of the clause (e.g. *the man that I live with*). This very un-Latin construction caused 17th and 18th-century writers of erudition to prefer types with preposition + *wh*- pronoun (e.g. *the man with whom I live*). In the later editions of his 'Essay on Dramatick Poesie' (1668) Dryden zealously weeded out clauses with *that* and end-placed preposition.

4. Down to about 1800 relative clauses, defining and non-defining alike, were generally introduced by a comma.

5. Only its possessive form *sīn* struggled into recorded speech, and is found sporadically in poetry. Beowulf has *Higelāc ongan sīnne geseldan ... fægere fricgean* 'Hygelac began to ask his retainers politely'.

   The MnE reflex of *sik* in *busk* (dialectal) and *bask* is from Scandinavian, cp. ON *baða sik* 'bathe oneself', *bua sik* 'get oneself ready'.

6. The OE form was *ēow*, so the initial *y-* calls for a word of comment. It has been varyingly explained as due to the shift of accent *éow > eów*, or to the initial sound of the subject form *ye* having been carried through the whole paradigm.

7. The origin of the new feminine *s*-form has never been satisfactorily explained. A widely accepted view is that it has sprung from the OE demonstrative pronoun *sēo* (Anglian *sīe*), which through shift of accent could be reflected by the earliest recorded form *scæ* in the East Midland. It could also by a similar shift of accent be derived from OE *hēo > heó > ʒho*, another early form. The Scandinavian demonstrative pronoun *sjá* has also been considered a contributory factor.

   The swift adoption of the feminine *s*- form is probably due to the often intolerably ambiguous older *h*-forms. In many ME dialects it often requires contextual aid to decide whether a *he* stands for 'he' or 'she'.

8. The old dative *him* was replaced by the accusative *it* in late ME. *It*, originally the unaccented variety of *hit*, is universal by EMnE. Chaucer has *hit* as the preferred form, but in Caxton *it* is the more common of the two.

9. The *Þ*-forms are of Scandinavian origin and made their earliest appearance in the North, whence they spread southwards. Chaucer has *they*, but retains the native *here* and *hem* for possessive and object forms. By the close of ME *they* and *their* had become practically universal, but the old object form *hem* could be found sporadically as late as about 1600 and survives colloquially in phrases like *take 'em, stop 'em*.

10. For the voiced fricatives and their dialect, see p. 72.

11. Since *you* took over the reference to both numbers the language has in many ways tried to establish compensatory singular-plural distinctions. These attempts, however, have all remained non-standard or dialectal, as e.g. Irish *you* (sing.) – *youse* (plur.) which also recurs in American idiom. American are also plural markers like *you guys*, and in the South *you-all*. Many dialects distinguish by means of the verb: *you is/was – you are/were (Bess, you is my woman now!)*. The latter distinction gained wide recognition even in cultivated circles of the 18th and 19th centuries. Boswell uses it consistently in his 'London Journal', and Dr Johnson sometimes in his letters.

12. However, the Quaker *thou* is sometimes curiously distorted, *thee* being used for the subject case, sometimes even combined with the third-person form of the verb *(thee comes ..)*. This is doubtless due to the analogy of other subject pronouns in [i:], *he, she, we*.

13. Dialectal reflexes of older forms are *ourseln, ussens* (both from ME *seluen*). Possessive forms like *hisself, theirselves*, formed on the analogy of *myself, herself*, etc. are also common and have existed since ME. (Two shepherds watching angler) Shepherd: 'Mon, Sandy, He's got nae flee on the end o' the line'. Sandy (sotto voce): 'Haud yer tongue, mon! He does no ken, an he's better withoot it. He was aye catching hisself and other trash!' (Punch).

Notes to chapter X

1. Cp. PE reflexes: *owe,* and from the preterite *ought.* The adjective *own* has been derived from the past participle of *owe* in all Germanic languages (*eigen, egen*).

2. Also commonly referred to as -*mi* verbs, because in IE they all had -*mi* in the first person of the present indicative (cp. Sanskrit *asmi* 'I am', Greek *eimi,* Latin *sum,* PE *am*).

3. The root-vowel was protected from the influence of the -*jan* suffix by a formative element -*ō*-, inserted in this class between root and suffix (*lufian < *lufejan < *lufōjan*) absorbing the umlaut. Verbs like *herian* 'ravage' and *clǣnsian* 'cleanse' are formed from words which had i-umlaut already.

4. Cp. Danish and German: *holde – erholde; stå – bestå: klare – forklare; horchen – gehorchen; fliessen – zerfliessen; gehen – entgehen,* etc.

5. *Till* and *at,* from Scandinavian, were frequent infinitive particles in the North: *till late thame byrnand on hir fall* 'to let them fall burning down on her', *we have othere thynges at do* 'we have other things to do'. *At* is obsolete in PE except in the dialects, and in the phrase *Much Ado.*

6. The agent of the passive (in OE introduced by *fram*) was in ME currently expressed by *of*: *He was cursed of God* 'He was cursed by God'. PE *by* in this function is first recorded in the 14th century and is universal by 1600.

7. Other ME causative auxiliaries are *make, let,* and in the North *ger* (< ON *göra*).

8. The shortened forms *I'll, you'll,* etc. represent historically a contraction of *will,* and not of *shall.* They have been in evidence since the 16th century and were originally written -*le* (*youle, hele,* etc.).

9. As in Shakespeare: *he's a birding, sweet Sir John.* This type with reduced preposition became substandard or dialectal after 1700: *She's a takin' me 'ome.*

Books for further reading

Albert C. Baugh/Thomas Cable: *A History of the English Language.* Prentice-Hall, Inc., third edition 1978.

Karl Brunner: *Die englische Sprache* I-II. Max Niemeyer Verlag, Tübingen 1960-62.

Robert Burchfield: *The English Language.* Oxford University Press 1985.

David Crystal: *The English Language.* Penguin Books 1988.

Otto Jespersen: *Growth and Structure of the English Language.* Basil Blackwell, Oxford 1946.

Thomas Pyles/John Algeo: *The Origins and Development of the English Language.* Harcourt Brace Jovanovich, Inc., third edition 1982.

J.A. Sheard: *The Words We Use.* Andre Deutsch 1962.

Barbara M.H. Strang: *A History of English.* Methuen & Co Ltd 1970 (with bibliography).

Elisabeth Closs Traugott: *The History of English Syntax.* A Transformational Approach to the History of English Sentence Structure. Holt, Rinehart and Winston, Inc. 1972.

Index

154